TEEN LIFE IN
ASIA

TEEN LIFE IN ASIA

Edited by Judith J. Slater

Foreword by Richard M. Lerner

Teen Life around the World
Jeffrey S. Kaplan, Series Editor

GREENWOOD PRESS
Westport, Connecticut • London

Library of Congress Cataloging-in-Publication Data

Teen life in Asia / edited by Judith J. Slater, foreword by Richard M. Lerner.
  p. cm.—(Teen life around the world, ISSN 1540–4897)
  Includes bibliographical references and index.
  ISBN 0–313–31532–9 (alk. paper)
  1. Teenagers—Asia—Social conditions. 2. Teenagers—Asia—Social
life and customs. I. Slater, Judith J. II. Series.

HQ799.A75T44   2004
305.235′095—dc21   2003045529

British Library Cataloguing in Publication Data is available.

Library of Congress Catalog Card Number: 2003045529

ISBN: 0–313–31532–9
ISSN: 1540–4897

First published in 2004

Greenwood Press, 88 Post Road West, Westport, CT 06881
An imprint of Greenwood Publishing Group, Inc.
www.greenwood.com

Printed in the United States of America

The paper used in this book complies with the
Permanent Paper Standard issued by the National
Information Standards Organization (Z39.48–1984).

10   9   8   7   6   5   4   3   2   1

CONTENTS

FOREWORD: TOWARD A WORLD OF POSITIVE YOUTH DEVELOPMENT

In these early years of the twenty-first century a new vision and vocabulary for discussing young people has emerged. Propelled by the increasingly more collaborative contributions of scholars, practitioners, advocates, and policy makers, youth are viewed as resources to be developed. The new vocabulary is legitimated by scholarly efforts at advancing what are termed "developmental systems theories." These models emphasize the plasticity of human development, that is, the potential for systematic change in behavior that exists as a consequence of mutually influential relationships between the developing person and his or her biology, psychological characteristics, family, community, culture, physical and designed ecology, and historical niche.

The plasticity of development legitimizes an optimistic view of potential for promoting positive changes in human life and directs emphasis to the strengths for positive development that are present within all young people. Accordingly, concepts such as developmental assets, positive youth development, moral development, civic engagement, well-being, and thriving have been used increasingly in research and applications associated with adolescents and their world. All concepts are predicated on the ideas that *every* young person has the potential for successful, healthy development and that *all* youth possess the capacity for positive development.

This vision for and vocabulary about youth has evolved over the course of a scientifically arduous path. Complicating this new, positive conceptualization of the character of youth as resources for the healthy development of self, families, and communities was an antithetical theoretical approach to the nature and development of young people. Dating within science to, at least, the publication in 1904 of G. Stanley Hall's two-volume work on adolescence, youth have been characterized by a deficit view, one that conceptualizes their behaviors as deviations from norma-tive development. Understanding such deviations was not seen as being of direct relevance to scholarship aimed at discovering the principles of basic developmental processes. Accordingly, the characteristics of youth were regarded as issues of "only" applied concern—and thus of secondary scientific interest. Not only did this model separate basic science from ap-plication but, as well, it disembedded the adolescent from the study of normal or healthy development. It also often separated the young person from among those members of society that could be relied on to produce valued outcomes for family, community, and civic life. In short, the deficit view of youth as problems to be managed split the study of young people from the study of health and positive individual and social development.

The current scholarly and applied work that counters the historical, deficit view of adolescence, and in turn builds upon developmental sys-tems theory to advance the new, positive vocabulary about young people and the growing research evidence for the potential of all youth to de-velop in positive ways, is both represented and advanced significantly by the *Teen Life around the World* series. More so than any other set of re-sources currently available to young people, parents, and teachers, the volumes in this series offer rich and engaging depictions about the diverse ways in which young people pursue positive lives in their families, com-munities, and nations. The volumes provide vivid reflections of the energy, passion, and skills that young people possess—even under chal-lenging ecological or economic conditions—and the impressive ways in which adolescents capitalize on their strengths to pursue positive lives during their teenage years and to prepare themselves to be productive adult members of their families and communities.

Across the volumes in this series a compelling story of the common hu-manity of all people emerges, one that justifies a great deal of hope that, in today's adolescents, there exist the resources for a humane, peaceful, tolerant, and global civil society. To attain such a world, all people must begin by appreciating the diversity of young people and their cultures and that, through such diversity, the world possesses multiple, potentially pro-ductive paths to human well-being and accomplishment. Readers of the *Teen Life around the World* series will be rewarded with just this informa-tion.

Ultimately, we must all continue to educate ourselves about the best means available to promote enhanced life chances among all of the world's youth, but especially among those whose potential for positive contributions to civil society is most in danger of being wasted. The books in this series constitute vital assets in pursuit of this knowledge. Given the enormous, indeed historically unprecedented, challenges facing all nations, perhaps especially as they strive to raise healthy and successful young people capable of leading civil society productively, responsibly, and morally across the twenty-first century, there is no time to lose in the development of such assets. The *Teen Life around the World* series is, then, a most timely and markedly important resource.

Richard M. Lerner
Eliot-Pearson Department of
Child Development
Tufts University
Medford, Massachusetts
September 3, 2002

SERIES FOREWORD

Have you ever imagined what it would be like to live in a different country? What would it be like to speak a different language? Eat different foods? Wear different clothes? Attend a different school? Listen to different music, or maybe, the same music, in a different language? How about practicing new customs? Or, better yet, a different religion? Simply, how different would your life be if you were born and raised in another region of the world? Would you be different? And if so, how?

As we begin the twenty-first century, young people around the world face enormous challenges. Those born to wealth or relative comfort enjoy technological miracles and can click a button or move a mouse and discover a world of opportunity and pleasure. Those born without means struggle just to survive.

Education, though, remains a way out of poverty and for many privileged young people it is the ultimate goal. As more and more jobs, including those in the manufacturing and service sectors, require literacy, numeracy, and computer skills, brains are increasingly valued over brawn: In the United States, entry-level wages for people with only a high-school education have fallen by more than 20% since the 1970s. Job prospects are bleaker than ever for youths who do not continue their education after high school. And, to be sure, while there are exceptions—like the teenager who starts a basement computer business and becomes a multi-millionaire—working a string of low-paying service jobs with no medical insurance is a much more common scenario for those with limited education. And this seems to be true for adolescents in most post-industrialist countries around the world.

Adolescent girls, in particular, are at a disadvantage in many nations, facing sex discrimination as an obstacle to obtaining even basic education and social skills. In the Middle East and South Asia, girls are more likely to be pulled from school at an early age, and are thus less likely to develop critical literacy skills. Across most of the world, girls face more demands for work in the home and restrictions on movement that constrain their opportunities to gain direct experience with diverse social worlds. Similarly, as rates of divorce and abandonment rise worldwide, so do the chances in the workplace lessen for young women who fail to obtain skills to function independently. And as adults, they are increasingly vulnerable to poverty and exploitation.

ADOLESCENCE AROUND THE GLOBE

Adolescent life is truly plagued by difficulties and determined by context and circumstance. Anthropologist Margaret Mead (1901–1978) may have been the first social scientist to question the universality of the adolescent experience. When Mead contrasted the experience of North American and South Pacific young people in terms of sexuality, she found their experiences and attitudes toward sexuality dramatically different (South Pacific adolescents were more tolerant), and, she contended, adolescence should be seen in the contexts in which people live and dwell. In fact, for Mead and other social scientists, the only definition that can best describe adolescence is at best, restricted to a "period of transition," in which young people are no longer considered children, but not yet considered an adult.

Adolescence is generally understood as the period between the ages of 15 to 19, with some scholars referring to it as up to age 24. The term *young adult* is the most apt term for this age group, and without doubt, the many biological, psychological, and behavioral changes which mark this age, make this a concept that is continually dynamic and fluid in its change. Depending on which region of the world, the concept of adolescence or young adult is either emerging, or already well established. Most Western European societies use legal markers to underline the passage to adulthood, commonly set at age 16, 18, or 21. Thus, from country to country, there are minimum legal ages for marriage, for consensual intercourse, and also for access to sexual and reproductive health services without parental consent.

In many developing countries, though, the concept of adolescence has either been non-existent or is relatively new in concept and understanding. Rather than define adulthood by age or biology, children become adults through well-established rites of passage—for example, religious ceremony, or marriage. In India, for example, especially in rural areas, many girls enter into arranged marriages before the onset of their first menstruation cycle, and then, have their first child at around 16 years of age. For these young Indian girls, there is no adolescence, as they shift so quickly from childhood to motherhood. Similarly, in traditional Sri Lankan society, young people—once they enter puberty—are expected to get married, or in the case of a male, wear the yellow robe of a monk. To remain single is not held in high esteem because it is considered "neither here nor there."

Yet, the world is changing. Traditional patterns of behavior for young people, and what is expected of them by the adults, are in a state of flux, and in more open societies, adolescents are emerging as a powerful force for influence and growth in Africa, Asia, and Latin America. In these regions, massive economic, institutional and social changes have been brought about by Western colonial expansion and by the move toward a global society and economy. With more young people working in non-agricultural jobs, attending school longer, delaying marriage, adolescents are holding their own with adults.

In Indonesia, for example, young boys in urban areas are no longer tied to the farm and have started forming peer groups, as an alternative to life spent entirely inside the immediacy of their family. Similarly, in the urban areas of India, many girls attend single-sex schools, thus spending more time with peer groups, eroding the traditional practice of arranged marriages at an early age. In Nigeria, young people attend school for longer periods of time, thus preparing for jobs in their now modern economy. And in many Latin American countries, where young girls were once also hurried into pre-arranged marriages, now, young girls are staying in school so, they too can prepare for non-agricultural jobs.

And yet, those without means can only fantasize about what they see of mainstream material culture. As always, money is the societal divide that cruelly demarcates and is unrelenting in its effects on social, cultural, and psychological behavior. Young people living in poverty struggle daily with the pressures of survival in a seemingly indifferent, and often dangerous world. And access to wealth, or the simple conveniences of modern society, makes a considerable difference in the development of the young people. In rural areas in Zimbabwe and Papua New Guinea, for example, simple changes such as building of a road or highway—enabling the bringing in of supplies and expertise—has had profound effects on young people's lifestyles.

When young people must leave their homes—either because of poverty, or increasingly, due to civil war—the result is often unprecedented numbers forced into engaging in bonded labor and commercial sex. For example, in the Indian cities of New Delhi, Mumbai, and Calcutta, thousands of young people take on menial jobs such as washing cars, pushing hand carts, collecting edibles from garbage dumps, or simply, begging. In Thailand, thousands of young girls earn their living as prostitutes. And in many countries of Eastern Europe, tens of thousands of young people are believed to be not attending school or formally employed, but instead, engaging in drug trafficking. Worldwide, the streets and temporary shelters are home to between 100 and 200 million children and adolescents, who are cut off from their parents and extended families (World Health Organization, 2000). What is it like to be them? What is it like to be young, scared, and poor?

Since the 1980s political and civil rights have improved substantially throughout the world, and 81 countries have taken significant steps in democratization, with 33 military regimes replaced by civilian governments. But of these fledgling democracies, only 47 are considered full democracies today. Only 82 countries, representing 57% of the world's population, are fully democratic.

Economically speaking, the proportion of the world's extremely poor fell from 29% in 1990 to 23% in 1999. Still, in 1999, 2.8 billion people lived on less than $2 a day, with 1.2 billion of them surviving on the margins of subsistence with less than $1 a day. In 2000, 1.1 billion people lacked access to safe water, and 2.4 billion did not have access to any form of improved sanitation services.

And armed conflict continues to blight the lives of millions: since 1990, 3.6 million people have died as a result of civil wars and ethnic violence, more than 16 times the number killed in wars between states. Civilians have accounted for more than 90% of the casualties—either injured or killed—in post–Cold War conflicts. Ninety countries are affected by landmines and live explosives, with rough estimates of 15,000 to 20,000 mine victims each year.

TEEN LIFE AROUND THE WORLD—THE SERIES

The Greenwood series *Teen Life around the World* examines what life is like for teens in different regions of the world. These volumes describe in detail the lives of young people in places both familiar and unfamiliar. How do teens spend their days? What makes their lives special? What difficulties and special burdens do they bear? And what will be their future as they make their way in their world?

Each volume is devoted to a region or regions of the world. For the purpose of this series, the volumes are divided as follows:

- Teen Life in Africa
- Teen Life in the Middle East
- Teen Life in Europe
- Teen Life in Central and South America and the Caribbean
- Teen Life in Asia

Readers can see similarities and differences in areas of the world that are relatively close in proximity, customs, and practices. Comparisons can be made between various countries in a region and across regions. American teens will perhaps be struck by the influence of American pop culture—music, fashion, food—around the world.

All volumes follow the same general format. The standardized format highlights information that all young people would most like to know. Each volume has up to fifteen chapters that describe teen life in a specific country in that region of the world. The countries chosen generally are representative of that region, and attempts were made to write about countries that young people would be most curious to learn more about.

Each chapter begins with a profile of the particular country. Basic political, economic, social, and cultural issues are discussed and a brief history of the country is provided. After this brief introduction to the specific country, an overview of teen life in that country is given, with a discussion of a teenager's typical day, family life, traditional and nontraditional foods, schooling, social life, recreation, entertainment, and religious practices and cultural practices. Finally, each chapter concludes with a list of resources that will help readers learn more about this country. These resources include nonfiction and fiction, Web sites, other sources to find information on the country, such as embassies, and pen pal addresses.

Although these chapters cannot tell the complete story of what it means to be a teenager in that region of the world and recognizing that perhaps there is no one typical lifestyle in any country, they provide a good starting point for insight into others' lives.

The contributors to this series present an informative and engaging look at the life of young people around the world and write in a straightforward manner. The volumes are edited by noted experts. They have an intimate understanding of their chosen region of the world—having either lived there, and/or they have devoted their professional lives to studying, teaching about, and researching the place. Also, an attempt was made to have each chapter written by an expert on teen life in that country. Above all, what these authors reveal is that young people everywhere—no matter where they live—have much in common. Although they might observe different social customs, rituals, and habits, they still long for the same basic things—security, respect, and love. They still live in that state of the half child/half adult, as they wait anxiously to become fully functioning members of their societies.

As series editor, it is my hope that these volumes, which are unique in publishing in both content and style, will increase your knowledge of teen life around the world.

Jeffrey S. Kaplan
Series Editor

REFERENCES

Baru, R. (1995). The social milieu of the adolescent girl. In S. Mehra (Ed.), *Adolescent Girl in India: An Indian Perspective*. Saket, New Delhi. MAMTA, Health Institute for Mother and Child.

Caldwell, J. C.; Caldwell, P.; & Caldwell, B. K. (1998). The construction of adolescence in a changing world: Implications for sexuality, reproduction, and marriage. *Studies in Family Planning*. 29(2), 137–53.

Dehne, K. L., & Reidner, G. (2001). Adolescence: A dynamic concept. *Reproductive Health Matters*. 9 (17), 11–16.

Deutsche Gesellschaft für Technische Zusammenarbeit (1997). *Youth in development cooperation: approaches and prospects in the multisectoral planning group "Youth."* Eschborn: GTZ.

Disanyake, J. B. (1998). *Understanding the sinhalese*. Columbo: Chatura Printers.

Larson, Reed. (2002). The Future of Adolescence: Lengthening the Ladders to Adulthood. *The Futurist*. 36(6), 16–21.

McCauley, A. P. & Salter, C. (1995). Meeting the needs of young adults. *Population Report*, Series J. 41:1–39.

UNAIDS (1999). *Sex and youth: contextual factors affecting risk for HIV/AIDS*. Geneva: UNAIDS.

UN Development Report (2002).

INTRODUCTION

Judith J. Slater

Teenagers all over the world have much in common. They are all on the threshold of adulthood, are busy with their friends, and are establishing the beliefs and values that will guide them in the future. *Teen Life in Asia* provides readers with an overview of a vast region of the world that is culturally very different from the United States. At first glance, many of the teens in the countries described in this book have the same desires, aspirations, and needs as do teens in America. But a closer look at the subtle and not-so-subtle differences in economics, social and cultural situations, and political orientations of each country reveals important differences. While the countries in this volume are part of one continent, historically each has been divided by colonization and historical suppression and repression of individual rights in many cases. This is a region of old surviving cultural distinctions that still influence the codes of behavior of the region. Teenage years are the time when cultures inculcate teens. Through education, governments prepare teens for citizenship. It is a time of tolerance for acceptable behavior and a time of intolerance for actions that are inappropriate to the perpetuation of the nation. Each country has a tradition and an emerging global position that it desires to fulfill, and teens are its hope for the future.

The countries included in this book are Cambodia, China, Hong Kong, India, Indonesia, Japan, Mongolia, Nepal, North Korea, the Philippines, Singapore, South Korea, Taiwan, Thailand, and Vietnam. In most cases, the descriptions were written by researcher/sociologists from the country, or by academics that have traveled to the country and talked to teens to get firsthand, up-to-date information about their lives.

Teens in Asia and teens in the United States tend to have similar desires and needs, to like similar foods, and to enjoy similar types of recreation. The differences between them tend to be cultural, religious, or economic/political. The more westernized and industrial the location, the more teen life looks similar to that in the United States. Activities that may be routine for people in industrialized societies are not available for many in poorer countries or those that are restricted by governmental rules and laws that limit teen behavior. Therefore, socialist countries such as North Korea and Mainland China (People's Republic of China) are very different from more affluent and politically open countries such as Japan and Taiwan (Republic of China) that tend to produce teens that appear to be more like American teenagers.

Regulations and rules dominate the ability of teens to have flexibility in their lives and in their social interactions in some locations. Countries that are focused on preparing teens for a competitive world are contrasted with countries where subsistence and industrialization as an economic competitor have not yet arrived. Some countries such as Cambodia, due to economic conditions, provide little educational opportunity for teens. Good economic conditions, such as in Hong Kong, Japan, South Korea, and Taiwan, provide more opportunity since there is a great emphasis placed on education by the government.

Schooling in Asian countries is also influenced by colonization patterns or effects of occupation and war. The model of education adopted is usually based on that of the host country, or it is some hybrid of the American or European system of education. Therefore, the European system of entrance examination for selecting students who will have the opportunity to get into the best high school or to advance into competitive fields depends on the system in place and on the economic conditions of the country. If teens are needed to go to work to help with subsistence income, education is not a priority. In other locations, education is a vehicle out of poverty, an opening of opportunity to advance, and many of these countries have vocational/technical programs geared directly toward their industrialization needs. The value the society places on education is also reflected in whether schooling for teens is compulsory, public, private, or government supported.

Probably the greatest similarity between Asian teens and U.S. teens is due to the worldwide phenomenon of consumerism, reflected in the tastes of most teens. Advertisements are for goods and services that may be produced in Asia but are marketed worldwide, and they influence the buying habits of teens everywhere.

The artifacts of a connected world are seen in the Americanization of food, clothing, music, television, and the Internet if available. These bring teens closer together worldwide and make them look and sound more similar. CNN Asia is broadcast in English and brings English language news, features, and sports to each of these countries. Sports, whether as competition or as exercise, is another area of similarity and forms a basis in many areas for the recreation and social life of teens.

Finally, the home life in each location, as in the United States, is influenced by the traditions of culture and/or religion that provide continuity to the country and perpetuate its unique character. While the similarities noted above provide a surface impression that teens in Asia are just like those in America, this is only partly true. Underneath the clothes that are familiar, beyond the food and recreation that they participate in, is a value structure built on the deeply rooted beliefs and customs of this ancient region. Asians are the largest population group in the world. All the locations described in this volume need to be thought of as independent areas because of the political and economic differences that are deeply rooted and entwined in cultures that have sustained themselves longer than those anywhere else on Earth. What remains to be seen is what teens do with their unique heritage and how they, tomorrow's adults, propel their countries ahead.

Chapter 1

CAMBODIA

Aixa Perez-Prado

INTRODUCTION

In 2000, the World Health Organization estimated that 50 percent of the population of Cambodia was younger than 17. This country of young people currently has a population of approximately 12 million. With these types of statistics, it is easy to see what an important role teenagers can have in this Southeast Asian country. Young Cambodians are in a pivotal position to move their country forward after a very long and tragic history of war and civil unrest.

Cambodia, or the Kingdom of Cambodia, is part of the Indochinese Peninsula of Southeast Asia. It is a lush tropical country bordered by Thailand, Laos, Vietnam, and the South China Sea. Topographically, Cambodia has been likened to a shallow bowl, with the lowest regions in the middle of the country. Although much of the central land area of Cambodia consists of flat plains where rice, corn, and tobacco are grown, there are also some low mountains, gently rolling hills, and tropical rain forests.

In Cambodia there are two seasons, rainy and dry. The rainy season lasts from April to November and is characterized by daily rainfall in the afternoons. During this season much of the land is flooded, which is why the homes of many rural Cambodians are on stilts. So much rain falls during the rainy season that the Tonle Sap, an enormous lake in the middle of the country, increases to three times its normal size and overflows each year. During the dry season the lake shrinks back and the fertile land around it is used for agriculture.

In addition to varied tropical vegetation, Cambodia is the home of many different kinds of animals. These include such wild animals as elephants, panthers, and snakes as well as beautiful butterflies and brightly colored parrots. There are also many domesticated animals and animals raised for slaughter in this country. Pigs, hens, and sea animals provide much of the protein in the Cambodian diet.

The people of Cambodia are mostly Khmer in ethnic origin. This is also the name of the official language of Cambodia. However, there are groups of people within Cambodia who belong to different ethnic groups and who have their own languages and customs. These groups of people often live in self-contained communities in the mountainous areas. One such group is called the Pear.

The major religion in Cambodia is Buddhism, but Muslims, Christians, and Hindus also live in the country. Angkor Wat, one of the major tourist attractions of Cambodia, is probably the largest religious structure in the world. There are temples and other religious buildings with ornate engravings and statues featuring scenes from the Hindu Ramayana as well as Buddhist gods and carvings.

Most Cambodians have light brown skin and wavy or curly black hair. There are also many Cambodians who can trace their roots back to China and who tend to be lighter in skin color and to have straighter hair. In general, Cambodians are smaller than Americans. The average height of an adult male Cambodian is 5 feet, 4 inches.

Cambodia has a long and interesting history. This small country has been invaded and populated by outsiders on a number of occasions. All these outside groups have left some traces of their own cultures and traditions on the country and its people. Evidence of a strong influence and immigration from China and India thousands of years ago can be seen through the temples and statues that have survived in places such as Angkor Wat. Cambodia has also been influenced by Thailand and Vietnam, its close neighbors, and was under the control of the French for several decades in the nineteenth and twentieth centuries.

When Cambodia declared its independence from France in 1953, Prince Norodom Sihanouk of Cambodia became the ruling monarch. Although he was forced to flee the country because of political turmoil and civil war, he was reinstated in September 1993. The executive branch of the Cambodian government also has a prime minister as its head and a council of ministers appointed by the monarch.

Perhaps Cambodia is best known for its more recent history. In the 1970s Cambodia was rampaged by the Khmer Rouge, a group of revolutionaries who tried to create an ideal communist agrarian society in Cambodia. From 1975 to 1979 hundreds of thousands of Cambodians were killed or starved to death under the Khmer Rouge regime. Any citizen who was educated or considered an intellectual was highly suspect and very often killed. This included many doctors, teachers, and other professionals. It is estimated that only 50 of the over 700 university professors in Cambodia at the beginning of the 1970s survived the Khmer Rouge takeover. Even people who were not highly educated but wore eyeglasses were considered to be potential enemies of the Khmer Rouge and were sometimes put to death.

At this tragic time in Cambodian history, most of the inhabitants of cities were ordered to leave their homes and begin new lives in the country working on communal farms. Many of these people died of starvation or disease on their way to relocation areas in the country. Of those who survived these long and difficult journeys to relocation, many died shortly upon arrival to their new homes. Still others were murdered by the Khmer Rouge soldiers, either during their journeys or once they had begun new lives as farmers in the country. Virtually all schools in Cambodia were shut down, and the entire populace was ordered to grow food. Illiteracy in Cambodia climbed to over 40 percent.

During this period, many Cambodians lived in fear of their lives. Families were frequently separated, with some teenagers and younger children forced to train as soldiers or work as laborers away from their parents and youngest siblings. Many eyewitness reports of this time document the cruelty of the Khmer Rouge soldiers and the terrible suffering of the people. In addition to working all day for the war effort, either by growing food or by fighting, all citizens were required to attend daily or weekly propaganda sessions led by the Khmer Rouge. These lectures were designed to indoctrinate the people with the philosophy of the Khmer Rouge regime and its leader, Pol Pot. This powerful leader, considered to be an all-knowing father figure by the soldiers, was both idolized and feared. Meanwhile, the Cambodian people continued to die of disease, starvation, and murder.

Finally, Vietnamese soldiers invaded Cambodia and were able to defeat the Khmer Rouge. Although most Cambodians were relieved to see the Khmer Rouge soldiers defeated, they still were not pleased to be under the control of Vietnam. These two countries have long had a difficult and contentious relationship. After the Vietnamese takeover, guerilla warfare continued for some time in the hills and forests of Cambodia. To this day, there are thousands of undetonated land mines left over from the civil wars. Tragically, many Cambodians have lost their lives and their limbs because of unknowingly stepping on these land mines during the course of daily activities such as farming or even walking to school. Currently, there are thousands of amputees in this country, and the number continues to grow.

Cambodia is still a very poor country. Much of the population lives in poverty and does not have access to adequate health care or other basic needs. Also, most Cambodians have not been able to pursue an education beyond a basic primary level, and therefore the general population is not well versed in disease prevention and how to maintain a healthy lifestyle. Because of this lack of education and prevalent poverty, the life expectancy in Cambodia is quite low. The average Cambodian is not expected to live beyond the age of 58.

Although there are many daily newspapers in Cambodia, most Cambodians do not have telephones or television sets. People get their information mostly from the radio or the newspapers. This includes a great deal of information about the rest of the world, as well as Cambodia. Because of this, most Cambodians probably know a lot more about the United States than most Americans do about Cambodia.

Cambodians usually travel on foot. This is due to the poverty of much of the population as well as to the lack of available vehicles. Many people, including teenagers, also get around with bicycles and motorbikes. Another way to go from place to place in the city is to use the pedicabs, or bicycle taxis. Rural people, and occasionally some city dwellers, may use an oxcart for transportation. The great majority of Cambodians do not own cars.

TYPICAL DAY

Most teenagers in Cambodia attend school for as many years as they can. In the city, kids get up and sometimes do housework or go over their homework before school. After breakfast teenagers usually go to school. Kids who live in poorer homes often have more duties in the house than do those who live in wealthier homes that may have maids to do the housework for them and to prepare meals. Teens who live in the country generally get up earlier in the morning. They are often involved with helping their parents do farm or household chores in the morning before going off to school. Girls generally help in the house with cooking, cleaning, washing, and taking care of pets. Boys help their fathers by finding firewood for cooking and doing other chores that require more physical strength, such as farming and fishing.

Teenagers in Cambodia normally help their parents in the home and sometimes outside of the home as well by working. Because of the poverty level in Cambodia, there is not as much free time for teenagers to just

A Cambodian daughter helps her mother sell food and drinks in Kampuchia.
Photo © B. A. Dixie Dean/TRIP.

hang around; they must concentrate on their studies and help their families in any way they can. Very often, the older children will work outside the home to help support the younger children. When this happens, teens may need to drop out of school.

Among those teenagers who drop out of school are a group of teenagers who end up living on the streets of urban areas, especially in Phnom Penh, the capital city. These street kids live dangerous and difficult lives that might include prostitution and drug addiction. One of the major problems among teens that live on the streets in Cambodia is glue sniffing. Teens who become addicted to glue sniffing spend their days in a kind of stupor that leaves them as potential easy victims for all kinds of people who might want to take advantage of them. Many of these teens are orphans, while others are from very poor families from whom they have run away. Still others are special-needs teenagers who are deaf or mentally disabled and who have been abandoned by their families. While some religious and humanitarian organizations in Cambodia today are trying to help these young people get off the streets and start better lives, many teens do not receive any help.

One place where there are many teenagers working instead of going to school is Stung Mearchey, a garbage dump on the outskirts of Phnom

Penh. Several hundred people a day, many of them teenagers, scavenge through the hazardous waste at this dump looking for recyclable materials that they can sell or trade for food and other necessities. The perils in this type of work include the threat of injury because of inadequate footwear, hazardous medical and chemical waste, and toxic smoke. Most of the teens working here come from families that are not intact and in which they may be the only source of income for younger siblings.

Despite the unfortunate realities of poverty, ignorance, and war, most teenagers in Cambodia do go to school every day. Those who live in the countryside usually walk to school. Often there are no high schools nearby, so teenagers have to travel to other villages to attend school. They may have to walk for long distances and through areas with no roads or pathways. Other teens ride bikes to school, or if they live in towns they may own a motorbike that they drive to school. Some kids go to school in a school bus or a private moto taxi (*moto doub*) or pedicab. Still others may get a ride from a family member or friend who has a car.

A Cambodian teenager typically has a large amount of homework that needs to be completed daily. Therefore, after-school activities are usually limited to getting homework done and helping with chores around the house, including caring for younger brothers and sisters. However, when teenagers do have some free time, they can often be found hanging out together.

FAMILY LIFE

Teens in Cambodia usually have a very close relationship with their families. Children are considered to be a great blessing in a family, and young infants and toddlers are given a great deal of physical affection and attention. Brothers and sisters often grow to be like best friends. Many games played by Cambodian siblings and friends emphasize cooperation and socialization rather than winning and losing. This may be one reason that families seem to work well together and family members tend to support one another so much in Cambodia.

Teenagers are very important members of the family in Cambodia. They have special relationships and different roles with all members of their families. With their close-in-age siblings, teens will often confide their personal experiences and problems. Parents are highly respected and teens usually are too shy or embarrassed to tell their parents about some of the problems they might be having, especially when these problems involve romantic relationships. Teens who have younger siblings often take on roles of responsibility with the caretaking of these siblings. They may be responsible for making sure that their little brothers and sisters get fed, do homework, get to school safely, and accomplish other tasks throughout the day. Younger siblings are taught to respect their older siblings as well as all older people. Grandparents and older aunts and uncles are also highly respected members of the family, and teens often have good relationships with them. In the Khmer language, special words that denote respect for elders are used in addressing family members and friends.

In most families in Cambodia, both parents work outside the home. The great majority of Cambodians work in agriculture, growing crops to sell or trade. Many Cambodians are also merchants who sell goods and products in the cities and towns. Although many mothers work, many also stay home to take care of younger children and do housework. Family roles and responsibilities are very important to Cambodians. The whole family works together to support one another, with teenage boys and girls having many responsibilities within the family. Because parents and grandparents are highly respected in this country, teenagers usually follow the rules provided within the family home. Although new generations of Cambodian teens are more Americanized than previous generations because of the influence of movies and television shows, there is still a very traditional way of life that is respected by most teens. Nevertheless, there are always some areas in which teens and parents disagree. This is especially true when it comes to how much freedom teenagers are allowed outside the home.

The country permits teens to drive and to consume alcohol beginning at age 18, but these age limits are not strictly enforced. Quite a number of people who drive in Cambodia do so without a license. However, this is not a major issue for teens since very few of them own their own cars. Those teens that are allowed to go out at night, primarily the males, often do drink beer in bars and clubs. Females are more likely to go to friends' houses or school events, where alcohol does not tend to be available.

TRADITIONAL AND NONTRADITIONAL FOOD DISHES

In Phnom Penh, the smells of Cambodian food fill the air in many places because of the large quantity of food stands. Many of these stands feature Cambodian favorites, such as rice or noodles and soup. Also, grilled fish and meat, fried vegetables with meat, fried eggs, porridge, or fish curry in coconut milk sauce (*amoc*) can be found everywhere. Curry is commonly eaten in Cambodia, especially during holidays. Cambodian food is similar to Thai cuisine but not as spicy. Much of the food has the flavors of fish sauce, lemongrass, coconut milk, and tamarind. A popular snack food in Cambodia is *um som choo*, a sticky rice preparation with soybeans and pork, all served inside a bamboo tube. Other snacks include dragon fruit, palm fruit, mangoes, and papaya. Cambodian teens also enjoy eating candy bars and junk food whenever they get a chance.

A favorite drink in Cambodia is sugarcane juice. This is widely available in street stalls. Another popular drink is *dteuk rolok*, a milky fruit shake to which locals often add an egg. Many Cambodians also enjoy Western soft drinks as well as coffee, tea, and beer.

Generally, everybody in the family eats together in Cambodia. However, in some traditional families, children eat only after their parents are finished. Because of the poverty in Cambodia, many people do not get enough vitamins in their diet, and this results in some health problems. Under the Khmer Rouge, many people suffered from malnutrition because of the scarcity of food rations. Since then there have been some international efforts in food donation to Cambodia and the situation has improved.

SCHOOLING

School is considered extremely important among teens in Cambodia. They tend to spend a lot of time studying and trying to get the best education they can. This is because education is seen as a way out of the cycle of poverty that has gripped so many of the families in Cambodia for such a long time. Parents normally pay for teens' school fees unless they are too poor to do so. Occasionally, impoverished students in Cambodia will receive sponsorship from a person or persons in another country that will allow them to continue studying. In addition to this kind of support, teens may find jobs to help pay for their own books and school supplies.

In Cambodian high schools, students take a wide variety of subjects. Those subjects most commonly taught in high school include biology, language, math, art, history, chemistry, physical education, other physical sciences, and cultural and moral studies. Teachers normally lecture to students, and there is quite a bit of rote memorization in the curriculum. Also, there is a lot of dictation in Cambodia: teachers read lessons and students copy them down in notebooks. When students do not understand something about a lecture, they raise their hands and ask questions. Teachers are usually receptive to student questions. They try to explain further and clarify course content for students.

Teenagers in Cambodia often have a great deal of homework. This means that they have to spend a large amount of additional time after school studying and completing their lessons. One reason for this is that there are challenging high school exams that must be passed in order to graduate and be allowed to apply to universities in Cambodia.

Some young people in Cambodia might also attend technical private schools to learn a trade. These programs often last from three to six months and allow teenagers to start working as soon as they are finished. The trades that can be learned include auto mechanics and electronics.

Students in Cambodia with special needs and disabilities usually attend the same schools as everyone else. Teachers and classmates try to help them out whenever they can. Because of the land mine problem in Cambodia, many teenagers and other people are amputees needing special assistance to get around.

SOCIAL LIFE

Just like teens from other countries, Cambodian teens enjoy hanging around and talking. Cambodians are shy, especially the girls. Parents try to make sure that their daughters do not wear skirts that are too short or other clothing that is too revealing. However, times are changing in Cambodia, and parents are usually not as strict as they used to be regarding their daughters' clothing choices. Nevertheless, girls are expected to always look neat and well put together, with their hair tied up and without too much makeup.

Teenage boys in Cambodia are expected to keep their hair short and to look respectable in their dress and appearance. Parents discourage boys from dressing in ways that associate them with slackers or persons who operate outside the law, despite what might be in fashion. In general, however, Cambodian parents seem less concerned with the appearance of their sons than they are with the appearance of their daughters.

Teenagers in Cambodia enjoy socializing both inside and outside of school. Sometimes there are school activities, such as dances and parties, where teens can get together to talk, dance, and have fun. They may listen to popular Cambodian music or music from the West. Some parents and teachers are usually present at these activities.

In addition to school activities and parties at friends' houses, some teenagers in Cambodia also go out on dates. These teens often like to go outside of town to rice and corn plantations where soft drinks, fruit, and other refreshments are sold. This gives couples a chance to be alone and to talk for an extended period of time in order to get to know one another better without family or other friends being around. There are also places for teens to go and enjoy looking out over the landscape. These scenic lookout areas are often in the hills around rivers or lakes, or at the beach areas. Girls and boys can go there with groups of friends in order to relax and socialize. Couples also enjoy going to these lookouts to be alone and get away from their parents for a while.

At night teenagers and young adults like to go to karaoke bars and nightclubs. Teen boys have more of a chance to do these things than do girls. Also, these are more common activities among teens that can afford to spend money on entertainment. Since so much of the general population in Cambodia lives in poverty, many teens do not have access to these types of recreational activities.

In Cambodia, boys generally are the ones who take the initiative in asking girls out. Boys and girls often meet at school and arrange to go somewhere together after school or on the weekend. There are not many friendships among teen boys and girls because of social customs that tend to discourage these types of friendships in adolescence. However, this too has been changing, and now there are more girl-boy friendships in Cambodia than there were in the past. One time during which there is a lot of socialization between adolescent girls and boys is during festivals, such as the New Year Festival. The group games and interactions that take place during these events provide one way for teens to start meeting potential mates.

In Cambodia it is not uncommon for wealthy and poor teenagers to become friends and to date. However, it becomes more difficult for them to marry, especially if the girl is wealthy and the boy is poor. Wealthy parents want their teenage daughters to marry into other wealthy families so that they will be well taken care of. Currently, approximately half of all marriages are pre-arranged. Families, friends, or matchmakers can make these marital arrangements. However, these matches are often initiated by the young man, who decides on a particular girl that he likes and then asks his parents or someone else to arrange a marriage.

Most Cambodians marry in their twenties, although it is not uncommon for teenagers to marry. After a match has been made and each family is satisfied with the match, presents are normally exchanged and the families consult a priest (achar) to set a wedding date. Traditional weddings are long, sometimes lasting several days, and full of ritual and ceremony. Parts of these ceremonies may include passing a candle around a circle of married couples to bless the newlyweds and tying threads soaked in holy water around the wrists of the bride and groom. Nowadays, especially in the cities, it is more common to have shorter weddings that include some rituals along with a religious blessing and a banquet for family and friends.

According to Cambodian social customs, it is unacceptable for teens to engage in premarital sex, which is considered a blemish on the family's honor. Virginity is a highly valued commodity, especially in brides. Nevertheless, some teens have premarital sex, usually without the knowledge of their parents. This is not a topic that is normally discussed in the home.

RECREATION

The two most popular sports among teens in Cambodia seem to be soccer and volleyball. These are more popular for boys to play and to watch than they are for girls. Cambodian girls do not play many sports because it is not customary for them to do so. However, both boys and girls enjoy swimming in the lakes and streams throughout the country, as well as the beaches and swimming pools available. School teams often compete.

ENTERTAINMENT

One of the things that teens and their families do for entertainment in Cambodia is to visit the natural outdoor attractions in the country. There are a number of beautiful, unspoiled beaches in Cambodia where young and old alike can enjoy a day of fun in the sun. Other outdoor places to visit in Cambodia are the volcanoes and the rain forest.

In addition to traveling, teens enjoy listening to music together on the radio and on CD players. Sometimes there are concerts on weekends at local Cambodian television stations that teens enjoy participating in. Boys and girls dance together to rock music from Europe and the Americas, as well as to Cambodian rock. One Cambodian dance, performed only by women, is called *lathem*. This type of dance is very ritualized and difficult. Students of lathem study for years to master intricate hand and arm movements. When performing, these dancers wear very elaborate and detailed costumes.

Young people also like to go to the movies and to watch television shows. Many of the movies and television shows that are shown in Cambodia come from the United States. Since not everyone has a television set in Cambodia, teenagers often gather at the house of a friend who does have a TV in order to watch shows together. In general, boys have a lot more freedom to go out than teen girls do, especially on weekends and in the evenings.

Teens also enjoy playing video and computer games when they have an opportunity to do so. This is an activity that is normally reserved for those in families that have a higher income level than the majority of Cambodians.

Although most Cambodians do not have a computer at home with access to the Internet, there are some cybercafes in urban areas where they can surf the Internet and enjoy many of the same on-line activities that American teens enjoy.

Other forms of entertainment in Cambodia include motorcycle and boat racing. These activities are becoming more popular among teens and young adults. Yet another form of entertainment in this country is cock-fighting. This is a traditional form of entertainment that has been practiced for decades. People of all ages go to cock-fighting matches. Some teenagers and adults gamble on the winners of these races and fights, while others attend just for fun. Despite the popularity of these events, this is another area in which there is much more participation from men and boys than from women and girls.

RELIGIOUS PRACTICES AND CULTURAL CEREMONIES

The state religion in Cambodia is Theravada Buddhism. This type of Buddhism teaches the notion of harmony and peace with one another and with the world. Although most teens and their families are Buddhists, there is not a large amount of religious participation or activity that takes place on a regular basis among Cambodian young people. Nevertheless, some teenage boys do become Buddhist monks for a year or more as part of their educational and coming of age experiences. In addition to Buddhists, there are also a large number of Hindus and Muslims in Cambodia. Each of these religions has its own customs, practices, and holidays.

One of the major holidays in Cambodia is ancestor's day (*P'chum Ben*), which usually takes place in late September. This day marks the beginning of the festival season that runs through April. A highlight of this season is the water festival (*Bon Om Dteuk*). This occurs when the current of the Tonle Sap River reverses and flows into the Mekong River. Festivities are centered on Phnom Penh's riverbanks, where people gather from all over the city and countryside to watch boat racing, parades, and fireworks. Teenagers enjoy these festivities with their families as well as their friends. These events offer many opportunities for teens to socialize and enjoy themselves.

CONCLUSION

Teens in Cambodia hope to see their country prosper in this coming century. They wish for peace and stability and the job opportunities they will need as they become adults and heads of their own families. This is a time of renewed hope in Cambodia after many years of civil unrest, poverty, and war. Many teenagers today are working hard to be part of the positive change in Cambodia.

Cambodians use the expression "I have a road" ("*mien plou*") to describe a stroke of good luck. This means hope and the possibility of a positive outcome or future. That seems to be the message of modern Cambodia, especially for the young people, who make up the majority of the country's population. Although there is still rampant poverty in this area of the world, along with ongoing consequences of civil wars, many Cambodians are hopeful about their futures and the future of their native land.

RESOURCE GUIDE

Nonfiction

Chandler, D. (2000). *A history of Cambodia*. Boulder, CO: Westview Press.

Claude, J. (1999). *Cambodia—Report from a stricken land*. New York: Arcade.

Coday, D. (2002, June 30). Young and searching in Cambodia. *National Catholic Reporter, 156*, 14–16.

Gilboa, A. (1990). *Off the rails in Phnom Penh—into the heart of guns, girls, and ganja*. Bangkok: Asia Books.

Him, C. (2000). *When broken glass floats: Growing up under the Khmer Rouge*. New York: W. W. Norton.

Ray, N. (2000). *Lonely Planet: Cambodia*. 3rd ed. Oakland, CA: Lonely Planet Publications.

The road to riches: After three decades of turmoil, Cambodia is trying to repave its way back to peace and prosperity. (2000, August 21). *Time International, 156*, 80.

Ung, L. (2001). *First they killed my father: A daughter of Cambodia remembers*. New York: Harper Collins.

Welaratna, U. (1993). *Beyond the killing fields: Voices of nine Cambodian survivors in America*. Stanford, CA: Stanford University Press.

Fiction

Lipp, H. (2001). *The caged birds of Phnom Penh*. New York: Holiday House Press.

Webber, E. (1990). *The saving rain*. Boston: Branden Publishing.

Web Sites

http://4j.lane.edu/Kelly/Cambodia
http://talesofasia.com
http://www.btinternet.com/~andybrouwer
http://www.yale.edu/cgp

More Information

http://www.embassy.org/Cambodia
http://www.phnompenhpost.com

Pen Pal/Chat

http://www.itisnet.com/english/asia/cambodia/e-cam-tap.htm

Chapter 2

CHINA

Leiping Bao

INTRODUCTION

China is a unique country with a long-standing and well-established culture and traditions that have existed for over five thousand years. It is in eastern Asia, west of the Pacific Ocean, has a territory of 9,600,000 square kilometers, and is the third-largest country in the world. China has 13 billion hardworking and enthusiastic people, one-fourth of them teenagers. Within its vast territory, China has magnificent natural scenery, abundant historical areas, and varied and colorful cultures.

China has diversified terrain. Mountains, hills, and plateaus occupy almost two-thirds of its territory; the remainder is plains. The highest mountain peak in the world—Qomolangma Feng (also known as Mount Everest), with an altitude of 8,848 meters—is located in southwestern China on the border with Nepal. The Yangtze River and the Yellow River flow from west to east across the country.

The Chinese civilization is one of the oldest in the world. Chinese historical records date back more than 4,000 years. There are abundant ancient codes and records about Chinese rites, formal attire, handicraft, and literature. The compass, gunpowder, and the techniques of printing and papermaking were originally invented and developed in ancient China.

China is a multiracial, multireligion country. The Han people compose nearly 92 percent of the population, and minorities compose about 8 percent. Chinese is the commonly used language. The official language is Mandarin, but the minorities have their own native spoken and written languages. Chinese people are free to choose their religion. Buddhism,

Taoism, Islam, Catholicism, and Christianity are the common religious sects in China.

The People's Republic of China was established on October 1, 1949. Formal diplomatic relationships exist with 160 countries, and there are governmental and nongovernmental economic cooperation, and trade and cultural exchange, relationships with many other countries in the world. The People's Republic of China is a socialist country with a foreign policy of peace seeking. Innovation and an open market are the main objectives of the political and economic policies since the 1980s, and this has resulted in remarkable efforts and accomplishments. The living standard in some big cities of the People's Republic of China is almost the same as that of the advanced Western countries.

TYPICAL DAY

"Ding, ding, ding, ding." The alarm clock rings at 7 A.M., as usual. Young Young, a 14-year-old junior high school student, reluctantly wakes up, with a strong desire to get back to sleep for a little while. His mother will not let him, though, and quickly lifts his blanket with a rapid warning, "Hurry up, or you will be late." Young Young knows his mother is right and does not wish to be criticized in front of his schoolmates or by his teacher for being late. He hurriedly jumps out of bed to go to the bathroom, washes his face, and cleans his teeth. Breakfast is already on the table. There are only several minutes left for him to finish. After breakfast, Young Young gets on his bicycle, which is a present from his parents, and rides fast to the school, which is not far from Young Young's home. Many of his schoolmates also go to school by bicycle. There is a parking lot reserved for bicycles at his school.

The classes begin at 8 A.M. Some schools require their students to arrive at school before 7:30, to allow an extra half-hour for individual study time. Young Young's school has cancelled this regulation to allow students to have more sleep. There are four classes in the morning. Large amounts of information will be presented as efficiently as possible. Students must concentrate well and quickly take notes so as not to miss any important information. There is a 10-minute break after every 50-minute class period. Between the second and third class periods, many Chinese elementary schools and high schools have meeting times, when teachers and students assemble in the playground, do exercises, and listen to announcements.

Lunch begins at 12 P.M. Students are free to eat either in the school cafeteria or at home, whichever is more convenient. In general, the cafeteria is cleaner, tidier, and less expensive than off-campus restaurants. Young Young has his lunch in the school cafeteria.

Lunchtime will last for one and a half hours. Students may take a nap or have some leisure activities, such as playing basketball or football, after their lunch. Classes resume at 1:30 P.M. Students have three more classes to take. After finishing all these classes, they finally are free to go home, but they have a lot of homework to do. With diligence and study, they can accomplish much. From the Chinese educator's point of view, more homework means more practice, and more practice means better performance. Some students will start to do their homework right after the end of the day's classes; others will have some leisure time first.

Young Young plays with his classmates for a little while before he starts to go home. He arrives home at 5:30 P.M. and has no leisure time after that except for a half-hour of cartoons or educational television programs. Young Young's mother will examine the homework and make sure he has mastered the day's lessons. Sometimes she will ask him to do extra exercises, such as practice calligraphy or practice spoken and written English. Although reluctant, Young Young will do what his parents ask. He understands that if he does not prepare himself well enough, he might not be able to get a good job and might not succeed. At 10:30 P.M., the day is over. Young Young goes to sleep. He works hard so he can pass the national entrance examination, which is his dream.

This is the typical daily life of most Chinese teenagers, although there are variations according to race, region, occupation, and season. The teenagers of Tibet, for example, might practice horseback riding or pray during their leisure time; the teenagers in rural areas might need to do farming; and the teenagers in vocational school might need to work in a hotel, a restaurant, or a factory for practical training. But in general, Young Young's daily life is quite common for Chinese high school students.

FAMILY LIFE

Most of the families in Mainland China are single-child families. The government of the People's Republic of China has been carrying out a birth control policy since 1978 that advocates that every married couple could have only one child. Most of the teenagers of this generation, as only children, have no idea about close relationships with other children. The "brothers" or "sisters" they mention mostly are their cousins or neighborhood children.

With only one child, the financial burden of rearing a family is greatly reduced. Chinese parents put much emphasis on children's education. Research indicates that children's educational expenditure occupies a large amount of the Chinese family's living expenses. Parents are willing to spend a great deal of money for their child to attend the best school in order to have an optimum educational environment. This would be difficult to do for more than one child.

Most Chinese families have double incomes. Both parents have full-time jobs and share household chores. It was quite different before 1949. For centuries, China was a feudal society in which women had no socioeconomic power and much less opportunity than men to be educated. Things have changed since the establishment of the People's Republic of China. Gender equity has been seriously considered. The rights of women are protected by laws. Women's socioeconomic status has improved substantially.

The trend of equal rights is reflected in the assignment of household chores. In an ordinary three-member Chinese family, the mother takes care of the cooking, the father deals with the grocery shopping and maintenance, and the child helps with the cleaning.

However, Chinese parents will assign only small household chores to their child. They prefer that the child focus on study and practice. Chinese teenagers, unlike American teenagers, do not have part-time jobs until they attend university. Sometimes they will take part in nonprofit community service activities under the direction of their school. The children are given full monetary support by their parents.

Chinese parents are strict with their children. They take good care of their children's daily needs and pay attention to their children's friends and reading matter. Although Chinese teenagers of this generation watch Japanese cartoons and American movies constantly, they still keep the traditional lifestyle. They are used to eating Chinese food, respect their elders, and work and rest regularly. On the other hand, they get special attention in the family because of their only child status. Parents are concerned about their children's thoughts and actions; they spend much time with them and patiently communicate with them.

The bicycle is the most convenient form of transportation for an ordinary Chinese family. It is usual to have more than one bicycle in a family. When children start high school, parents will buy them a bicycle if the school is within a reasonable distance of home. Children from wealthy families might have an expensive sports-style bicycle. Schools discourage parents from buying expensive bicycles for their children because it will cause unnecessary comparisons between students. Cars are not commonly used as transportation in Mainland China at present. Some parents who live in a big city drive their children to school. It is rare now but might be common within 10 years.

TRADITIONAL AND NONTRADITIONAL FOOD DISHES

Chinese food varies by region. For instance, rice is the most popular food in the south, while flour is the major food in the north. In addition, pork products are taboo in Islamic regions, and Buddhist families prohibit the consumption of all meats.

Aside from those extreme examples, generally speaking, most Chinese have similar dietary habits. The typical breakfast includes milk with bread, or vegetables with rice soup. Dinner is the most important meal since it is the time for the family to get together. During weekdays a household with three members is used to preparing three dishes of vegetables and meats and one pot of soup for dinner. For holidays, a dozen different foods may be served to celebrate the reunion with families and friends.

In a traditional family, the mother still plays a major role in the kitchen. However, there are an increasing number of fathers taking over the cooking. In big cities, a new profession has emerged: the personal chef. Some families may hire a professional cook paid at an hourly wage.

Most Chinese are used to shopping in a farmer's market because of the assortment of fresh and inexpensive food. By contrast, numerous young people, particularly the rich, single, white-collar groups, prefer either doing their grocery shopping in the modern supermarket or going out to eat with their friends.

Although a growing number of people are able to afford a luxurious meal at a romantic restaurant, many elders still enjoy spending plenty of time cooking. The types of Chinese cooking are so diversified that it is impossible to list each of them. Roughly speaking, Chinese food can be divided into major categories (regionalized, for example, as Szechwan, Canton, Hunan, and Shantung, among others). The history of these foods may be traced back hundreds or even thousands of years. For example, one of the famous Cantonese foods named "farewell my love" is associated with a well-known love story from two thousand years ago.

In addition, tea is a necessity in Chinese daily life. In a formal Chinese banquet, the first food offered is tea. Tea is more than a drink; it is an essential part of Chinese culture.

McDonald's and Kentucky Fried Chicken are very popular across the nation. With their smart marketing strategies, they have gained teenagers' loyalty. Japanese, Korean, and French food is also available. However, for most traditional Chinese, these foreign foods are served only to satisfy people's curiosity, not to replace Chinese food.

SCHOOLING

Traditionally, a high emphasis is placed on education in China. The government funds schools across all levels. A few private schools, known as noble schools, targeting rich families by offering an excellent learning environment have opened recently, but since these schools are not open to all, most students still stay in public schools. The structure of Chinese education includes elementary schools, junior high, senior high, and higher education (universities and vocational colleges). In public higher education, students are required to pay their tuition and living costs only. Most universities provide scholarships, student loans, and part-time job opportunities to alleviate students' economic pressure.

China implements nine-year compulsory education. Students are required to attend elementary and junior high schools but pay no tuition. In coastal regions and big cities, most students are able to enter into senior high and colleges. Nonetheless, some students in remote areas are

Chinese students in Tiananmen Square. Photo © Bryce Atwell/TRIP.

dropouts because either they cannot afford the learning materials or their family needs one more laborer at home. The mission of "Hope Engineering" is to raise funds to help these children stay in or return to the classroom.

Senior high schools, categorized into point schools and nonpoint schools, vary in terms of quantity and quality. Going to a point school almost guarantees that students will pass the college entrance exam, while students from nonpoint schools do not tend to perform well on the exam. Only those students who earn a high grade point average are able to register in point schools. To send their children to point schools, a number of parents are willing to pay large sponsor fees to the schools if their children do not meet the academic requirements. Indeed, Chinese parents devote themselves to their children's education without any hesitation. They will put up with a hard living in exchange for a better educational opportunity for their children.

On the other hand, China also places increasing emphasis on special education. China has had schools for deaf children and children with other handicaps for a long time. But now there is an increasing argument about whether disabled children should be separated from normal children. Many people believe that disabled children should be assigned to the normal classroom in order to gradually reinforce their ability to live in the real world.

The teaching model in Chinese classrooms centers on traditional lecturing, although in the past decade, more and more schools have begun to value the development of students' problem-solving skills, imagination, and creativity. Each school has strict teaching plans and teaching evaluations. The competition among students is intense. Each student's academic ranking is regularly issued at the school. Moreover, there is also the rank among schools based on students' academic achievement, which affect the school's enrollment, reputation, and revenues, as well as the quality of new students.

Chinese students take numerous exams. The most challenging exams are the entrance exams for senior high schools and colleges. The result of the senior high entrance exam determines which students are able to register in point schools. Years later, if students perform well on college entrance exams, they can choose a college and major. In Chinese society, vocational schools are considered to be the last choice; thus, only those students who fail the exams will study in vocational schools. For most undergraduates, the four-year college life still involves much study. They may prepare themselves for the tests of graduate schools and doctoral programs:

TOEFL and GRE tests. Consequently, studying at a better school means gaining access to a higher income and social status in the future.

SOCIAL LIFE

Chinese schools are coeducational. Teenagers have many chances to make friends. They are eager to chat on the Internet, but schools and parents do not support this interest in the Internet, and parents tell their children that spending time chatting on the Internet takes time away from the more serious pursuit of school studies. Under strict supervision, the social life of pupils and teens is relatively simple. Parents know their children's friends well. If children want to go out, they have to ask their parents' permission first. Most children look forward to the coming of summer vacation since they can participate in summer camps, go out with parents, or exercise with friends. Throughout the school days, schools offer diverse "interest groups" that are very similar to the American schools extracurricular activities, but children are not allowed to spend too much time on these activities since their major task is study. In vocational schools and colleges, the young possess more freedom to make friends. They can meet friends at parties, on the Internet, or on trips. They also develop their organizing as well as socializing abilities through participation in extracurricular activities.

Unlike pupils and teens, college students can decide what to wear. Most teen clothing is very Americanized. They prefer T-shirts, jeans, and sneakers but wear suits in more formal situations. As a matter of fact, Chinese clothing in big cities is similar to that in other international cities. Some individuals may wear clothing that is too bold, leading to critiques from elders and conservatives. It should be noted that just a century ago, women who showed their arms were perceived as unethical. The recent revolution has changed people's perception and attitude. Today's China is more open to new ideas; therefore, people have learned to tolerate the younger generation's clothing styles.

Many schools require students to wear uniforms. Unsurprisingly, the teens are interested in stylish clothing only. Movie stars are the teens' role models. They imitate the clothing, behavior, and speech of their favorite superstars. In addition, the discussion and interaction among peers strengthens their enthusiasm about fashion.

Ten years ago, those pupils and teens with girlfriends or boyfriends would get in trouble and encounter strong critiques from teachers. Teachers would do whatever they could to prevent children from falling in love at an early age. Possible approaches included asking for parents' intervention, evoking the whole school's critiques, and even making the student drop out. From a traditional Chinese standpoint, a naive child would become unethical if he or she fell in love. Today's teens are much luckier than their predecessors, though. Once a student falls in love, teachers remind the student to continue studying so as not to impede his or her future, but they do not try to end the relationship.

College students have close girlfriends and boyfriends, and living together has become common. Although a number of people no longer emphasize virginity, overtly sexual behaviors certainly bring about some social problems. This issue is the primary concern of sociologists and educators. When it comes to marriage, though, young lovers will ask for their parents' permission because marriage is a highly important decision in Chinese society. Most Chinese look forward to a stable marriage since for most of them divorce is too painful to bear.

RECREATION

Chinese teenagers like sports. Since the successful bid by Beijing to host the 2008 Olympics, their passion for sports has risen even further. Except for students training to be athletes, students in general do not have much time to exercise; they spend their time on study. However, they will make time for exercising and enjoy the fun of sports.

All elementary schools, middle schools, high schools, and colleges in China have three- or four-day sports meetings every year. Potential athletes will be found in these meetings and trained to participate in more professional games. The sports meetings are held every year to encourage students to exercise and to cultivate sportsmanship. Colleges have teams for all different kinds of sports, such as football, basketball, volleyball, Ping-Pong, and badminton. Middle schools may have only one or two types of teams because for middle school students, studying is more important than participating in sports. However, students with the talent to become professional athletes have more of a chance to go to better schools or get better jobs than other students.

Boys like to join soccer and basketball teams. Basketball is very popular in China; many schools have basketball courts and students can borrow basketballs to play. Soccer fields require more space; therefore it is harder to have a standard soccer field. Except colleges and several special middle schools, most schools do not have a soccer field. Teens play in any vacant lot they can find. Because of the lack of a professional coach and support, teens play soccer only for fun; they will not choose soccer as their career.

Not many girls play soccer, but the Chinese girl soccer teams are the best in the world. Girls like to play volleyball, badminton, and Ping-Pong.

Nowadays girls are not restricted to only certain kinds of sports. There is no girls-only or boys-only sport. Boys and girls often play basketball or other games together.

Heavily promoted in the media, skateboarding has become a popular sport lately. Both boys and girls like skateboarding; on the street, you can see many teenagers skateboarding. In contrast, kung fu is a traditional Chinese way of exercising. Young people are interested in kung fu because they like kung fu films. There are different types of kung fu; all are good for health and self-protection. Tai chi, traditional Chinese shadow boxing, is also popular, although among elders more than teens.

Many Chinese teenagers are fans of sports stars such as Michael Jordan or various Chinese sports stars. They will wait for hours outside the gym to see their idols. As in Western countries, in China sports stars are widely admired. Every four years, when Olympic champions return to China, they are treated as heroes and receive a hearty welcome from the whole nation. The leading gymnast Lee, who won three gold medals at the Summer Olympics in Los Angeles, is a hero to many young people.

For most young people in China, sports are an important part of life. Playing sports is a good way of relaxing, is good for their health, and is a good way of making friends.

ENTERTAINMENT

The MP3 music format that condenses music files, making them quicker to download, is very popular with Chinese teenagers who search the Internet for music. They can download music from the Internet and edit it by themselves. Most teenagers like popular songs; some like classical music. Songs from Hong Kong and Taiwan are popular among teens, but only older people listen to traditional Chinese songs. Teenagers like to dress like their favorite singers and are interested in their personal lives. They also collect stars' photos and signatures.

Teenagers also like to go to the dance hall, bar, and KTV (karaoke), but it is illegal for middle school students to go to these places because sometimes there are illegal sexual activities or drugs. Most Chinese teenagers do not do drugs because it is very dangerous and drugs can ruin their lives. Also, drugs are so expensive in China that ordinary people cannot afford them.

The teahouse is the other place where young people like to spend their leisure time. They can have a cup of tea with friends and play chess, play cards, or just talk. Young people who are in love especially like to go to teahouses because they are romantic.

Young people spend a lot of time watching television, especially kung fu films and Japanese and Korean soap operas. Most soap operas are about love stories. Some teenagers also like to watch the Discovery Channel. Middle school students like cartoons and mysteries. Most popular cartoons and mysteries come from Japan. Shops sell magazines, stickers, and toys associated with the popular cartoons.

Internet cafes, places where people can get access to the Internet for a relatively reasonable hourly fee, have become more and more popular. People who do not have a computer at home can come to these places to play computer games, send and receive e-mails, and chat with people online. However, parents and teachers worry about children spending too much time in Internet cafes; they also worry that children may have access to Web sites that contain inappropriate content. The government is making laws to take control of Internet cafes to avoid these problems. Generally speaking, parents and teachers are very strict with children; they do not allow children to go to these places.

RELIGIOUS PRACTICES AND CULTURAL CEREMONIES

The People's Republic of China is led by the Communist Party, which believes in Marxism and the principles of Mao. Communists are atheists; they believe in science. The government does respect different religions and cultures, however.

Many Chinese young people do not practice a religion. This is because they receive atheistic education from a very young age. Schools do not offer courses related to religion, so young people are not familiar with religion. There are many temples in China; most are Buddhist or Taoist. There are also churches in some big cities. But young people mostly go to those places for tours, not for religious reasons. Most of the nation's religious people are elders.

Different from Buddhism, Islam, Catholicism, and Christianity, Taoism is a local religion that originated in China. Taoism, created by Lao Tzu 2,500 years ago, has unique rites and thoughts, the most famous of which are the tai-chi and the Eight Diagrams. Tai chi, or shadow boxing, is the most recognized Chinese martial art. Baguazhang, or the Eight Diagrams, consists of spiral movements with sophisticated footwork and fighting angles used for both health and combat purposes.

Confucianism has more influence on Chinese culture than any other religion. Since the Han Dynasty (2,000 years ago), Confucianism has dominated Chinese culture. Confucius, the greatest thinker in Chinese history, founded Confucianism in about 500 B.C.E. He was deified after his death. Many temples, especially in his hometown of Shantung, were built to memorialize him and his thoughts, which have deeply influenced how Chinese people think and interact with others. Confucianism was the major influence in the country until 1949.

CONCLUSION

China is a very big country, and people in different parts of the country have different lifestyles. This chapter discusses the typical lifestyle of young people in big cities. Young people who live in villages have different lifestyles. They may have to help their parents with farming, they may not know much about the Internet, and they may not receive as much education as young people in cities.

Some tribes living on the borderland also have a very different lifestyle. For example, Mongol people ride on horses, the most popular sport for them is wrestling, and the most popular music for them is bucolic songs. There are 56 different tribes in China, and all of them have different lifestyles. These different ways of life and different ways of thinking enrich Chinese culture and will be passed on from generation to generation.

RESOURCE GUIDE

Nonfiction

CCTV. (1999). *The report on the China's urbanism*. Beijing, China: Chinese Statistic Publishing House.

Gunde, R. (2001). *Culture and customs of China*. Westport, CT: Greenwood Press.

Harper, D. (2002). *Lonely planet China*. 8th ed. Berkeley, CA: Lonely Planet.

Jie, Z. (2000). A perspective on the generation for cool. *China News Weekly*, 10. Retrieved from http://www.chinanews.com.cn/xinwenzhoukan/2000-10/new/(10)%201.html

Lieping, B. (2000). *The thinking on the virtual community with youth*. Paper presented at the meeting of the 5th International Symposium on Asian Youth Studies, Macao, China.

Lieping, B. (2002). Social stress and personal resilience in Shanghai sociey: A cross-section study. In Y. Juzhuo (Ed.), *The 2002 report on Shanghai society*. Shanghai, China: SASS Press.

Mead, M. (1978). *Culture and commitment*. New York: Columbia University Press.

Polo, M., & Latham, R. (Eds.). (1958). *The travels of Marco Polo*. London: Penguin Books.

Shuyan, S. (1999). *China readings*. Shengyang, China: Liaoning Education Publishing House.

Snow, E. R. (1968). *Red star over China*. New York: Grove/Atlantic.

Spence, J. D. (2000). *The search for modern China*. 2nd ed. NY: W.W. Norton & Co.

Weiner, R., Murphy, M., & Li, A. (1997). *Living in China: A guide to teaching and studying in China including Taiwan and Hong Kong*. CA: China Books & Periodicals.

Fiction

Buck, P. (1999). *The Good Earth*. New York: Washington Square Press.

Cheng'en, W. & Jenner, W. J. F. (2001). *Journey to the west*. Columbus, OH: Foreign Language Press.

Henshui, Z. (2000). *Romance of tears and smiles*. China: Tsai Fong Books.

Jin, B. (1992). *Family*. Williston, VT: Cheng & Tsui.

JingZi, W. (2000). *The scholars*. New York: Morningside Books, Columbia University Press.

Kuan-Chung, L., & Brewitt-Taylor, C. H. (Trans.). (2003). *Three kingdoms*. Boston: Charles E. Tuttle.

Nai'an, S., & LuoGuanzhong, L. (1987). *Outlaws of the marsh*. New York: Harper Collins.

Qian, Z. S. (1998). *Wei Cheng [Fortress Besieged]*. China: Shu Lin.

She, L. (2001). *Camel Xiangzi*. China: Tsai Fong Books.

Songling, P. (1982). *Selected tales of Liauzhai*. San Francisco, CA: China Books & Periodicals.

Xingjian, G. (2001). *Soul mountain*. New York: Perennial.

Xueqin, C. (2001). *A dream of red mansions*. New York: Acacia Press.

Yong, J. (1999). *Shediao yingxiong zhuan (The eagle-shooting heroes)*. China: Tsai Fong Books.

Web Sites

Government

http://www.china.org.cn/english/index.htm
http://www.online.sh.cn
Ministry of Foreign Affairs: http://www.fmprc.gov.cn/e/eframe.htm
Ministry of Foreign Trade and Economics: http://www.moftec.gov.cn/Cooperation

Youth

http://www.chinakids.net
http://www.cycnet.com/chinayouth/index.htm

News and Media

China Daily: http://www.chinadaily.com.cn/
China Internet Information Center: http://www.china.org.cn/

China Radio International: http://www.cri.com.cn/english/
Shanghai Daily: http://www.shanghaidaily.com.cn/
South China Morning Post: http://www.scmp.com
Xinhua News Agency: http://202.84.17.11/en/index.htm

Business

http://www.china-guide.com/
China Light Industry Information: http://www.clii.com.cn/clii-en/index.htm
Economic and Technological Development Zones: http://www.sezo.gov.cn/
    kfqwye.htm

Education

Chinese Academy of Social Sciences: http://www.cass.net.cn
Fudan University: http://www.fudan.edu.cn/English/ieindex.html
Nangjing University: http://www.nju.edu.cn
Peking University: http://www.pku.edu.cn/
Shanghai Academy of Social Sciences: http://www.sass.stc.sh.cn
Tsinghua University: http://tsinghua.edu.cn/
Zhejiang University: http://www.zju.edu.cn

Travel

China International Travel Service: http://www.bta.net.cn/travel.cn/tguolu.htm
China Travel Service: http://www.ctsho.com

Other

Chinese Culture: http://english.ccnt.com.cn
Chinese Film World: http://www.lnlib.com
International Channel of Tanfo Online: http://int.sc.cninfo.net
Map of China: http://www.go2map.com/
National Library of China: http://www.nlc.gov.cn
Near China: http://www1.nearchina.com

More Information

Embassy of the People's Republic of China

Yang Jie, Ambassador
2300 Connecticut Avenue NW
Washington, DC 20008
Web site: http://www.china-embassy.org

E-mail: webmaster@china-embassy.org
Telephone: (202) 328–2500, (202) 328–2551
Fax: (202) 328–2582

Pen Pal/Chat

http://www.0-100.com.cn/h/fudan/yjlb/bysq.htm
http://www.cyol.net

Chapter 3

HONG KONG

Tai-lok Lui

INTRODUCTION

Hong Kong is one of the leading global cities in the world. It is widely
seen as an example of an economic miracle in Asia in the postwar
decades. It has a total area of just under 1,100 square kilometers but a population of around 6.7 million. Formerly a British colony, it was returned to
China on July 1, 1997, bringing an end to some 150 years of colonial rule.
In the postwar decades, Hong Kong has quickly developed from an entre-
pôt (an intermediary commerce center) into an industrial city in the
1960s, and then into a financial center in East Asia since the 1970s. Its
economic success is well documented. Joining Singapore, Taiwan, and
South Korea, Hong Kong is one of the so-called Four Little Dragons in the
region. As a regional center of global financial and commercial activities,
its outlook is affluent and cosmopolitan.

The process of political transition as a result of the Sino-British Nego-
tiations of Hong Kong's future in the early 1980s has been one of the most
significant social and political changes in the past two decades. Equally
important are the process of economic restructuring (including the massive relocation of manufacturing production to Mainland China and a
changing socioeconomic structure largely shaped by a growing service
economy) and the collapse of the "bubble economy" built upon property
and stock speculations since late 1997. Such economic changes have
drastically altered the economic confidence of and career prospects for the
younger generation. Unlike their parents, who were brought up in the
more difficult days of the early postwar period but were able to take advantage of the rapid economic growth since the 1970s, today's Hong Kong

teenagers have to face the prospects of youth unemployment and an extended, and painful, process of social as well as economic reengineering. The economic security once enjoyed by their parents is gone. Teenagers encounter an environment of uncertainty that their parents have long forgotten.

TYPICAL DAY

A typical day for most teenagers in Hong Kong depends on whether they are students or young workers. The former follow the school schedule: attending a full day of school with about an hour's break for lunch, doing homework at home, and watching TV for entertainment. The latter have a longer day. As most of them are engaged in work in the service sector, they are likely to work from noon until the late evening. To some extent, one may say that they follow the daily schedules of other teenagers raised in highly urbanized areas. There is no morning ritual to follow. Nor do they have rest breaks in the afternoons. Hong Kong residents, including teenagers, are expected to move and work intensively. A typical day is fast-paced and hectic.

FAMILY LIFE

Most of the teenagers in Hong Kong are unmarried and are likely to be living with their parents. In 1996, 99.2 percent and 98.3 percent of men and women between the ages of 15 and 19, respectively, had never been married.[1] Almost 80 percent of them lived with their nuclear families. In the same year, the median ages at marriage for men and women were 31.2 and 29.1, respectively, indicating that Hong Kong residents are delaying marriage. It also suggests that, mainly because of the shortage as well as the high cost of housing, most teenagers in Hong Kong will live with their parents and siblings for some time.

Most Hong Kong teenagers' parents work full-time outside the home. With the average household size at 3.3 persons in 1996, they are likely to be living in small families. In 1996, about 60 percent of all households had no children under the age of 15. Moreover, about 20 percent of households had one child. With most adults having fewer children, teenagers are likely to benefit from the resources that their parents can afford to give them. Unlike teenagers of the earlier generation, who had a larger number of siblings, they do not need to worry about the thinning of household resources as a result of sharing with their brothers and sisters. How affluence is spoiling the younger generation—say, the decline of the spirit of sharing and group solidarity—has been a regular topic of discussion in the local media.

How affluent the young people in Hong Kong actually are remains debatable. But most observers would agree that, as a result of the reduction of the number of children born to local families, parents in Hong Kong today are prepared to spend more money on their children or to allow their children to purchase things (e.g., brand-name fashions) that previously would have been categorized as luxury items.

On the other hand, the teenagers are often perceived as the bearers of the hopes of their parents. Investments in children, particularly in terms of cultural capital (e.g., music lessons, ballet classes, and summer schools abroad), have become popular topics of discussion and a growing area of business. Both because of a cultural emphasis on education and the fear of dim economic prospects triggered by the Asian financial crisis, how to prepare the children for a more competitive world has been a concern of Hong Kong parents, particularly those of the middle class. Despite the fact that most parents work full-time outside the home, the teenagers are likely to find their lives rather closely programmed and monitored. That is, they are likely to find that they have been scheduled for different kinds of classes (from English classes to art lessons) in their after-school and weekend hours.

So far, there is no single study that is rigorous enough to allow us to probe the social values and inner feelings of the teenagers in relation to various domains of social life in Hong Kong. A study of young people's values, based upon telephone interviews with 573 persons ages 15 to 39, carried out by the Hong Kong Federation of Youth Groups in 1998, suggests that the younger generation still espouse strong family values.[2] The majority (i.e., over 90%) of the respondents agreed that they would get married, said that they would give birth to children, and found the idea of having brothers and sisters desirable. A significant portion (around 80%) of the respondents agreed that relationships with family members are more important than relationships with others and disagreed that the idea of children financially supporting their parents is obsolete. Also, almost half of them said that they would continue to live with their parents after marriage. These findings suggest that in contemporary Hong Kong, family and family values are far from falling apart. However, that said, it should be noted that the aforementioned survey also shows that some of the more traditional concepts—for example, the idea that filial piety is important and that divorce is absolutely undesirable—are starting to be questioned.

Generally speaking, there are signs of a change in family relations and family values. Teenagers do not comply simply on the grounds of tradition and traditional authority. Yet such changes should not be overstated. On the one hand, parents largely retain their authority within the family (parents' expectations of their children, whether in terms of educational attainment or moving ahead, continue to be the major source of pressure on teenagers). On the other hand, the status of the children has been significantly improved. This, however, does not necessarily reflect a liberalization of family values. The assumption that economic development, modernization, and growing affluence would change domestic life is only partially right. While it is quite true that more and more parents subscribe to the ideal image of "liberal parents," we have also regularly heard of teenagers complaining about being subordinated to the larger, and often grander, career development schemes imposed by their parents. Indeed, parent-child relations remain a constant source of tension and conflict. Cultural influence imported from abroad may expose both parents and teenagers to different patterns of family relations and family life. But, as mentioned above, such influence has a limited impact on the more basic family values. Perhaps the enhancement of children's status and bargaining power has more to do with the reduction of the number of children born to local families. Nowadays, children have come to be the focus of the family's attention. Though, of course, they cannot simply get everything they want, compared with teenagers of earlier cohorts, they are more likely to find their wants satisfied. At least their parents are more prepared to satisfy their children's material needs.

TRADITIONAL AND NONTRADITIONAL FOOD DISHES

Teenagers in Hong Kong eat fast food regularly, with 24 percent of the respondents to a survey eating fast food at least once a day.[3] The popularity of fast food among the younger generation reflects two issues. First, Hong Kong people in general have a rather open attitude toward food. They eat whatever they believe is delicious. So, Hong Kong has all kinds of restaurants, literally serving any food that one can imagine. It is quite common to find Chinese restaurants lining up side by side with Sushi bars, American cafes, and restaurants serving Italian pizza. Furthermore, Hong Kong residents are very practical about food. Many local dishes are actually indigenized Western or Asian food. Even Chinese food, which itself is very diversified according to origins from different provinces, is often blended—modified to suit the more southern tastes of the Hong Kong people. Although Chinese dishes remain very popular, they are hardly hegemonic. The food culture of Hong Kong itself is diverse. Teenagers are generally the targets of fast food chains' marketing campaigns. They are receptive to hamburgers, pizzas, and fried chicken. But they also show little resistance to Chinese, Japanese, Thai, Vietnamese, and broadly Western food in fast food format. Local fast food chains have begun serving Chinese dishes in fast food packages, with great success. Teenagers fond of fast food do not necessarily prefer Western food to local Chinese dishes.

It is also important to note that most students attending full-day schools buy their lunch from their school canteens or take-out services nearby rather than packing their own lunch. Some eat out in fast food chains or local lower-end restaurants. Eating fast food is an important part of the food culture for both teenagers and working adults. In response to a trend toward more frequent heart attacks among teenagers and young adults, there have been educational programs alerting young people to the health implications of their frequent consumption of fast food and the importance of a balanced diet. However, so far, this advice has not been taken very seriously and there are few signs that young people are becoming more aware of problems associated with their eating habits.

SCHOOLING

Since the introduction of free compulsory primary education (six years) in 1971 and compulsory lower secondary school education (three years) in 1978, school attendance rates for children under the age of 16 have been close to 100 percent. The mainstream educational channel for the teenagers includes three curricula: grammar, technical, and prevocational. These curricula are offered in five-year secondary courses leading to a public examination to be held at the end of the fifth year of secondary school education. Then, there is a two-year sixth-form course preparing the students for entrance to local colleges and universities. In 2000, enrollment in secondary schools offering the three types of curriculum stated above totaled about 456,000 students.

The government's initiatives in increasing educational opportunities for all schoolchildren are widely regarded as helping to equalize opportunities and the possibility of social mobility. Girls as well as poor children have significantly improved their chances of attaining higher education since the 1970s. However, while most schoolchildren (almost 90%) will have the opportunity to pursue studies at the senior forms (i.e., the fourth and fifth years) of secondary school, only about one-third of the teenagers in the appropriate age group are able to find spots for themselves in high school (i.e., the sixth and seventh forms in secondary school before entering university). Despite the expansion of educational opportunities, especially at primary and the lower levels of secondary education, education in

Hong Kong remains highly competitive at all levels. Competition starts from the kindergarten level, especially for the more privileged. Then, entrance to Primary One (lower elementary level) is widely perceived as another major hurdle for securing school places in local schools with good reputations. The competition continues at other levels. At present, about 18 percent of those aged 17 to 20 can proceed to local institutions of higher education. There are eight higher educational institutions funded by the government, offering almost 15,000 places for first-year first-degree courses.

Teenagers are expected to encounter a major transition between ages 17 and 19. The fortunate few will continue their studies and move on to university education. More of them, however, must find jobs in the labor market. So, there are two different patterns of life for a typical teenager in Hong Kong. First, many teenagers stay in school. Their school life is primarily shaped by the requirements of the public examinations for moving up to senior forms of high school and for entering university. Academic results in these public examinations determine how far these young students go in the institutionalized academic track. Because of this emphasis on attaining good results in open examinations, quite a significant number of secondary school students attend courses and classes offered by prep schools after formal school sessions. Private tutoring is not uncommon. Whenever and however possible, parents try to find the means to ensure that their children can perform well in these open examinations. Every year in the examination season, the atmosphere is tense and nervous. Parents' emphasis on success in examinations has come to constitute a major source (if not *the* source) of pressure on their children. Without overstating the extent of suicide among schoolchildren, there are regular news stories of examinees making suicide attempts before or after taking their examinations. In recent years, even the government called for a reduction of examination pressure (as part of its larger program of educational reform).

Schooling in Hong Kong is known for its emphasis on reciting text materials and on examination. To some extent, it is not an exaggeration to say that the schooling process is mainly driven by the examination system. Efforts have been made by local schools and the government to change the school organization and the curriculum for the purpose of enhancing the creativity of the students. Indeed, it is the government that has suggested that in order to enhance Hong Kong's economic competitiveness, there must be a change in the direction of local education. In view of the need for developing human resources to meet the challenge of the knowledge-based economy, it is suggested that more emphasis be given to creativity. So far more has been said than done. The call for a freer and more creative classroom is more rhetorical than real. Because of the economic downturn and the government's commitment to streamlining the bureaucratic structure of publicly funded organizations, schools in Hong Kong still find themselves short of the resources they need. Most of the subsidized schools are still running their classes with a high student-teacher ratio. Having a teacher lecturing in front of some 40 or more students in a classroom is by no means uncommon. The deplorable student-teacher ratio is a major hurdle to the creation of lively classroom interactions and activity-based teaching. Interactive teaching and learning cannot happen in such school settings.

Increasingly, parents and students, particularly those who can afford to do so, are thinking of exiting from the local schooling system. Some parents choose to send their children to international schools—schools originally targeted at expatriate families in Hong Kong. Others send their children abroad after they have finished three to five years of secondary school education in local schools. This is a popular educational strategy for schoolchildren coming from middle-class families. The number of applications for student visas to Britain has increased from around 13,000 cases in 1997–1998 to about 15,000 cases in 1999–2000. The number of students studying abroad is expected to continue to rise. This strategy is believed to give the children quality and a less examination-oriented education. But it must be pointed out that these are expensive options. Given their financial constraints, most local parents and teenagers, often reluctantly, have to stay in the competitive local school system and be prepared for the open examinations.

Quite a significant number of teens start to work after realizing that they cannot go any further in formal channels of schooling. In 1996, about 110,000 young people (less than one-fourth of the population in this age group) ages 15 to 19 were economically active. They formed less than 4 percent of the total labor force. Most of these teenage workers take up jobs in the service sector, namely the industries of (following the official classifications in Hong Kong) "wholesale, retail and import/export trades, restaurants and hotels" and "community, social and personal services." They are relatively less likely to be found in "financing, insurance, real estate and business services." In terms of occupation, most of them worked as "service workers and shop sales workers" and "clerks." Only 1,870 of these young people were self-employed. The great majority of them worked as employees. Given their lack of working experience and formal qualifications, these teenage workers, compared with adult workers working in the same sector and/or in comparable jobs, are paid less and are likely to be found engaging in so-called McJobs (low-pay, dead-end jobs in the lower tiers of the service sector).

More critically, recent years have witnessed a trend of rising youth unemployment. In 1996 the unemployment rate for youth workers aged 15 to 19 was 12.5 percent. It rose to 26.9 percent in 1999. The economic downturn since late 1997 has, no doubt, further restricted the opportunities for teenage workers to secure employment once out of school. Indeed, problems like the increase in the number of young working poor and the rise of youth unemployment are becoming alarming. Many teenage workers have to work long hours to make a living. Furthermore, their jobs offer them limited career prospects.

These problems of youth employment reveal the tensions and contradictions emerging in Hong Kong in its transition to a service economy. Previously, the manufacturing sector provided relatively less educated young people with employment opportunities and a reasonably stable working life. The growth of small businesses also encouraged the young workers, suggesting that they could rely on diligence and entrepreneurship to help them climb the social ladder. The hopes of becoming one's own boss had for many years provided young workers who lacked the credentials for managerial and professional careers with the prospects of higher personal achievement. While credentials mattered, there were still other channels for mobility for those who were not strong academically. Those were the days. The shift to services does not open a lot of new opportunities for those who leave school as teenagers. Most of them work in low-paid service jobs rather than in jobs that would lead to gradual promotions and higher income. In other words, they are likely to find themselves working in jobs that lead nowhere. The deepening of the economic restructuring process will further widen the gap between well educated and less educated young people.

SOCIAL LIFE

Living in a global city, different generations of teenagers in Hong Kong have long been exposed to cultural influences from different parts of the world. Hong Kong was a British colony before its return to China in 1997, so British culture is quite prevalent. Yet the British cultural influence has not been dominant in the sense that the locals, perhaps with a few exceptions among the elites in the upper hierarchy of Hong Kong society, proudly espouse British colonial symbols (say, the royal family) and culture. This partly reflects some subtle resistance to colonial superiority by the people, 98 percent of them Chinese, in Hong Kong.

Competing with British cultural influences have been those of other countries. American culture has shaped youth culture in Hong Kong since the early postwar years. Hollywood movies and rock music were well received by the postwar baby boomers. Also, Japanese culture has quietly built up its influence in Hong Kong. Japanese movies and TV programs have been popular since the 1960s, the same decade that the first Japanese department store in Hong Kong was established. Chinese versions of Japanese comics had been published locally around the same period. Then in the late 1970s and the early 1980s, reflecting the rise of the Japanese economy in the world economic order, Japanese pop culture and consumption culture displaced earlier American and British dominance. So, long before PlayStation and Pokemon, Japanese pop culture had a presence in Hong Kong. Icons of Japanese pop culture can be found literally everywhere in Hong Kong, from the fashion columns of local youth magazines to the wide (partially underground, partially public) circulation of pirated DVDs of Japanese TV dramas to the posters of Japanese idols on students' message boards.

However, despite such exposure to the cultural influences from Japan, the United States, Britain, and many other countries, teenagers in Hong Kong retain strong ties to their local popular culture. Popular culture with a strong Hong Kong identity and style emerged in the 1970s. Its emergence went hand in hand with the growth of the postwar baby boomers, reflecting a desire to search for a local identity among the young people of a generation that grew up Chinese in a colonial setting. While their parents were migrants from Mainland China and saw Hong Kong as a lifeboat in the sea of political turmoil in the early postwar years, the baby boomers who grew up in Hong Kong rather than in China had a very different perception of their society. They were alienated both from the British colonial culture and from the Mainland Chinese culture and politics. A local culture developed out of this gap and grew rapidly with the proliferation of TV sets in local households and the rise of youth culture since the late 1960s and early 1970s. Phenomenal economic growth and the resultant material affluence in the 1970s further facilitated a sense of belonging to Hong Kong among the younger generation. In the 1970s there was drastic growth of local cultural production in local TV stations, the film industry, and the music industry. Now people from different parts of the world are no strangers to pop culture with a strong Hong Kong flavor. Indeed, Hong Kong pop culture has become a cultural product for export. It makes its presence in the United States, Britain, and Europe. It is influential in Asia in general, and particularly in Mainland China. Despite language (more precisely, dialect) barriers, Hong Kong pop culture (from gangster movies and comedies to Cantonese pop songs to comic books) is not only a profitable export item but also a powerful public relations tool, projecting Hong Kong's image to the wider world.

Hong Kong is a rather open society on matters related to teenagers' social life. Teenagers are largely free to choose their own religion or be an atheist. Co-education in most secondary schools means that young boys and girls have lots of opportunities to make friends with the opposite sex. This is, of course, not to say that Hong Kong is a permissive society. Premarital sex among teenagers is still a topic of heated public discussion and a source of moral panic. Students are still expected to concentrate on their academic studies and not to start dating when they are still in secondary school. However, there is no formal code of conduct or more institutional practice to deter young people from developing friendships with the opposite sex.

There is no reliable source of statistical data on young people's sexual behavior. Both overreporting and underreporting are expected in studies by concerned groups and services organizations. The popular perception is that the younger generation is getting more casual about sex. But how sexually liberated the young people are remains unknown. While it may be true that they are more exposed to sex in the mass media than the earlier cohorts, there are few signs indicating a more open and liberal attitude toward sex. Sex education has gradually been introduced in schools, yet many teenagers continue to whisper when they talk about premarital sex or homosexuality.

Before concluding our discussion of teenagers' social life, it should be pointed out that despite the stereotyped image of Hong Kong's teenagers as affluent, spoiled, and carefree, many of them do take an active part in volunteer work. More than 100,000 young people participate in the uniform groups like the Boy Scouts and the Red Cross. Youth service centers had a membership of more than 130,000 teenagers (aged 10–19) in 1994.[4] Many more have participated in various kinds of volunteer work and social services, in varying degree and depth, through school-based activities. Any one-sided picture of the Hong Kong youth would be misleading.

RECREATION

Compared with teens from Australia, India, Japan, Korea, Malaysia, and other countries along the Pacific, teens from Hong Kong are the least brand-conscious. According to a survey, only 17 percent of them (compared to 84% in India and 42% in Japan) believe that owning designer brands is very important or quite important.[5] This finding has been interpreted in rather different ways. On the one side, it is suggested that young people in Hong Kong are becoming less brand-conscious because of their affluence—that their ability to buy brand-name products and to spend a lot reduces their interest in brand names. The survey suggests that young people in Hong Kong have an average amount of H.K. $14,999 (about U.S. $1,925) a year as their pocket and gift money.

Some suggest that the notion of designer brands is vague and may have been inconsistently interpreted among young respondents from different countries in the Pacific. Hong Kong respondents' familiarity with lower- and middle-market brands may have led them to assume that they were being asked about their attitudes towards the top and very expensive designer brands not targeted at their age group. So, their response does not necessarily imply a low level of brand consciousness. Indeed, a short tour to shopping malls for young consumers in Hong Kong is enough to show that the daily life of the young people has been saturated with brands. There are too many rather than too few brands. This brand saturation phenomenon leads to one plausible explanation that, although hit items from certain designers may still create a fashion trend or attract a lot of young followers, young consumers are increasingly moving away from designer brands. The popularity of the so-called retro style does point to the new development that young consumers are becoming more demanding—that their fashion sense and preferences are more finely tuned. Brand names and fashions are not dead. They are still alive. But mass fashion is dead. No fashion lasts long enough to command the same following as one found in the 1970s and 1980s. Hong Kong's young people have not abandoned brand names, but they change their styles more frequently.

Also, it is important to note that their consumption is no longer confined to young fashions, pop music, and trendy accessories. For one thing, Hong Kong teens are becoming more body conscious. A survey of 4,765 girls between the ages of 11 and 20 suggests that, although schoolgirls in Hong Kong are relatively slim compared to their Western counterparts, many of them (almost 65% of all respondents) still want to lose weight and the majority of them (more than 80%) are concerned about their weight and shape.[6] Those in their late teens are more likely than the younger girls to worry about the shape of their bodies. No doubt, they are becoming the targets of various commercial products that promise to help them lose weight and enhance their figure. Nevertheless, at present, it is still relatively rare for teenage girls to use substances like laxatives to lose weight. That said, it should be noted that survey findings tell us that young girls will do extra exercise or put themselves on a diet in order to keep their bodies slim.

The other popular (probably most desired) consumption item is the mobile phone. The aforementioned survey suggests that 54 percent of young people between the ages of 16 and 18 own a mobile phone, and most respondents expected to own one by the age of 19.[7] Mobile phones are quickly becoming the most important and significant status symbol among teenagers. For teenagers, the mobile phones are a fashion statement. For their parents, who must purchase mobile phones for teens younger than age 18, the mobile phone is a means to maintain close contact with their children—at least, they can locate and reach their children while the parents are away from home for work or other pursuits.

But more drastic changes in teenagers' leisure life are found in their cross-border adventures on weekends and public holidays. In Hong Kong, it takes around an hour to travel by train or coach to reach Shenzhen Special Economic Zone in China. As a result of further economic reform and liberalization in China, Shenzhen is becoming one of the most popular destinations for the people of Hong Kong to relax and have fun. Because of the proximity of Shenzhen and the ease of getting into and out of the region (it takes only minutes to go through the immigration control), many young people now go to Shenzhen on day trips. There they find consumer goods (ranging from visiting karaoke to buying pirated brand-name handbags and CDs) much cheaper than what they can get in Hong Kong. Some even stay overnight and spend their money going to discos. Cross-border travel is becoming part of Hong Kong residents' leisure activity. Teenagers are joining the crowds on weekends. Indeed, teenagers' cross-border leisure activities are becoming an issue of public concern. They are exposed to soft drugs and the sex industry there.

ENTERTAINMENT

When Hong Kong children between the ages of 7 and 18 were asked to identify the best thing about their lives, the most common answer (accounting for more than one-third of all answers) was "nothing." This is part of the findings of a lifestyle survey called the New GenerAsians commissioned by the cable TV Cartoon Network and released in 2000. This "nothing" response is not easy to interpret. Some suggest that the kids in Hong Kong are spoiled, having been showered with material goods, and therefore appreciate nothing. Others argue that it simply indicates a refusal to answer (or to think of an answer). Perhaps a lot of young people do feel unfulfilled.

According to the findings of this survey, the favorite leisure activities for young people in Hong Kong are watching TV and playing video games

Hong Kong teens going to a concert at City Hall.
Photo © Eric Pelham/TRIP.

at home. Other choices include listening to music, shopping, and reading comics. Such findings are not surprising. More than 60 percent of the respondents spent at least two hours a day watching TV. These descriptions fall rather closely to the stereotyped image of teenagers in Hong Kong. While this may be a reasonably accurate picture of the leisure activities of local teenagers, it does not explain why they are so domestic and passive in their leisure life. Two points merit our attention here. First, the emphasis on home-based entertainment perhaps reflects the constraints imposed upon the teenagers by their school schedules. For teenagers attending secondary schools, their lives, both school life and social life, are essentially structured by their school schedules. The burden of homework means that a lot of teenagers are either at school or at home for most of their daily life. In other words, a lot of their so-called leisure hours are likely to be spent at home, where watching TV and playing video games are viable options.

This generation of teenagers grew up in the context of a mature and highly commercialized local pop culture. Most of them listen to Cantonese pop songs, watch locally produced TV dramas, and (in spite of a recession in the local film industry in recent years) still have rather strong attachments to local movies and their movie stars. However, at the same time, they have plenty of pop culture products to choose from. So, for a weekend hangout, they probably sing Cantonese pop songs in karaokes, watch Hollywood movies, and shop for cute Japanese accessories or European fashions. In the world of popular culture, the sky's the limit.

RELIGIOUS PRACTICES AND CULTURAL CEREMONIES

Teenagers in Hong Kong can fully enjoy freedom of religious practice. Many schools and social services in Hong Kong are organized by Christian and Catholic churches and groups. So, teenagers are likely to have had access to and contacts with these religious organizations since childhood. While it is fair to say that the influence of the Christian and Catholic churches is quite significant, other religions are equally active in Hong Kong. Chinese religions like Buddhism and Taoism, despite their links with the traditional culture, are able to recruit followers among the teenagers. New-age groups have also gotten teenagers' attention in recent years. However, generally speaking, many teenagers are rather eclectic in their approach to religion. In other words, many of them would worship any god or any combination of gods that they believe would bring them luck and fortune. But Hong Kong teenagers are most likely to be influenced by Catholicism and Christianity.

As regards cultural ceremonies, Hong Kong is a hypermodern city that has kept few traditional cultural practices intact. Even the Chinese New Year, probably the biggest festival among the Hong Kong Chinese, has been significantly tuned down and has become only a longer holiday. Teenagers are not required to attend any special ceremony signifying their passage to adulthood. Nor is there any important traditional religious practice or cultural ceremony that targets teenagers. On the whole, cultural ceremony plays a very small part in the social life of Hong Kong.

CONCLUSION

Teenagers in Hong Kong are feeling the changes in their living environment. Like it or not, they have to put up with a very competitive schooling system. The opening of more opportunities for advancing to high school does not immediately ease the pressure to attain good results in public examinations. Teenagers still feel that to move ahead they need to remain competitive. Otherwise, they will have to start working early. Prospects in the job market look dim, both for finding job security and for locating jobs with good career prospects.

As a global city, Hong Kong offers its teenagers a colorful cultural and social life. There is no shortage of new consumer goods to create new desires among the younger generation. Nowadays, the mobile phone is the most popular item. Before long, new trends could take over. Teenagers are rather free in the cultural domain. They are free to make friends with members of the opposite sex, to choose their own religion, to buy what they want, and to eat what they find delicious. Their leisure activities are not particularly exciting, but many of them do participate in volunteer work.

The scope of teenagers' activity has been expanding. They are becoming more mobile. Many of them are enjoying their weekends across the border. Yet this also means that they are increasingly exposed to a world they find unfamiliar. Teens' exposure to drugs and commercial sex worries parents, teachers, and social workers alike.

Changes in social life and development in the region are reflected in the lives of Hong Kong teens. The local culture and traditions continue to affect teenagers' daily lives. Yet the local culture and traditions are always changing. Economic development and affluence have brought new options, like the local fast food. And the teenagers enjoy their freedom to choose. However, upon closer scrutiny, the local culture remains tenacious. Hong Kong teenagers are affluent and cosmopolitan without giving up their own local identity.

NOTES

1. Demographic data reported in this chapter are drawn from a report compiled by Chor-fai Au, *Youth in Hong Kong: A Statistical Profile 1997* (Hong Kong: Commission on Youth, 1997); and Census and Statistics Department, *1996 Population By-Census: Main Report* (Hong Kong: Government Printer, 1997).

2. Hong Kong Federation of Youth Groups, *Youth Trends in Hong Kong 1999* (Hong Kong: Hong Kong Federation of Youth Groups, 1999).

3. Katherine Forestier, "Our Spoilt Children, with Everything and Nothing," *South China Morning Post*, 2 April 2000.

4. Au, *Youth in Hong Kong: A Statistical Profile 1997*.

5. See note 3.

6. Freedom Leung, Sharon Lam, and Iris Chan, "Disorder eating attitudes and behavior among adolescent girls in Hong Kong," *Journal of Youth Studies*, 4 (2001). Retrieved October 24, 2003, from www.hkfyg.org.hk/yrc/english/yr-jys-e.html

7. See note 3.

RESOURCE GUIDE

Nonfiction

Au, C. (1997). *Youth in Hong Kong: A Statistical Profile 1997*. Hong Kong: Commission on Youth.

Hong Kong Federation of Youth Groups. (1999). *Youth trends in Hong Kong 1999*. Hong Kong.

Leung, B.K.P. (1996). *Perspectives on Hong Kong society*. Oxford, England: Oxford University Press.
The book reviews sociological studies of contemporary Hong Kong society.

Film

Chan, F. (Director). (1997). *Made in Hong Kong* [Motion picture]. Guardian Unlimited.
The film addresses young people's sense of alienation in 1990s Hong Kong.

Web Sites

http://www.gov.hk
A good source for information on Hong Kong is this official Web site constructed by the Government of Hong Kong Special Administrative Region. It is the official source of information on governmental organizations and offers links to local universities and public bodies as well as summaries of social statistics.

http://www.hkta.org
This Web site provides information for tourists.

http://www.hkfyg.org.hk
This Web site of the Hong Kong Federation of Youth Groups is quite helpful and useful. It gives information on its own organization profiles and activities. It also posts relevant information on many surveys it has carried out on matters related to teenagers and youth.

Chapter 4

INDIA

Veronica Gesser with Rimjhim Banerjee

INTRODUCTION

India, known officially as Republic of India or Bharat, represents the greater area of South Asia. It is located between Pakistan, China, and Nepal. India consists of 25 states, each of which has a significant degree of control over its own situation, and 7 union territories with less power to control their own affairs. India's capital is New Delhi. With roughly 15 percent of the total population in the world, India is the world's second most populous country.

India's high-density population averages 216 people per square kilometer, but great variation exists in different areas. For instance, Bombay and Calcutta, India's biggest cities, have a population density of nearly 4,000 per square kilometer, but in hilly areas the density is as low as 50 to 60 per square kilometer. The dominance of the rural to urban population is characteristic of India's demographic density, attaining a proportion of 70 to 30, regardless of the fact that India is one of the 10 most industrialized countries in the world. Population stabilization is a major challenge for India today. As a result, the government in India has announced a new policy on population growth that encourages the poorest Indian couples to have no more than two children.

India's dizzying topographical variations include the world's highest mountain ranges (the northern Himalayas and adjoining mountains to the west and east), tropical rain forests, plateaus, and sandy deserts in the northwestern areas. The landmass of India is a subcontinent of Asia and ranks, in area, as the seventh largest country in the globe. It covers 1,222,559 square miles (3,166,414 square kilometers) of the earth—a bit more than 2 percent of the earth's land surface. The country comprises four main regions that are classified as follows: the great mountain zone, the Indus and Ganges plains, the desert zone, and the southern peninsula. The Himalayas, which are located in the north of India, stretch roughly 1,500 miles and have the highest mountain peaks in the world, including Mt. Everest, Mt. K2, and Mt. Kanchenjunga. The Ganges and Brahmaputra are two of the longest rivers in the world.

India's frontier stretches 9,425 miles, of which 3,533 miles is coastline. India borders six countries, and three are of particular interest. India has difficulty managing its borders with Pakistan, which is located to the northwest, and China, to the north. Bangladesh is surrounded by Indian territories on three sides. India is also bordered by Nepal and Bhutan, located between India and China, and Myanmar to the east.

The land in India is very diverse, and much of its territory lies within a big peninsula that is surrounded by the Arabian Sea on the west and the Bay of Bengal on the east. Cape Comorin represents the southernmost area of the Indian mainland and marks the border between these two sources of water. The Sea of Mannar and the Palk Strait, which are situated off the extreme southeastern coast, isolate India from the island nation of Sri Lanka. Two Indian territories composed wholly of islands are Lakshadweep, which is located in the Arabian Sea, and the Andaman and Nicobar Islands, which are surrounded by the Bay of Bengal and the Andaman Sea.

After years of domination by Great Britain, India finally achieved independence in 1947. India's independence became reality due to pressures exerted by a well-organized movement for freedom under the leadership of Mahatma Gandhi and under the banner of the Indian National Congress. Thousands of Indians sacrificed their lives for the cause of freedom under the leadership of various prominent leaders, including Subhas Bose, Lajpat Rai, and Bhagat Singh. With the division of the country into Pakistan and India, after the loss of many human lives, India became a republic on January 26, 1950, when Dr. Rajendra Prasad was designated as the first president of the Indian republic.

India has experienced a mixed economic and political system through which the government, legally characterized as socialist, works as the major planner, regulator, investor, manager, and producer. The decision-making process in India is highly political, in particular with regard to its attempts to invest equally in the several states of the nation. Besides the major role of the government in India's economic enterprise, major companies such as Tata, Birla, and Reliance control various spheres of the modern and advanced economic activities, and the bulk of employment is offered by millions of small businesses in all areas, including agriculture.

Approximately one-fifth of India's labor force works in organized sectors of the economy, such as mining, agriculture, industry, utilities, modern transportation, commercial enterprises, and services. This small
fraction contributes a disproportionate share of the nation's gross domestic product, supports the middle- and upper-class population, and gener-
ates the largest share of the economic growth. Even though India has
evolved socially and economically since its independence, it is still among
the poorest countries in per capita gross national product, and a large percentage of the population lives below the poverty line. Low educational
level and illiteracy contribute to these social and economic conditions.

India is one of the most ethnically diverse nations on the planet. The
variety of races, religions, cultures, and languages in the Indian society are
the result of successive waves of immigration and invaders, including the
Aryans, Greeks, central Asians, and Mughals, who came into the country
and mixed with the native population.

Within this diversity of races, India has a great number of castes and
tribes. The caste system has been a controlling classification for many
years. A caste, usually categorized by the word *jati*, which means "birth,"
is a highly controlled social community into which a person is born. The
relationship between caste and occupational specialization is generally
very limited. Marriage is usually restricted to someone within the same
caste. This means that a person is expected to follow the same set of rules
and values for appropriate behavior (including kinship, occupation, and
diet) and to act within the community based on the group's position in
the social hierarchy. Although today caste discrimination is illegal in
India, it is still a part of daily life.

In India all nontribal Hindus and many followers of other religious
faiths belong to one of these hereditary social groups or communities.
Among Hindus, members of a regulated social community (jatis) are normally designated to one of the big caste groups (*varnas*), each of which
developed a traditional social role. For instance, Brahmans (priests)
belong to the top of the social hierarchy and, in descending order, there
are Ksatriyas (warriors), Vaishyas (initially peasants, but later merchants),
and Shudras (serfs). What determines a jati's relative level of purity, particularly for varna, is the community's traditional relationship with any of
a number of "pollutants." These may include menstrual flow, saliva,
leather, dirt, and hair. Restrictions between castes were imposed to protect the relative level of "purity" of a specific jati from being influenced by
the impurities of a lower caste.

The Panchamas, a fifth group, were literally expelled from the system
because their occupations and lifestyle usually brought them in close

contact with pollutants. Originally called the "untouchables" (because their touch, transmitting pollution, was avoided), they were renamed Harijans (children of God) by Gandhi, who officially designated them as Scheduled Castes. Those classified as Harijans are usually landless, are extremely poor, and do most of the agricultural work and a number of ritually polluting caste occupations. Collectively, they account for about one-sixth of India's population. In certain parts of India where ignorance reigns supreme, they are subordinated to and avoided and frequently abused by higher castes in the hierarchical classification.

India's linguistic composition also represents the multicultural aspects of its culture. It has frequently been called a Tower of Babel, since nationally, India's constitution has recognized 15 languages that are spoken in more than 1,600 dialects. The official language in India is Hindi (different dialects are spoken according to each geographical area) with more than 300 million speakers. English, however, is the official working language and the first language for a large number of well-educated Indians. For a great number who are bilingual or multilingual, English is usually the second language. English is highly emphasized in Indian schools and universities, and there is a conflict growing among Indians because for some, English is generating a society division.

Although Hindi and English are predominant in the country, the other spoken languages include Urdu, Telugu, Oriya, Punjabi, Marathi, Tamil, Sindhi, Bengali (the third most dominant language), Konkani, Kashmiri, Kannada, and Gujarati. The majority of the Indian languages have their own script and are spoken in their states of origin along with English. Such a high level of diversity is observed in very few other countries.

Today India reflects a picture of unity in a multicultural context that historically cannot be compared to other nations. It includes social and economic hardships that Indian families face in their daily lives. Young people and children can experience tremendous difficulties and have considerable responsibilities. At a very young age, they are physically, morally, and psychologically challenged to make their way out of their community and attain certain levels of social mobility, dignity, and success. In this sense, various aspects of a teenager's life (e.g., family life, schooling, social life, recreation, religious and cultural ceremonies) are affected by the social and cultural conditions of India.

TYPICAL DAY

India's teenagers usually go to high school and then to college to pursue bachelor's degrees. Schools usually start at 8 A.M. in India, and the academic year stretches from April to March. An Indian teenager would most likely start the day by getting ready for school and then taking a school bus or a public bus to reach school. On certain days, schools start with an assembly period where the students are given some moral education along with an update on current affairs. A school day usually consists of eight periods lasting 40 minutes each. In the middle of the day, there is a short break of 15 to 20 minutes. Different subjects are taught in the different periods, and the student usually remains in the same classroom while the teachers move from room to room to teach their respective subjects. Class sizes in Indian schools are usually around 50, and classrooms are provided with a blackboard and chalk only. A lecture method is used in most subjects. In science, students can conduct practical experiments in the laboratory. Physical education is compulsory for teenagers in schools, and once a week they have the opportunity to learn exercises and play games in the school. Schools also have various events (such as concerts, competitions, plays, etc.) in which students are encouraged to participate, and sometimes these students spend time after school hours to practice for these events. Teenagers are also required to be members of various clubs and organizations in the school such as student government, the drama club, and the music club.

The typical school in India lasts from kindergarten through 12th grade, unlike the United States, where elementary, middle, and high schools are usually different. After school is over for the day, the teenagers either go back home by school bus or by public transport or are picked up by their parents. They have lunch as soon as they reach their home, which usually consists of rice, lentils, and some sort of nonvegetarian dish. Following lunch, teens either start studying or play some games with their neighborhood friends depending on whether exams are approaching. However, even when exams are not imminent, teens still study or go to tuition centers to gear up for major exams like the Indian School Certificate Exam (ISCE) given in 10th grade and the Indian School Certification (ISC) given in 12th grade. These exams, similar to the U.S. PSAT and SAT, are given by the Council for the Indian School Certificate Exams and serve to document high school completion as well as provide scores for entrance into programs in higher education institutions. The standards of these exams are extremely high, and teens start feeling pressure to perform well in these from eighth grade on. These exams are held all over India, and even average universities demand high scores on these exams for admission. To gear up for the exams, teens go to tuition classes immediately after they reach home. Some teens do not even have time to go to their houses because their classes are scheduled right after school ends. There are very few teens who get to play every day after returning from school. Compared with American teens, Indian teens seem much more stressed out. Teens even go to tuition classes for subjects that are not related to these major exams, for example, music and cricket. Most Indian parents want their children to excel not only in academics but also in other fields. This puts additional pressure on the teens.

With all this stress, most Indian teens feel the need to escape some-times. At the extreme, this desire can lead some teens to threaten to commit suicide. An average teenager is often found returning home around 9 P.M. after spending a hectic day clad in a school uniform, having eaten only junk food because there is no time to return home from school before going to other activities. The teen's day starts with school and ends late in the evening with little time left for self-study, family life, or hobbies.

FAMILY LIFE

Family is the most important social institution in India. Family struc-ture, size, and life in India differ significantly from those in other conti-nents and countries. For instance, there is a strong tendency in India for extended families that consist of two or more married couples, or of mul-tiple generations, to share finances and a common house and kitchen. This joint family structure is mainly influenced by socioreligious beliefs and practices. Indian families have a patriarchal structure based on Hin-duism. Inequalities between sexes and occupations are normally accepted. The patriarch of the family is a protective, respected authority figure. This family structure is found in the majority of Indian families, but in the south, there are some states (Kerala, Karnataka, and tribal societies) where families were once matriarchal and matricentered. Today, these societies are also moving toward a patriarchal configuration.

This patriarchal family consists of all male members (including hus-band, elder son, and father) who make decisions involving the physical and moral protection of the rest of the family. All family members have to obey the family seniors and elders. This family structure is changing slowly among the well-educated, urban population, becoming more egal-itarian, but in some rural settings, families continue to function in the conservative, traditional fashion. Any sacrifice of one's life is considered a religious duty in order to maintain the family name and tradition. For instance, a brother cannot marry until his younger sister is married off. Also, if the father is absent or unable to make decisions for the family, these duties fall to the eldest son.

The Indian family structure (joint family or extended family) reflects part of the religious belief system that is still in practice. The family god, a small statue or icon, is commonly worshiped by all married brothers. Along with the care of the family property, this is transferred to the eldest son at the time of the father's death. In case of migration of the eldest son to the city for a job, the family god is kept in the ancestor's homes. In fact, this tradition is common not only in rural areas or lower castes. It is a common feature in urban families and also in higher-level hierarchical castes.

Indian families have maintained this tradition through their family cycle rituals. In early traditions, every individual (every male in particular) has to experience 16 life cycle rituals called "Sanskaras," or purificatory rituals. These rituals begin when a woman gets pregnant. There is a ceremony by a priest to contemplate a celebration for the birth of a male child. Then, as part of the ritual, family members and the whole community offer the pregnant women special meals, fruits, and presents. The other important life cycle rituals include the start of student life, the end of studenthood, sexual abstinence, marriage, and so on, ending with the death rite. For females, the most important rite is marriage. The lower the caste classification, the lesser the number of life cycle rituals.

Besides these family traditions, some changes have been introduced because of social and economic transformations and demand. For instance, families join with others to save money when young adolescents leave the home for jobs. For certain, in some families women's roles have changed. Women no longer work in only agricultural activities or domestic duties; some are becoming part of the workforce outside of the home, especially in urban families, and women now help run the household.

Religion is a way of life in India, and the family is believed to exist mainly for the fulfillment of religious obligations such as worshiping ancestors, begetting a male child, and passing socioreligious traditions to the next generation. Marriage is part of the fulfillment of religious obligation. Family life for teens in India is significantly different from that of other societies. Religious beliefs play a major role in defining a hierarchical relationship among family members. Women, adolescents, and children basically obey orders from their elders, which makes Indian families greatly different from Western families.

TRADITIONAL AND NONTRADITIONAL FOOD DISHES

The food available in India is as diverse as its culture, its geography, and its racial composition. It is said that the secret to Indian cuisine is the correct use of aromatic spices. The spices are used to enhance rather than overwhelm the natural flavor of a dish. The spices both enhance the food's flavor and aid digestion. Along with spices, other major ingredients of Indian cuisine are milk products, lentils (*dals*), and vegetables. Their use is based on regional preferences, and availability differs across the regions and with seasons.

The Hindu and the Muslim traditions are the two cultures that have had the greatest influence on Indian cooking and foods. For instance, vegetarianism, a Hindu practice, is widespread in India, whereas the cooking of meats is most apparent in the Muslim tradition. The Hindus believe in the existence of God in humans, animals, and natural forces. A cow represents a Hindu god; therefore, meat or beef is not part of their traditional menu, except for special ceremonies. For most higher castes, meat is rarely part of their menu, except on special rituals or occasions. Fish, fresh milk, and vegetables, however, are usually widely consumed according to regional and seasonal availability. In terms of beverages, tea is preferred in northern and eastern India, whereas coffee is preferred in the south. In the Indian tradition, a meal is normally finished with the after-dinner paan or betel leaf, which consists of a mixture of digestive spices such as anise, cloves, cardamom, and areca nut.

Teens eat the same types of foods as their parents. Yet official documents report that there is inadequate nutrition, usually for girls and women, due to the discriminatory gender attitudes that persists in Asian countries, including India. Because of the low status of women in the country, adolescent girls usually lack good nutrition. Malnutrition affects a significant number of people in India, especially children, adolescents (girls in a higher percentage), and women in general. It is said that mothers and sisters normally skip meals in poor families or communities in order to provide more than their share to husbands, sons, and brothers.

In India, nutrition represents one major indicator of teenagers' health and general status. Appropriate nutrition is vital for adolescent growth. Based on this indicator, poor nutrition is usually indicated as the major reason for the delay in the onset of puberty in Indian adolescents. As a result of gender discrimination in India, the levels of undernutrition are higher in girls. Indian females receive only 88 percent of the required nutritional components as compared to boys. Even though the average protein and energy intake is low in all groups at age 15 due to the low socioeconomic condition of many residents, in adolescents girls it gets more complicated because of early pregnancies and anemia that can result from early marriages and high fertility rates among females.

Adolescents who come from poor families have little or no choice with regard to favorite foods because they rarely have enough to eat. Teenagers in the middle or upper class seem to have more choice. Their favorite foods include hot dogs, pizza, and hamburgers. When it comes to beverages, they can have carbonated soft drinks. Indian food is also popular among Indian teenagers.

SCHOOLING

Education is free and compulsory for all children under the age of 14 in India. Even though India offers some adult education, among people aged 15 and over, illiteracy is common. For instance, about half of the population and approximately two-thirds of all females are illiterate. Attempts to provide adult education have had little success. The educational system is structured as follows: early childhood education (2 years), elementary education (8 years), and secondary education (2 years).

In the upper primary stage (grades 6–8), children study three languages (mother tongue or regional tongue, modern Indian language, and English). Additionally, they learn regular subjects such as mathematics, science and technology, social sciences, work education, art education, and health and physical education. In the secondary stage (2 years, grades 9–10), adolescents also have three languages and the regular subjects mentioned previously.

In the secondary education or higher secondary (classes 11–12), classes assume greater significance as adolescents move toward diversification. Students are given a chance to develop their own thinking and independence of mind. For instance, they can choose courses that will enable them to prepare for their future. A typical curriculum at this stage would include two languages (English and the student's mother tongue); vocational and technical courses such as computers, typing, electronics, woodworking, and bookkeeping; and a choice of subjects in the science stream, commerce stream, or humanities stream.

There are two types of schools in India. Public schools are tuition-funded schools usually with a private trust of their own and some government grants. They are normally for the middle and upper classes, and English is often the language used for instruction. These schools are considered to provide the best education. Government schools are tuition free, but books are paid for by the parents. Boys and girls usually go to separate classes in both types of schools.

Indian students must pass difficult examinations in order to proceed with their studies. After grades 10 and 12, for instance, students must take examinations if they wish to advance into the school or college of their choice. Students face extreme pressure and anxiety before taking the examinations. Pressure usually comes from parents.

Class size is a problem in India. Classes are usually very large, and having 45 students in a class is common. Discipline is excellent; students sit up straight and pay attention most of the time. The teachers lecture frequently and rarely ask students to participate in research-based activities.

SOCIAL LIFE

While people from Western cultures tend to be individualistic, with a moral orientation towards autonomy, individual rights, and personal prerogative, individuals from non-Western cultures are more collectivist, morally connected to others, with a strong sense of social duty and interpersonal responsibility. This non-Western orientation influences India's family structure and religion and is the basis of social relationships. Teenagers' social life is a matter of family decision and not a matter to be decided at a personal level. For instance, dates and marriages are usually arranged by the patriarch or elders of the family. Because marriages are arranged, sons are frequently given the right of veto but daughters are not.

India has a variety of types of marriage systems and mate selection. Marriage is one of the most important life cycle rituals in the Hindu tradition. Marriage basically entails an obligation to produce a male child. If a man does not get a son from his first marriage, he is encouraged to have a second wife. In some religions, such as among Muslims, a man can have up to four wives; however, monogamy is prevalent throughout India. In the Hindu tradition, marriage unites two families, not only two individuals. Thus, a marriage is arranged on the basis of caste, socioeconomic status, education, and astrology. Non-arranged marriages or "love marriages" are becoming more prevalent among the elite.

Besides being an important ritual, marriage is a very significant social event in the life of the individuals who marry, as well as the family and community. For Hindus, marriage is a lifetime commitment, a purificatory ritual and sacrament. For other major religions, it is also a sacrament, but for Muslims, marriage is a contract. A traditional feature of Indian marriage is called "dowry." Dowry is a stigmatic tradition through which cash, gold, and other modern luxuries such as cars, videos, and other valuable objects are given by the girl's parents to the boy. Well-educated boys with government positions or professionals such as doctors and engineers are so highly valued that they can name their prices. This is a practice that is present regardless of education level. However, law in India bans taking dowry. In some cases or families, parents look for choices for their child throughout the nation via newspaper and magazine advertisements.

The legal age for marriage is 18 for females and 21 for males. Nevertheless, early marriage continues to be common. In general, teens get married during adolescence; by the age of 15, as many as 26 percent of females are married. By the age of 18, this figure rises to 54 percent. In rural areas the percentage of early marriages is higher, and so is the fertility rate among adolescents. In rural areas, teenage marriages are common, but in modern cities teens tend not to marry before completing their education and developing the economic capacity to support a family. Early marriage among adolescents is highly correlated with fertility rates. Most Indian adolescents who have children do so when wed. For instance, 36 percent of married teenagers aged 13 to 16 and 64 percent of those aged 17 to 19 are already expecting or have already had a child.

Teen sexual activities usually start with marriage, especially for females. Premarital sexual activity is more common among boys, among whom it is more accepted. This behavior toward sexual relationships reflects India's family structure. Girls are trained from childhood to be nice, docile, chaste, and separated from boys. That is why in the Hindu tradition, for a girl, marriage is prescribed before puberty because maintaining virginity is a major goal. As a result, well-educated girls do not see marriage as a satisfaction of passion but a promise of lifelong economic stability that parents alone can arrange.

Sex education and information associated with health and birth control are very limited. Parents and teachers do not play a major role in educating children and adolescents about these topics. Generally, information on sexuality and reproduction comes from peers. Contraceptive use is low and information about it is practically nonexistent. Information on HIV/AIDS, safe sex, and preventive behavior is not common. Teenage women have little or no choice about whom and when to marry, and they are normally not in a position to negotiate contraceptive use. Due to this lack of information, in India, adolescent girls suffer major consequences associated with unwanted pregnancies, abortion (legal since 1972), and high maternal mortality rates.

Under the Hindu tradition, marriage is a sacrament and divorce should not be considered. Lately, under extreme situations like barrenness, impotency, or upper class membership, divorce has become an option. In lower castes, divorce was accepted and practiced especially when a woman was childless, but a divorced woman with a child could never remarry regardless of her age. A divorced man of any caste or class would be allowed to remarry even a virgin of lower group, whether he had children or not and regardless of his age. While Indian law prohibits polygamy, men in rural areas often get remarried even without divorce, while women from disastrous marriages rarely remarry, remain celibate, and depend on their parents, uncles, brothers, or other family members.

Teenage boys and girls in modern urban India go out together but normally in groups. They do not kiss, hold hands, or otherwise display affection in public. Even though marriages are still arranged, some changes have been observed. For instance, in middle- and upper-class families the young couple today is given time to meet and to get to know each other. In some cases, they may even refuse to marry if they do not like each other. In general, this is not the rule in India, but it is an exception within these families or classes.

RECREATION AND ENTERTAINMENT

India is well known for its festivals and festivities. India's festivals are mainly celebrated to express gratitude to the main forces of nature that provide protection and help to human beings in the production of food and in the procreation of healthy offspring, and to all resources from nature such as water, air, and the sun. Therefore, festivals are part of the recreation and entertainment for all people. They are also part of prayer and worship of several gods and goddesses. Among the many festivals that are celebrated in India are Baisakhi (the Harvest Festival), Holi (the Festival of Colors, celebrated in spring), and Diwali (the Festival of Lights). Baisakhi has a rural flavor to it, and rural teenagers are more involved in it than their urban counterparts. The teenage boys are usually involved with their fathers while harvesting the rice in the fields. Since it is a harvest festival, a major part of the festival is associated with making different kinds of sweet dishes with the newly harvested rice. Teenage girls help their mothers prepare these dishes. The preparation is usually an elaborate affair, and women of the community often come together, sing songs, and take up various roles in the preparation. Holi is a beautiful festival that is celebrated in honor of spring. According to Hindu mythology, this is also the festival for lovers to express their love for each other through the use of colors. The application of different kinds of powdered colors and watercolors expresses the vivacity of the people's moods in the spring and harmony with nature. Teenagers look forward to this festival especially since this is perhaps the only day in the year when the society is not so restrictive and boys and girls can freely express their feelings for each other.

Indian girls walking through Calcutta. Photo © H. Rogers/TRIP.

Diwali, the other major festival, is marked by decorating one's home by lighting numerous oil lamps and placing them on windowsills, terraces, and doors. It is also associated with beautiful fireworks and the bursting of firecrackers. Teenagers and children are most excited about this festival and plan well in advance for the kind of fireworks they are going to purchase.

Besides festivals, Indian boys and girls have other forms of recreation and entertainment after school and on the weekend. Middle- and upperclass teenagers practice some favorite sports for fun. The most popular sports are cricket and soccer. Tennis, volleyball, basketball, and softball are also enjoyed and played by teenagers. Additionally, they watch Indian and American movies. Indian movies are longer (about three hours long) than American movies; have a lot of music, dancing, action, and romance all together in a single plot; and usually have a happy ending. American movies are usually recent releases and are watched on VCRs. Television is also a source of recreation, but Indian teenagers do not get to watch more than an hour a day due to the pressure of studies. Televised cricket matches and soccer matches are a big draw for teenagers. Indian teenagers are not so interested in classical Indian music. Their favorite music includes the current hits on MTV and Indian film music. Interestingly enough, girls also learn traditional dancing. Upper- and middle-class teenagers learn Western dancing and often go to parties where they dance to Western

tunes. Schools and colleges in the urban areas arrange interinstitution cultural contests, and these events are big attractions for teenagers. Since girls
and boys often go to separate schools, they look forward to these events to
meet and socialize with members of the opposite sex. They get to participate in various events such as debates, quizzes, dance, music, painting, and
plays and watch these events at these interinstitutional festivals. Teenagers
usually do not have jobs after school or on the weekends. As one can see,
recreation and entertainment for teens in India is much more controlled
and limited than that of teenagers in many Western countries.

RELIGIOUS PRACTICES AND CULTURAL CEREMONIES

India's roots go back to many, many years before Christ. It has a rich
religious and cultural heritage that extends back to about 5000 B.C. The
population of India is multiracial, multireligious, and multilingual.
Archeological evidence has shown that the Indus Civilization, a highly
sophisticated, urbanized culture, exerted great influence and basically
dominated the northwestern area of the subcontinent from roughly 2600
and 2000 B.C. India basically worked as a self-contained cultural and political system that promoted a significant tradition that was related essentially to Hinduism, the origin of which stems largely from the Indus
Civilization. India's religion, Dharma, is not a narrow term as in the Western sense but is an all-encompassing way of life. Religions such as Buddhism and Jainism also stemmed from ancient India, but they are not
often practiced in India today.

In India, religion represents a vital aspect of cultural identity for the
majority of the population. Much of India's history can be understood
through its multiple religious groups. Most Indians (more than 80% of the
population) follow Hinduism, which is a diverse religion with many doc-
trines, sects, and ways of life. Hinduism is the predominant faith in India,
and religion is an intrinsic component of the Indian tradition and way of
life. Even though Hindus represent the majority of the population, the
most evident religious group that is perceived as an integral part of the
Indian society is Muslims. In fact, India has the second-largest population
of Muslims on the planet, lagging only behind Indonesia.

India has other important religious minorities, including Christians.
They are highly concentrated in the northeast and Kerala. Buddhists
are found in Maharashtra, Sikkim, and Kashmir. Jains are concentrated
in Maharashtra, Gujarat, and Rajasthan. Considering religion as a way
of life, Indian common rituals mark most religious faith in India, and
all groups celebrate many of the festivals of music, dance, and feasting

each year. Each festival has its own heroes, legends, and culinary specialties.

CONCLUSION

Teen life in India is very different from teen life in other countries (especially in Western countries), and the problems of Indian adolescents are multidimensional. The invisibility of teenagers in policy and in service delivery comes out as the most critical problem. There is a lack of information and studies regarding adolescents in India. Several main aspects became clear throughout this chapter. The level of poverty throughout India makes life for teenagers very difficult. Due to the growing population of adolescents in India, their situation is becoming even more difficult. Nutritional aspects (especially for girls) are major problems, and when associated with the high rates of early marriages, high fertility rates, and pregnancies, they become even worse. As a consequence, India has high levels of mortality among children and adolescents, especially among girls.

Indian adolescents have a very restricted social life. It is limited to movies, festivals, and a few sports. Arranged marriage by parents at an early age is still common, as is early childbearing. Even though education is free and mandatory until age 14, illiteracy is still high among adolescents and the population in general, especially girls and women, due to gender discrimination. In general, family is the most important institution in India because it is used to impart religious values and principles. In India almost everything, such as rituals, festivals, family values, and social behavior, is led by faith or religion.

RESOURCE GUIDE

Nonfiction

Henderson, C. E. (2002). *Culture and customs of India*. Westport, CT: Greenwood Press.

Indian Department of Education. (2001). *Organization of curriculum at elementary and secondary stages*. Retrieved from http://www.nic.in/vseducation/ncert/cfchap2.htm.

India Travel Guide. (2001). *India travel information*. Retrieved from http://india-travel.org.

Kitts, C. (1989). *Middle and upper class teenage life in urban India*. Washington, DC: Center for International Education, United States Educational Foundation in India, 1–30.

Lak, D. (1999, November 19). India's malnutrition crisis. *BBC News*. Retrieved November 19, 1999, from http://news.bbc.co.uk/hi/english/world/south_asia/newsid_528000/528485.stm.

Lak, D. (2000, February 15). New Indian initiative on population growth. *BBC News*. Retrieved February 15, 2000, from http://news.bbc.co.uk/hi/english/world/south_asia/newsid_643000/643894.stm.

Leela, M. (1995, spring). Families in India: Beliefs and realities. *Journal of Comparative Family Studies*, 26. Retrieved from http://newfirstsearch.altip.oclc.org/webZ/FTFETC...entityemailftfrom = WilsonSelectPlus_F.

McGivering, J. (2001, May 10). India's language divide. *BBC News*. Retrieved May 10, 2001, from http://news.bbc.co.uk/hi/english/world/south_asia/newsid_1323000/1323234.stm.

Neff, K. D. (2001). Judgments of personal autonomy and interpersonal responsibility in the context of Indian spousal relationships: An examination of young people's reasoning in Mysore, India. *British Journal of Development Psychology*, 19, 233–257.

Podger, C. (2001, August 16). India rejects caste racism debate. *BBC News*. Retrieved August 16, 2001, from http://news.bbc.co.uk/hi/english/world/south_asia/newsid_1495000/1495052.stm.

Shah, C. S. (2001). *Festivals of India*. Retrieved from http://www.boloji.com/festivals/festivals.htm.

Shah, S. Y. (1996, October–December). Literacy accelerates the pace of development: Indian scenario. *Indian Journal of Adult Education*, 20–30.

United Nations Population Fund—UNFPA. (2001). *Adolescents in India: A profile*. Retrieved from http://www.unfpa.org/facetoface/docs/adolescentsprofile.pdf.

Web Sites

http://dmoz.org/Kids_and_Teens/School_Time/Social_Studies/History/By_Time_Period/Ancient_History/India/

http://www.boloji.com/festivals/

The World Factbook 2000—India: http://www.odci.gov/cia/publications/factbook/geos/in.html
    An overview of the country's government, economy, population, system of transportation, and military.

The Electronic Passport to the Indian Subcontinent: http://www.mrdowling.com/612india.html
    A brief, illustrated guide to the land and its people. Created for middle school students.

Pitara Kids Network: http://www.pitara.com/
    Kids portal based in India features news, folktales, and in-depth information about the land and its people. Also offers stories, books, poems, activities, a forum, and school sections.

PBS Online: http://www.pbs.org/edens/anamalai/
Introduces the wildlife sanctuary where Asian elephants live in safety. Also provides information on the elephants and explains why this creature is considered sacred by many people of India.

An Introduction to India: http://www.interknowledge.com/india/
General information about the country, its geography, and its people and culture.

Welcome to India: http://www.welcometoindia.com/home.asp
Provides an assortment of information about the country, including history, arts, culture, and cuisine.

India—National Facts—Top Education: http://www.top-education.com/gk/nationalfacts/
Provides brief information about National Facts of India.

India—The Great Ocean of Heritage: http://library.thinkquest.org/28853/
Gives a brief description of the country, along with information on its history, religion, people, culture, environment, and architecture.

India: After the British: http://library.thinkquest.org/17282/
Filled with the memories of a young girl's life in contemporary India. Discusses traditions, festivals, animals, transportation, food, clothing, and makeup. Also includes numerous photographs.

50 Glorious Years of Indian Independence: http://library.thinkquest.org/22678/
This site tells about India's progress since 1945 and the leaders who helped move the country forward.

India: http://encarta.msn.com/find/Concise.asp?z=1&pg=2&ti=761557562
Article from Encarta Encyclopedia provides a basic introduction to the land and people of India.

Learning about Indian Culture: http://library.thinkquest.org/11372/
Introduction to India's fascinating 5,000-year-old culture, including facts about languages, religion, music, film, politics and government, history, economy, and sports.

Pen Pal/Chat

http://in.lycosasia.com/dir/Home_and_Family/Teens/
http://members.tripod.com/indianteens/
http://youngstersonline.com

Chapter 5

INDONESIA

David Callejo-Perez

INTRODUCTION

The Republic of Indonesia, known as Indonesia, is the world's largest archipelago. Indonesia achieved independence from the Netherlands in 1949. Indonesia has always been an important island for the United States because it has a strategic location between the Indian and Pacific Oceans in Southeast Asia and it has been staunchly anticommunist. Indonesia is composed of 17,000 islands, of which 6,000 are inhabited. It is about three times the size of Texas. It borders Malaysia and New Guinea. The climate of Indonesia is a tropical humid climate, with more moderate temperatures in the highlands. The terrain is mostly coastal lowlands, although the larger islands have interior mountains. The highest point is Puncak Jaya at 16,500 feet.

Indonesia produces petroleum, tin, natural gas, nickel, timber, bauxite, copper, crops, gold, and silver. Most of Indonesia is tropical forest, like the Amazon. Indonesia has several hazards that make living difficult, including floods and severe droughts. The most worrisome hazards come from the oceans and mountains. Indonesia is susceptible to tsunamis or tidal waves and hurricanes, as well as volcanoes and earthquakes. Along with these natural disasters, Indonesia is facing environmental problems such as deforestation, water pollution from industrial wastes, and air pollution in urban areas. The population of Indonesia is over 228 million: 30 percent are under 14 years of age, and 65 percent are between 15 and 64 years of age. The census estimates that there are 52,000 people in Indonesia living with HIV/AIDS. About 40 percent of the population is Javanese. Other major groups include Sudanese, Madurese, coastal Malays, and various tribal groups. It is one of the most diverse nations in the world. It is also the world's largest Islamic country, with over 88 percent of the population practicing the religion. Islam was brought there by Arab merchants from North Africa over 500 years ago.

Indonesia is a republic based on Roman law, modified by traditional practices. There are 27 provinces. The Republic claimed independence on August 17, 1945, which is now the national holiday. The voting age in Indonesia is 17, meaning that older teens can vote. Like the U.S. government, the government of Indonesia is divided into three branches. The executive branch is composed of the chief of state and the head of government, who are the same person. The president and vice-president are elected separately by the 700-member People's Consultive Assembly, or MPR, for five-year terms. The assembly meets every five years to elect a president and a vice-president, and to approve the broad outlines of national policy. The judicial branch, or Mahkamah Agung, is appointed by the president from a list of candidates approved by the legislature.

There are severe economic problems in Indonesia caused by the secessionist movements and the low level of security in the outer regions like East Timor, lack of legal recourse for the people regarding government corruption, and a weak banking system. The average Indonesian earns $2,900 in one year. About half of all Indonesians work in agriculture, and about 20 percent of all workers are unemployed. The major industries are rice, cassava (tapioca), peanuts, rubber, cocoa, coffee, palm oil, petroleum and natural gas, textiles such as apparel and footwear, mining, cement, chemical fertilizers, plywood, rubber, and tourism. Indonesia has made headlines because of its use of child labor in the textile industry, especially the manufacture of shoes. The Nike Corporation has been widely criticized for its use of child labor in the making of the Air Jordan series. Also, the major agricultural products are illegal. Cannabis and heroin are the two major cash crops produced in Indonesia.

Indonesia is very spread out, so communications are a big problem. There are over 10,000 islands. However, there are only 3 radio stations and 41 television stations, and the latest reports show that only 400,000 persons use the Internet in the country.

In August 1999, Indonesia made headlines across the world when the people of Timor overwhelmingly approved a provincial referendum for independence. Indonesia's national legislature approved the measure under world pressure and gave the region the name East Timor. This action led to a bloody civil struggle on the island, and the United Nations was asked to mediate. Australia led the international force that helped quell violence that had led to the death of thousands. Indonesia is facing similar problems from its other minorities.

As Indonesia is going through several changes, it must address those issues for its youth. Schools have recently become central in dealing with those problems, especially religion and ethnicity. Regional minorities have asked that their children be educated in the ways of their people. The government is dealing with those issues as well as trying to maintain a national system of education. The problems have escalated since the economic situation has worsened and led to violence in many parts of Indonesia. The police force is no longer under the military, although police are still being used to fight the separatists. The police's salaries are low, about a dollar a day. Street justice has become a reality: last year a man was found guilty of stealing a motorcycle, nabbed by locals, doused with gasoline, and set on fire. The issues of poverty and religion have led to people dying for 100 rupiahs, or less than 10 cents. People with money have begun to build extra walls around their homes and communities to keep the poor out. More and more poor are moving into urban areas from the countryside.

TYPICAL DAY

The following is what a typical day would be like for teenagers in Jakarta who come from middle-class families. They wake up at 5 A.M. and pray. Indonesia is the world's largest Islamic country. Most teens begin their day with prayer, even though many adults are complaining that fewer teenagers are "religious." Then at about 5:30, they take a bath and have breakfast, which is usually milk and bread, fried rice, or noodles. At about 6:30 they go to school. It takes about an hour to get to school by bus. Jakarta is a crowded city, and traffic is an immense problem. Everyday, students can be in traffic jams. School starts at 7:30. Lunch at the school cafeteria is at about 10:30. As in American schools, lunch is hurried. If they do not have time to eat rice, students can simply order burgers. American food is becoming very popular in Indonesia. Schools do not like that their students are eating such foods, especially fast food. Students go home at 2 P.M. The ride home is shorter since the afternoon traffic jam has not begun. Some of the students take naps because they get up so early; others play with friends. It is very hot sometimes, so many stay indoors. Students there do some of the same things that U.S. students do: play video games, work on computers, play soccer, or just hang out. Some teenagers go to the mall and shop. Mall life has become a reality for many

Indonesian teenagers, like those in the United States. Many malls welcome the teenagers and their money. At 7:30, it is time for dinner, usually eaten with the family. The mother cooks dinner for the family with the help of the daughters, or the grandmother. This tradition has also begun to change. The younger daughters have different values. Also, as more mothers have begun to spend time working outside the home, dinner is beginning to resemble dinner in an American household. Many Indonesian companies sell packaged traditional meals for the families who can afford them. Poorer families still cook traditional meals. They usually cook rice, vegetables, and side dishes.

After dinner, many teenagers eat tropical fruits and relax. Sometimes the family eats at Western restaurants; McDonalds is very popular. The McDonalds meals are adjusted to Indonesian taste. Unlike in the United States, where over half of all teenagers have jobs, in Indonesia many students do not work. There is not much work for teenagers in Indonesia. Of the many children who work, the majority are not in school or are forced to work to help support their families. Human rights groups have asserted that Indonesia is one of the leading violators of child labor laws and has numerous sweatshops. Because it is such a poor country, many families need the children to work, and sweatshops are some of the few places that hire teenagers.

FAMILY LIFE

There are some cultural differences between the United States and Indonesia, especially in the family structure and relationships. In Indonesia, the relationships between family members are very close. Most families try to have dinner together almost every evening during the week, and all the relatives often eat together once a week. Indonesians, unlike Americans, try to gather together the entire family as many times as possible. The role of the children is to serve the family. Boys are encouraged to continue their education. Girls, however, are expected to find a husband at an early age and then become part of their husband's family. A girl moves from serving her family to serving her husband's family. This has brought great criticism from many women who believe they have as much right as men to an education. This subject is discussed at length below.

Many teenagers are no longer spending as much time with their families. As more Western distractions and television have come into the country, teenagers have begun to change their behavior. The end of the dictatorship lifted many of the bans on secular life, leading many to experiment with alternative lifestyles. Skating and raves have become very popular. Many of the perceptions of the world for teenagers come from video games and satellite television.

Families have been challenged in the past few years with the influence of Western clothing and styles, as seen on television, in movies, and on the Internet. Indonesia is an Islamic country, and wearing revealing clothing can lead to staring, ultimately embarrassing a family. Teenagers have found ways to push the boundaries of society by mixing traditional clothing with more Western styles. Most teenagers are very poor and make meager wages that have to support the family. The capital is home to thousands of homeless children. Also, tourists serve as a perfect target for theft. Child prostitution is now more common, especially in resort areas. As the crackdown on Thai child brothels has increased, many have opened in Indonesia, offering "sex vacations" to brothels where the prostitutes are as young as 11. Facing a poor economic situation, the government has left the sex trade alone because it attracts tourists.

In traditional Indonesian culture, it is impolite to call an older person by his or her name. It is polite to use Mr. or Mrs. before their first name. It is a sign of appreciation and respect to a person who is older. On the other hand, in the United States, older persons are usually referred to by their first name or by a name indicating their relationship to the speaker (e.g., Grandpa, Grandma). This has also changed. Many government agencies are blaming the economic downfall on the decadence of teenage culture and Western influence. According to teenagers, these are easy excuses for the problems of the country.

TRADITIONAL AND NONTRADITIONAL FOOD DISHES

Many foods can be found in nearly every corner of the Indonesian archipelago today. Rice is a national staple, even in areas such as eastern Indonesia, where the main source of most starch was once corn (known as maize), cassava, taro, or sago. On ceremonial occasions—modern weddings, funerals, or state functions—small pieces of meat roasted on a skewer (*sate*), fried shrimp or fish-flavored chips made with rice flour (*krupuk*), and highly spiced curries of chicken and goat are commonly served. These foods are placed on a table and served at room temperature. Guests serve themselves buffet-style. Rice is placed in the center of the plate, with meats or other foods on the edges. Food is eaten rapidly and without speaking, with the fingertips or with a spoon and fork. Water is generally drunk only after the meal, when men (rarely women) smoke their distinctive clove-scented *kretek* cigarettes.

As stated before, American foods, especially fast food, have become popular. It has become a sign of wealth to be able to serve hamburgers at a party along with the traditional foods. Since most Indonesians are Muslim, pork is not eaten. Teenagers' meals have become less rigid and more sporadic. Many parents have protested the advertisements for fast food, alcohol, and cigarettes. Getting together is still very important for most teenagers, but they have begun to separate into their own groups instead of playing the traditional role of serving adults at parties. Poverty determines in large part what food is eaten. The many poor of the country are malnourished, some eating scraps whenever they can. There are many missions, mostly religious, that provide food for the poor. Evangelical religions are on the rise among young Indonesians, especially as more question Islam, mainly because it is associated with the old government.

SCHOOLING

Indonesians of between 7 and 12 years of age are required to attend six years of primary school. They can choose between state-run, nonsectarian public schools supervised by the Department of Education and Culture or private/semiprivate religious (usually Islamic) schools supervised and financed by the Department of Religious Affairs. However, although 85 percent of the Indonesian population is Muslim, less than 15 percent attended religious schools in 1990. The number is even lower today. Enrollment figures were slightly higher for girls than boys and much higher in Java than the rest of Indonesia. The terrain in the rest of the country and the role of agriculture (children are needed to work the fields) lead to many dropping out of school or never attending.

The main goal of the national education system was not only to impart secular wisdom about the world but also to socialize children in the principles of participation in the modern nation-state, its bureaucracies, and its moral and ideological foundations. Since 1975, a key feature of the national curriculum was instruction in the Pancasila. Students age six and above learn its five principles (belief in one God, humanitarianism, national unity, democracy, and social justice) by rote memorization and are instructed daily to apply the meanings of this key national symbol to their lives. The failed attempt at a communist coup in 1965 provided a vivid image of an attack on the Pancasila. To prove their rejection of communist ideology, all teachers and all members of the Indonesian state have to swear allegiance to the Pancasila and the government party of functional groups. This is similar to the U.S. Pledge of Allegiance. Since the change in government, teachers and students have publicly challenged the government's dictates. Many teenagers say they just recite the right answers but do not believe what is said.

In the public schools, pedagogy emphasizes rote learning and deference to the authority of the teacher. Although the youngest children are sometimes allowed to use the local language, by the third year of primary school nearly all instruction is conducted in formal Indonesian. A standard teaching technique is to narrate a historical event or to describe a mathematical problem, pausing at key junctures to allow the students to fill in the blanks. By not responding to individual problems of the students and retaining an emotionally distanced demeanor, the teacher is said to be patient (*sabar*), which is considered admirable.

Nationally, the average primary class size is about 27, while upper-level classes include between 30 and 40 students. Ninety-two percent of primary school students graduate, but only about half continue to junior high school (ages 13–15). Of those, 87 percent go on to a senior high school (ages 16–18). The national adult literacy rate remains at about 84 percent, keeping Indonesia and Brunei at the lowest literacy levels among the six member nations of the Association for Southeast Asian Nations.

After completion of the six-year primary school program, students choose among a variety of vocational and preprofessional junior and senior high schools, each level lasting three years. There are academic and

A classroom in Jakarta, Indonesia. Photo © TRIP/TRIP.

vocational junior high schools that can lead to senior-level diplomas; also, "domestic science" or home economics junior high schools for girls exist. Many girls are placed in these involuntarily. At this level, the student is not allowed to pick where he or she wants to go. The teacher or the supervisor usually makes the choice. At the senior high school level, there are three-year agricultural, veterinary, and forestry schools open to only students who graduated from academic junior high schools. Special schools at the junior and senior levels teach hotel management, legal clerking, arts (sculpture, carving, pottery, and weaving), and music. Students are funneled into schools as needed by the economy. If mechanics are needed, students are sent to learn mechanics.

Teaching is different in the United States and in Indonesia. In the United States, a teacher needs at least a college degree. But in Indonesia, for example, in the 1950s anyone completing a teacher-training program at the junior high level could obtain a teacher's certificate. Since the 1970s, the teaching profession has been restricted to graduates of a senior high school for teachers in a primary school and to graduates of a university-level education course for teachers of higher grades.

Education is quite different for boys and girls. For example, only 1 out of every 100 women is a university graduate, and half of them have not finished elementary education. In major urban centers, only 7 out of every 100 women hold university diplomas, while one-third of them have not graduated from elementary school. This is not the case for men, who are sent off to pursue higher education by their families when possible, and often at the expense of their female siblings. As government records show, the number of women in rural and urban areas who have not gone to university is more than double the figure for men. This underlines the gender stereotypes, which continue to reinforce among both girls and boys the traditional domestic role of women. The belief is that women cannot think like men and that their role is to bear children and raise families. As more teenage girls begin to demand their right to go to school, or leave Indonesia to study abroad (for college), that is changing. There is still much to be done, however.

There are around 173,000 primary schools all over Indonesia, and every village has one or two, including religious primary schools (madrasah). In universities, most women take humanities or social science subjects rather than engineering or science courses, which the job market demands. In areas of study like engineering and information technology, for instance, there are very few women enrolled. Because so many women are kept away from schools, it is no wonder that two-thirds of the number of illiterate Indonesians are females. In many parts of the country, child marriage is still common. Data from a 1998 national socioeconomic survey show that in eight provinces, 10 percent or more of married women aged 25 to 34 years married before reaching the age of 16. Two provinces— West Java and South Kalimantan—had more than 15 percent child marriages, while in the remaining six, child marriages ranged from 10 to 14 percent. Nationally, Indonesian girls marry at around 16. To some Indonesian parents, sending their sons instead of their daughters to universities is like making an investment. In the Indonesian culture, sons are expected to continue helping their parents even if they are already married and have their own children. Daughters, on the other hand, are expected to marry and live with their husbands' families. To improve the education of women, the ministry of national education is providing informal education, including literacy, life-skills programs, and income-generating activities. This program has not been as successful, because many teenagers do not trust the government and its motives. There are some 1,600 community learning centers in the country providing informal education. The ministry also gives scholarships, ensuring that 50 percent of the recipients are women. For 32 years under the Suharto regime, the so-called Ibuism or housewife position ideology was applied in Indonesia, and it is clearly stipulated in the country's marriage law. To popularize gender equality in Indonesia, the ministry of national education involves women in writing textbooks. However, gender discrimination is very visible in elementary school textbooks. Pictures of mothers and daughters working in the kitchen and photos of fathers working in the office both exemplify and perpetuate the stereotypes.

SOCIAL LIFE

Indonesia has a wealth of arts and culture since the country has more than three hundred ethnic groups, each with its own culture and traditions. Social life in Indonesia for teens has been influenced by the ancient traditions and customs (*adat*). Its rules depend on where the teen is from. Each ethnic group has different social practices. Also, urban and rural teenagers see their world differently. Whereas urban areas in Indonesia are overcrowded, rural areas are sparsely populated. Culture in Indonesia— rituals, ceremonies, and restrictions—also depends heavily on the influence of religion. The ethnic diversity of Indonesia attracts visitors. The Western media and culture have done to Indonesia's culture what the 32-year reign of Suharto could not: begin to bridge cultural gaps among teenagers. At the same time, it has awakened many issues of ethnic identity. Teenagers see the Western culture as allowing them to express themselves. This probably has less to do with Western culture than with the end of the dictatorship, as in Eastern Europe.

Tourism has also been spurred by darker trends in Indonesia: increasingly easy access to drugs and more widespread prostitution. Ecstasy abuse is a major problem, especially in urban areas. Methamphetamines arrived in the Jakarta nightlife in 1998, mainly from Australians in other Asian countries. Many of the pills are sold as ecstasy in Jakarta nightclubs but are actually methamphetamines that come from other Asian countries. The Indonesian government is wary of the Australian and Japanese tourists that come to the archipelago for vacation. Marijuana is produced in remote areas of northern Sumatra, primarily for domestic consumption. There has been an increase in clandestine methamphetamine and ecstasy laboratories. The government has noticed a drastic increase in methamphetamine use in Indonesia among teenagers, young professionals, and prostitutes. In recent years, official concern over designer drugs, first ecstasy and now methamphetamines, has eclipsed concern with more traditional narcotics, such as marijuana. The government has begun instituting tougher penalties, as well as educational programs in schools for teenagers. Teenagers use drugs as an escape for several reasons. First, it allows them to experiment with an identity that is different from theirs. Their lives are controlled by traditions that they do not feel connected to. Second, the high poverty rates have led many to use drugs, which are cheaper and more available than alcohol or cigarettes. Third, the unsupervised homeless children see using drugs as a ritual, as a rite of passage, and as their right as adults.

The government has blamed the rise of the popularity of Western culture and the decline of traditional values for the drug use among teens. Medical doctors and psychiatrists say much has to do with the instability of life in the country. Many teenagers do not feel connected to their parents' culture or the state. The recent uprisings and the economic disparity have left many teenagers wondering about their future. The rise of poverty and the increasing discrimination in schools of the poor has led many teenagers to abandon traditional culture. Tourism has also brought money that can be easily accessed by teenagers who serve as guides or prostitutes. The rise in prostitution is attributed to the popularity of Indonesia as a place for sex vacations. Although most Indonesian teenagers are not prostitutes, the rise in the number of troubled teenagers has worried the state. The issue of mental health care is now taken seriously, as the teenage suicide rate has multiplied rapidly. Many girls have taken to killing themselves rather than being married to a particular person. The lessons taught in schools have alienated the teenagers, because they are very different from the lessons they learn on the streets.

Most Indonesian teenagers spend time at the mall or watching movies. Movies and video games can be bought for less than a U.S. dollar. These are pirated. Any marketplace sells anything from G-rated movies to pornography. In a nation where Western and Japanese movies, video games, and music were once banned, teenagers are glad to be able to watch these freely in the home. Although the government censors movies and television, it has no control over pirated DVDs and videos. In the countryside, teenage life is much different. Most children have to work on farms or with their parents. There are fewer problems with drugs but also fewer drugs available. Many children do not attend school past the primary level unless their family can afford to send them to one. The government has tried to help, but tradition is very hard to break. Many programs, such as those for girls, have been dropped because of the economic and political crisis.

RECREATION AND ENTERTAINMENT

Entertainment in Indonesia is a combination of traditional, modern (local), and nonlocal. Traditional entertainment includes puppet shows (*wayang*), comedy shows, and traditional dances. One such example is *conglak*, a game that came to Indonesia from Africa via the Arab merchants who brought Islam. The game includes a board with holes, and the design is usually in the shape of a dragon. As in checkers, the goal is to get your pieces (marbles) to the "home bases" at the end of the board. In poorer areas, players use the ground and dig holes. It was played originally by young girls of Javanese nobility. In most regions it is a game for young and teenage girls, and it connects mothers and daughters. Unlike many other traditional pieces of culture that have become absorbed into the Western cultural landscape of video games and television, *conglak* still remains popular in its traditional form. It is one of the most popular games in Indonesia, mostly among girls.

Local entertainment is similar to entertainment in other countries but with local flavor and traditions. In music, for example, there are pop bands and singers, rock bands, country singers, jazz groups, and rappers. Famous Indonesian songwriters are Titik Puspa, Guruh Sukarnoputra, Chandra Darusman, Rhoma Irama, and Iwan Fals. Nteve, a television station, devotes enormous blocks of time to pop music shows, some produced by the Nteve staff but most produced by MTV Asia, all of which, regardless of the national identity of the performers, employ Western styles of music, rock, country, rhythm and blues, and mild forms of rap. Another station, TPI, emphasizes the throbbing sounds (similar to reggae and techno) of Indonesia's popular *dangdut* genre, which is also featured in several shows on Indosiar but rarely heard on private stations. Rajawali Citra Televisi Indonesia (RCTI) and others have produced and broadcast glitzy shows in which top-selling pop music stars perform in collaboration with performers of ethnic music (*musik etnik*). *Pop daerah*, popular songs in regional languages (Javanese, Minang, etc.), are not usually included on MTV, although Televisi Republik Indonesia (TVRI) and Indosiar broadcast entire shows devoted to *pop daerah*. The use of satellites has brought other forms of U.S. MTV into the home. Through the Internet, pop stars from the United States—Britney Spears, NSync, and Eminem—have gained popularity.

There are also nontraditional music styles, such as *kroncong* and *dangdut*. They use regular musical instruments, although *dangdut* is closer to Indian music from India. Other entertainment includes music and movies from outside Indonesia. For movies, Chinese kung fu or martial arts and Indian films are among the most popular. There have been complaints that many of the new Indian movies have strong sexual content and sexually suggestive titles. Although the government has attempted to ban or edit them, they thrive in pirated videos. Indonesia has made the copyright infringement list, only second behind China, because of the widespread use of pirated music, movies, and video games. Imported movies are either subtitled in Bahasa Indonesia or dubbed with Bahasa Indonesia when shown in theaters. The theaters are popular because they provide a place where teenagers can go without parental supervision.

Urban Indonesian nightlife in the early 1990s centered around visiting night markets, shopping in Chinese stores (*toko*), patronizing food stalls called *warung*, and going to the Indonesian cinema. Although they were an important part of Indonesian national culture in the early 1990s, films did not necessarily mirror Indonesian life accurately. Most Indonesian-made films were set in cities even though the population was largely rural, and most films employed Bahasa Indonesia even though most viewers were Javanese. There was rarely mention of religion or ethnicity, even though most of the population had a religious affiliation. The social class depicted was almost always middle class, even though Indonesia's middle class was small. Westerners were presented as modern, as having no tradition whatsoever, and Western women as having no constraints on their sexuality. The audiences for films consisted almost entirely of teenagers and young adults, more males than females. Many theaters have become empty. The night markets are selling movies and drugs, and teenagers can go back to a house, use drugs, and stay up late watching pirated movies.

People in Indonesia prefer television rather than cinema, and the number of television sets in Indonesian households rose dramatically in the 1980s. Nearly every corner of the archipelago had television relay stations permitting reception of one or more channels of tightly controlled government programs. These programs generally featured education, entertainment, and some unsubtitled foreign serials such as *Kojak* and *Dynasty*. At the same time, advertisements for consumer goods appeared on television. National and international news was very popular, even in remote areas, and contained many descriptions of government development programs. Nearly all of the programming in the early 1990s was in Bahasa Indonesia, although some local arts programs were conducted in regional languages. The most popular televised programs are sporting events, such as soccer, boxing, and volleyball. Today, that is still true. Many new programs are starting to appear as the restrictions of the previous government have been lifted. Also, satellite television has introduced U.S. and European television.

RELIGIOUS PRACTICES AND CULTURAL CEREMONIES

In Indonesia, five religions are recognized by the government: Islam, Christianity (Protestant and Catholic), Hinduism, and Buddhism. Islam is the largest religion in Indonesia (88%), followed by Protestant Christianity (5.8%), Catholic Christianity (2.9%), Hinduism (2%), and Buddhism (0.9%). Religion is an important part of life in Indonesia. It influences politics, culture, and economics, and it should not be taken lightly. Most of the great monotheistic world religions are present, and also a number of tribal religions and beliefs among the cultures in Kalimantan, Irian, and Jaya. There are specialized strains of religious beliefs among communities in Java, Bali, and Sumatra. This section will focus on the most common in the archipelago.

Islam

Islam came to the northern tip of Sumatra sometime during the twelfth century and spread south and east until it had conquered the whole Indonesian archipelago. It supposedly came with Muslim merchants that were trading with the courts on the coastline. Thus, through trade it became popular. The traditional religion of the area was a Hindu-Buddhist religion adhered to by kings and princes. The merchants and traders as well as the poor became attracted to Islam. It was not until Islam came to the inland courts on Java that it spread. At the end of the fourteenth century, all kingdoms on Java were Muslim; the remaining Hindu kingdom fled to Bali. Today, the most fundamentalist Indonesian Muslims live in Aceh, the northern tip of Sumatra, where Islam first took hold. The inhabitants of this area have always been fierce fighters, giving both the Dutch and the Indonesian state constant opposition. Aceh pressured the Indonesian government for many years to become an independent Islamic state and has today special status as an autonomous region.

In the south, Java has the largest Islamic organization today. Nadhlatul Ulama is a version of Islam that is more relaxed in its beliefs, building on the traditional values of Java as much as on Islamic scripture. Generally, Islam was an important political force during the period of nationalism, after 1900. One of the most important movements during that time was modernistic Muhammadiyah (established in 1912). The modernistic school wanted to purify Islam from local tradition (*adat*) and return to its original source, the Koran and the *Hadith* or *Sunnah*. Its supporters also believed in modernizing the Islamic world, often with ideas from Western science. Muhammadiyah took on their ideology to work in the modernist direction but met resistance everywhere. The organization was too small and unorganized to follow through on its agenda. The organization almost fell apart in 1925 but was able to recover, and in 1935 it boasted 250,000 members.

During both the Sukarno and the Suharto regimes, the demand of an Islamic Indonesian state has been thoroughly subdued, even though uprisings and violent riots have occurred from time to time. Today, the situation can be described as unstable. During the demonstrations that began in 1997 and continued until Suharto's resignation, a lot of violence occurred. Most of this violence was directed at the Chinese, who were considered religious infidels and economic oppressors. The Indonesian government did not react until it was threatened. But it was too late. The demonstrations grew from the indiscriminate beating of the Chinese to a general uprising against the appalling economic situation facing many of the Indonesians today. Today, Islam is still a political force.

Many teenagers were raised in an Islamic household. Many learned the history from the schools and their parents. However, in the last 10 years, teenagers have become less "religious." Attendance at religious events is down. Public prayer is not common among school-aged children. The secularization of religion left many without a devout sense of belief. Still, many aspects persist as cultural realities: no pork in the diet, the role of women, and religious holidays. As more teenagers question these things, religious observation is diminishing. The bad economic crisis has led many young men to join the extreme Islamic movements at the fringes of the island. The lack of jobs, the crackdown by the government, and the alienation from school and society have left them searching for answers, and the orthodox movements offer answers that the adults and government cannot.

Christianity

The Dutch introduced Christianity to the Indonesian archipelago, and the Portuguese had a strong influence in East Timor. No other people brought Christianity to the country. The introduction of a religion reflects the intent of the people who spread it. The behavior of the Dutch toward the people of Indonesia was never good. Thus, very few persons ever associated Christianity with anything but harsh treatment by the Dutch. However, during the Suharto takeover in 1965, everybody had to have a religion. Those who refused were labeled Communists. According to the law, all Communists had to be terminated, and thus, many who refused to take a religion were shot. Many Chinese adopted Christianity, which further fueled the conflict between them and the indigenous Indonesians. There are some Christian enclaves in the Moluccas and on Kalimantan. The island of Flores is also mostly Christian. Since the mid-1990s, many missionaries have come to Indonesia. Evangelical Christianity is growing quickly among the young. The message of hope offers a vital connection to an institution in a country with very few stable institutions. The newness and Western feel of Christianity has attracted many. Also, missionaries have begun to be the doctors and teachers in rural areas, converting many as they work in hospitals and help farmers.

Buddhism

Buddhism has very few, if any, followers today. It has been an exclusively Chinese religion over the last few centuries. But it was a prominent religion before Islam arrived, and it controlled the courts on both Sumatra and Java. The Borobudur temple is said to be the center of Buddhism on the archipelago. Few teenagers practice this religion. Many teenagers from Australia, Europe, and the United States, however, come to Indonesia to see the monuments to Buddha. They feel a connection to them and are usually the only persons at local shrines.

Hinduism

On the island of Bali, most people adhere to Hinduism, although it is very different from the Hinduism practiced in India. In Bali, unlike India, religion is not separated from everyday life. At one time Hinduism, along with Buddhism, was the predominant religion in Indonesia (as seen by the many great Hindu monuments in Java), but it died out with the spread of Islam through the archipelago. The final great Hindu kingdom, the Majapahits, evacuated to Bali, taking its religion, rituals, art, literature, and music. Religion in Bali has two features: it is absolutely everywhere and it stresses good fun over the worries of life. A person cannot escape religion in Bali. There are temples in every village, shrines in every field, and offerings being made at every corner. This way of life has made Bali the most popular vacation spot in all of Asia. Tourists love the idea of the spirituality and emphasis on good living. Over half of Australia's population under the age of 21 has been to Bali. It is becoming a popular spot for U.S. college students and for European teenagers after they graduate from high school. The rise in foreign tourism has led to a rise in drugs. Local teenagers have become major suppliers to visitors who are seeking to have a good time.

CONCLUSION

With the rise of the Internet, satellite television, and other forms of modern communication, teenagers in Indonesia now experience some of the same things as U.S. teenagers. However, Indonesia is very different from the United States. Each island culture influences how the people take in Western culture. The adults and government are trying to preserve their culture, not become Western. The government is facing the huge task of keeping the country together in the face of rising ethnic violence. Teenagers are very involved in this type of action. As they grow up, they begin to realize that they have a unique culture that they believe the government does not respect, and they become angry.

Schooling has undergone some major changes. Just like in the United States, the Indonesian government has begun to include ethnic minorities in textbooks. Education for girls has seen a dramatic change as the government has begun to help parents pay to educate women.

Indonesia faces a tough road ahead, given the current economic instability and ethnic violence. Also, the rise of drugs has become a concern for teenagers.

RESOURCE GUIDE

Nonfiction

Alexander, P. (Ed.). (1989). *Creating Indonesian cultures*. Sydney, Australia: Oceania Publications.

Cribb, R. (Ed.). (1990). *The Indonesian killings 1965–1966*. Victoria, Australia: Monash University, Centre of Southeast Asian Studies.

Cribb, R. (2000). *Historical atlas of Indonesia*. Honolulu, HI: University of Hawaii Press.

Dalton, B. (1995). *Indonesia handbook*. Emeryville, CA: Moon Publications.

Daws, G., & Fujita, M. (1999). *Archipelago: Islands of Indonesia, from the nineteenth-century discoveries of Alfred Russell Wallace to the fate of forests and reefs in the twenty-first*. Berkeley, CA: University of California Press.

Dawson, B., & Gillow, J. (1994). *The traditional architecture of Indonesia*. London, England: Thames and Hudson.

Harding, P. (2002). *Lonely planet Australia*. 11th ed. Berkeley, CA: Lonely Planet.

Turner, P., Delahunty, B., Greenway, P., Lyon, J. (1995). *Indonesia*. Lonely Planet Indonesia. Berkeley, CA: Lonely Planet.

Fiction

Bloem, M., & Boeke, W. (1996). *The cockatoo's lie*. Seattle, WA: Women in Translation.

Conrad, J. (1963). *Almayer's folly: A story of an eastern river*. New York: Nelson Publishers.

Conrad, J. (1989). *Lord Jim*. New York: Penguin Books.

Koch, C. J. (1995). *The year of living dangerously*. New York: Penguin Books.

Lingard, J. (Trans.). (1996). *Diverse lives: Contemporary stories from Indonesia*. London, England: Oxford University Press.

Lubis, M. (1989). *The outlaw and other stories*. New York: Penguin Books.

Multatuli. (1995). *Max Havelaar or, the coffee auctions of the Dutch Trading Company*. New York: Penguin Books.

Roskies, D.M.E. (Trans.). *Black clouds over the Isle of Gods and other modern Indonesian short stories*. Armonk, NY: M.E. Sharpe Publishing.

Toer, P. A. (1996). *A heap of ashes*. New York: Penguin Books.

Toer, P. A. (1996). *Child of all nations*. New York: Penguin Books.

Toer, P. A. (1996). *Footsteps*. New York: Penguin Books.

Toer, P. A. (1996). *This earth of mankind*. New York: Penguin Books.

Toer, P. A. (1997). *House of glass*. New York: Penguin Books.

Van der Post, L. (1997). *The admiral's baby*. New York: Morrow/Avon Publishers.

Van Dis, A. (1996). *My father's war: A novel*. New York: New Press.

Web Sites

http://commdocs.house.gov/committees/intlrel/hfa45910.000/hfa45910_0.htm U.S. policy toward Indonesia. A 1998 hearing before the Subcommittee on Asia and the Pacific of the Committee on International Relations in the House of Representatives

http://newton.uor.edu/Departments&Programs/AsianStudiesDept/indonesia.html
    East and Southeast Asia: An Annotated Directory of Internet Resources
http://www.cia.gov/cia/publications/factbook/geos/id.html
    CIA fact book on Indonesia, the most comprehensive information site on
    Indonesia
http://www.cgtd.com/asia/indonesia.htm
    Trade and marketing information on Indonesia from the Center for Global
    Trade Development.
http://www.fe.doe.gov/international/indonesia.html
    Department of Energy Web site with links to Indonesia and other federal sites
    that have links to Indonesia
http://www.middleeastnews.com/indonesianews.html
    News and information resources on Indonesia
http://www.state.gov/g/drl/rls/
    Report on Indonesia from the U.S. Department of State's Bureau of Democ-
    racy, Human Rights, and Labor
http://www.worldwide.edu/ci/indonesia/
    WorldWide classroom is an international organization that offers information
    exchange between schools. This is a great site that discusses schools and uni-
    versities in Indonesia

Pen Pal/Chat

http://users.skynet.be/sky91849/indonesia.htm.

Chapter 6

JAPAN

Eric Dwyer and Risako Ide

INTRODUCTION

There is a famous song that all Japanese know called "Sakura." *Sakura* means "cherry blossom," and both the flower and the song named for it are perhaps the best-known symbols of Japanese culture in the world. People recognize this melody all over the world. For today's Japanese, the cherry blossom is a symbol of renewal and optimism. The cherry blossom is one of the first flowers to bloom in the spring. Since some buds are bright white with soft pink edges and its tree is large and round with broad, out-stretched branches, the first cherry blossom bloom after an icy three months of leafless and flowerless wintry grayness is certainly a breathtaking sight.

Contrasting with the cherry trees yet equally impressive is the view of a Japanese downtown. As Japanese teenagers walk out of any city train station in their country, they're bound to see some of the most modern and brightly lit buildings in the world. Busy, crowded city centers of even smaller towns are adorned with neon signs and the fluorescent lights of department stores. Today's Japanese teenagers experience the latest and cleverest of the world's most recent technology and architecture in an essentially low-crime society.

Sharing the trains and the streets with the teenagers are their grand-parents. Japan certainly did not look like this when they were kids. They were born into one of the most secluded cultures in the world. Little did they know that their Asian neighbors were being subjected to war, death, and misery, instigated by Japan's emperor and military through the first 40 years of the twentieth century. When the world finally retaliated during

World War II, these innocent grandparents suffered the destruction of their country from its most southern island to the northern extremes of Honshu. They endured the pain of being the only country in the world to have suffered atomic bomb attacks. Even when World War II was finished, those who had escaped the bombings on the far northern island of Hokkaido immediately had to deal with volcanic eruptions and earthquakes destroying some of their farms. With a new postwar American-written constitution as a foundation, these grandparents began a new era of progress in the second half of the century, grasping their newly attained postwar power and placing it into the hands of the businesses. The product as the twenty-first century gets underway is the second-largest economy in the world. And while today's immediate look of Japan from the train platforms is of modernism and flashy lights, the identity of the common person rooted in ancient Japan—a culture of literacy, art, community, and detail—has survived. The grandparents have asserted that this is the case, and the teenagers reap the benefits of community commitment, retention of what worked in ancient times, and acceptance of what helps the world today. As for the Japanese grandparents, no one their age in any other place on Earth has witnessed as many material and ideological changes as they have. And while less than a handful of war criminals who supported Japanese imperialism up through World War II still live out their elder years in a secret and quiet in-country exile, the remainder of Japan, young and old, has joined the world as an economic giant and benevolent leader in world progress.

This is the country that today's Japanese teenagers have inherited. And in the spring, teenagers and grandparents head to the breeze and warmth of the parks and countryside to see the cherry trees ablaze with light pink.

TYPICAL DAY

For teenagers, the first cherry blossom indicates not only that nature has refreshed itself but also that the new school year is about to begin. (The Japanese school year begins in April; it consists of three terms separated by short holidays in spring and winter and a one-month break in summer.) School is the centerpiece of a Japanese teenager's life. The typical school week goes from Monday to Friday. Until 2002, many Japanese schools had classes on Saturday until noon, but schools have recently decided to give students a two-day weekend. Today's teenagers are the first to experience such long weekends, yet students still spend a considerable amount of their everyday life, even on weekends, in and around schools.

Japanese teenagers are usually responsible for their own transportation to and from school. Through the third year of junior high (equivalent to the ninth grade in the United States), the majority of students attend public schools in their district that are usually within walking distance of home. Students may ride their bicycles or take buses or trains if their schools are farther away. Additionally, most Japanese schools do not have parking lots due to limited land; even the teachers depend on public transportation to commute.

Teenagers are not allowed to drive to school. First, the age for receiving a driver's license is 18. Second, the price of driver's education is prohibitive, and many kids take driver's education during college. As a result, there are a number of adults who do not have driver's licenses simply because it is too expensive to obtain one. If one does get a driver's license, though, some driving rules are notably different from those of other countries. Driving in Japan is on the left. No turn on red lights is permitted, even if no one is coming, and all people must stop at railroad crossings, as opposed to just slowing down. Still, at least in cities, driving is so impractical that it deters anyone from choosing to drive to school. The roads are narrow, the traffic is heavy, and one may actually get to school faster on foot or by bicycle than with a car. On the other hand, since public transportation is so widely available, traffic is not all that bad in the countryside. Knowing that crime is low in Japan and that adults and older kids help younger people, families allow their children to travel long distances to school and social events on their own. It is not uncommon to see children as young as 9 or 10 years old traveling on trains on their own, even in the largest cities.

However, this is not to say that families implicitly trust their children to be on the streets all night. Curfew is a common and strict practice with families, and teenagers adhere to curfew rules. If the curfew is broken, the children may suffer punishments such as a lowered allowance or no TV and Nintendo games for a while.

Club activities are a vital part of school life. Many club organizations fall into one of two categories: *taiikukei* and *bunkakei*. Taiikukei, meaning "physical education type," is where one finds baseball, basketball, volleyball, gymnastics, swimming, tennis, softball, and so forth. Kendo (Japanese fencing), judo, and other traditionally Japanese forms of physical practice are also popular clubs, especially among male students. Bunkakei, meaning "culture type," is where one finds clubs for music (woodwind ensembles and string sections are popular), chorus, art, and drama. There are also science clubs and English Speaking Society (ESS), where students practice English conversation or watch Hollywood movies together. It is in bunkakei that the traditional Japanese games of Go and Shogi (Japanese-style chess) inspire clubs as well as calligraphy, which is the brush painting of Chinese characters. There are also clubs related to modern popular culture, particularly Japanese comic books (*manga*) and animation (*anime*).

Clubs meet as many as two or three times a week and on Saturdays, depending on the intensity of their activities. Some taiikukei club activities, such as baseball and tennis, often meet early in the morning before class for *asa-ren*, or "morning practice." They also have daily practice sessions before sport tournaments as well as public performances for music and drama clubs. Many events are found in a schoolwide festival held in the fall known as *bunkasai,* or the cultural festival. During bunkasai, each class uses its classroom to display the result of its research or create food and game stands. During this time, club activities are displayed for the school and students' families, as well as the school's surrounding community, whose members are often holding their own tournaments, assemblies, concerts, and productions.

Not all teenagers choose to attend university. For those who choose not to, options remain at vocational schools known as *senmon gakko*. Attending these schools often leads, just as attending universities does, to life-long careers at famous companies. Many children's families work for a business or organization that has contributed to its town or neighborhood for generations. As a result, the teenagers' career has been chosen for them; they have been born into it.

Nevertheless, whether it is a senmon gakko or a university, approximately half of all Japanese teenagers will go to some form of college. Families support children in school and are often willing to spend large sums of money for their education, spending well over $2,000 a year just for tuition for their children. Additionally, parents may let their children take other lessons such as piano, violin, and English lessons from as early as the age of 3.

While studying is the primary activity Japanese teenagers are expected to engage in, teenagers can hold part-time jobs, known as *arbaito* (from the German word *arbeit,* meaning "to work"). However, these are exceptions rather than norms; usually parents discourage their junior high and senior high school students from part-time work unless they are in financial need. As a result, teenagers usually wait until they graduate from high school to engage in part-time jobs. Due to the lighter study load required for Japan's university students compared to U.S. university students, many freshmen at universities choose to take part in arubaito. They may work in fast food restaurants or convenience stores. Many choose to work in stores that hone in on their hobbies. For example, it is not uncommon to see students working in stores that address their interest in clothes or music. Some teenagers work in their family businesses.

The following interviews are examples of students' schedules:

Nagaizumi Kita Junior High School, 2nd year, Shizuoka (female, age 13)

(1) Everyday schedule: I wake up at 6:30 and leave home at 7:00. I come home around 4:30. When I have club activity (brass band club), I come home at around 5:30. At school, I have 50-minute classes with a 10-minute break in the morning. After lunch, we have a 30-minute break. Club activity will be about three or four times a week (four or five times a week during summer), and the time varies according to the season. During summer, we practice till 6 P.M. and 5 P.M. during the winter. Everyone must attend some club activity.

(2) Breakfast menu: Rice, miso soup, fruit, bread.

(3) Weekend schedule: The morning hours are usually spent doing club activities. When I do not have club activities, I go out with friends or relax at home.

(4) Favorite food/fast food: Fruit, hamburgers.

(5) Outings with friends: I go out on trains and go to bookstores, visit small shops, and go window-shopping for clothes.

(6) After-school fashions/fads among friends: When I stay at home, I wear pants and *toreenaa* (school sweatsuit), or denim skirts or *paakaa* (windbreaker-style tops with hood).

(7) Hours of TV and favorite programs: About three hours per day. I like animation and entertainment programs.

(8) Fads among friends: All my friends are into the boys' comic magazine *Shonen Jump*.

(9) Do you have somebody you like (including celebrities)? No.

(10) What is the source of stress these days? Studying is troublesome.

(11) What would you do if you had all the time and money you could use freely? I'd like to buy manga and my favorite PC software and play all day.

(12) Do you have future dreams? Do you want to get married? I'd like to study archeology or geology and get a job in that field. As for marriage, I do not want to get married for now.

Shimizu Shiritsu Daiichi Junior High School, 2nd year, Shizuoka (male, age 13)

(1) Everyday schedule: I wake up at 7:10 and leave home at 7:50. Classes start at 8:10. At school, I have a 50-minute class with a 10-minute break. Club activity will be about 2 hours a day. I am in the basketball club.

(2) Breakfast menu: Rice, miso soup, fruit.

(3) Weekend schedule: The morning hours are usually spent with club activities. During the afternoon, I play games and watch TV, relaxing at home. I study a little bit during the evening.

(4) Favorite food/fast food: ramen noodles, fish, and clams. McDonalds (cheeseburger), Kentucky Fried Chicken.

(5) Outings with friends: I go to Game Centers and Animate (they sell lots of manga and stuff).

(6) After-school fashions/fads among friends: I basically stay in the same clothes I wore at school. I sometimes change into regular clothes. Among my friends, the Internet site called Samurai Tamashii (samurai spirit) is really popular.

(7) Hours of TV and favorite programs: I do not know how much TV I watch. My favorite types of shows are dramas, variety shows, and comedies.

(8) Do you have somebody you like (including celebrities)? No.

(9) What is the source of stress these days? Weird things that my "kohai" [junior; or inferior to "senpai," or superior] do.

(10) What would you do if you had all the time and money you could use freely? I'd just want to play!

(11) Do you have future dreams? Do you want to get married? I want to become a voice actor (*seiyuu*) but my parents say "you better not." As for marriage, I'm not sure.

Example schedule for senior high schooler: Shimizu Higashi High School, 2nd year, Shizuoka (male, age 13)

(1) Everyday schedule: I wake up at 7:00 and leave home at 8:05. When there are club activities on weekends, I wake up at 7:30 but without I wake up at 11:00. Classes start at 8:10 (it is a one-minute walk to school). At school, I have 65-minute classes with 10-minute breaks. Morning schedule is 8:25 to 9:30, 9:40

to 10:45, and 10:55 to 12:00. Afternoons are 12:50 to 13:55, and 14:05 to 15:10. Club activities last two or three hours. I am in the gymnastics club.

(2) Breakfast menu: Rice, miso soup, fruit.

(3) Weekend schedule: The morning hours are usually spent with club activities. During the afternoon, I listen to music and watch TV, relaxing at home. Sometimes I go to karaoke and movies and I study a little bit during the evening. (Actually, I have a lot of weekend homework.)

(4) Favorite food/fast food: Ramen noodles, fried rice, Japanese BBQ (*yakiniku*). McDonalds, Kentucky Fried Chicken.

(5) Outings with friends: I go to the movies and sometimes to game centers for a change of pace. I also go to karaoke. Shouting loudly lets go of my stress.

(6) After-school fashions/fads among friends: I basically stay in the same clothes that I wore at school (in *jaaji*, sweats worn as school uniforms for physical activities).

(7) Hours of TV and favorite programs: Regular days, about 2 hours. On weekends, about 3 hours (favorites include basketball and other sports, dramas, and variety shows).

(8) Do you have somebody you like (include celebrities)? Yes. In celebrities, Domoto Tsuyoshi in Kinki Kids. Miki Mizuno (actress).

(9) What is the source of stress these days? Studying!

(10) What would you do if you had all the time and money you could use freely? I'd like to own a racehorse and eat all my favorite foods.

(11) Do you have future dreams? Do you want to get married? No particular dream yet. I'd like to marry at around 24.

FAMILY LIFE

On spring Sunday afternoons, families often go on picnics to parks where they may see cherry blossoms or any of the many flowers that bloom throughout the country. The nuclear family is the usual family group, although grandparents may also be included. However, other relatives usually do not live too far away, and grandparents occasionally live with families or next door.

Many children grow up without seeing too much of their fathers. The father often works for a firm that demands full commitment and dedication from its workers. And many Japanese *salarymen,* or office workers, make their job a higher priority than their family. A typical Japanese father leaves early in the morning around 7:30 and arrives home late at night. It is not rare for fathers to come back home as late as past midnight when they must accompany customers and colleagues to dinner and evening business entertainment. Meanwhile, teenagers themselves have obligations of their own, spending their weekends doing club activities and homework, leaving little time to spend with family, especially with their fathers. Sundays are the optimum day to spend time together, and often this is done with an outing, such as eating a meal at a restaurant, visiting nearby places, or simply watching TV together. The old Japanese proverb "kids grow up watching their parents' back" (*kodomo wa oya no senaka o mite sodatsu*) still holds true. A positive interpretation of this proverb is to say that as long as parents work hard, their children will understand them. However, the proverb can also point to the decline of intimate communication between the generations.

As a result, as one might expect, the mother is the main person who has access to and control of the kids. The mother may talk with the teenagers more frequently compared with the father and usually reports to the father about the kids' progress. Many Japanese mothers are referred to as education mothers (*kyooiku-mama*) because they put a priority on seeing that their children do well in school in preparation for a better future. However, this is not to say that Japanese mothers are constantly on their children's backs coaching them to study. Approximately 70 percent of all mothers work part-time once the kids reach junior high. They may work up to six hours a day, usually arranging their schedules to be at home when their children return for dinner.

Children stay home until they are married. Kids that enter into jobs that take them away from their homes can occasionally expect a company to pay for their housing. Men, in particular, are generally not expected to cook; hence, food services are provided to them along with the company housing. Traditionally, the eldest child is revered in a Japanese family, particularly if the child is a boy. For other siblings, hierarchies exist, based usually on age and occasionally on gender, with the older children given more responsibility and honor than younger siblings. Simultaneously, the older child is expected to look after the parents when they reach retirement age. However, as families choose to have fewer children, such hierarchies and responsibilities among siblings are diminishing.

Japan has many houses, particularly in smaller towns and in the country, but they are never very big. Other Japanese live in apartments. The size of an apartment is often defined by the number of rectangular mats made of straw (*tatami*) a living room holds. Each tatami mat is numbered as a *jo*. A small apartment may support only a 6-jo room, while larger apartments may have rooms that are 12-jo or even bigger. In smaller apartments, the living room doubles as a bedroom. A light mattress, called a *futon*, is kept in the closet for each person. At night, each person may open sliding closet doors called *fusuma*, take the futon out of the closet, and lay it flat across the tatami floor. Entire families may share the floor at night if they are all sharing such an apartment. Other teenagers that live in larger apartments or houses may have their own rooms, and a handful even use beds. For those who share the floor with their family, they wake up in the morning and place the futons in the closet and put back the sparse tatami floor with a single small table as the centerpiece. Often families will sit around this table for dinner or conversation. In accordance with the emphasis on school, kids almost always have their own study desks and chairs once they enter elementary school.

Most Japanese households do not have centralized heating or air conditioning. As a result, in the wintertime, a special table (*kotatsu*) equipped under the table with a heating element as well as an accompanying blanket is used. People then place their legs under the table and blanket to keep warm. If electric heaters are not used, families may use a modern kerosene heater. Often this heater also serves as a stove in which people may place a teakettle, which families use to keep rooms humidified and to make green tea. It used to be that the same stove was also used for cooking miso soup for dinner or breakfast. In spite of the crowded conditions, friends are often invited over for tea or meals. However, it is rare that they are invited to stay the night.

TRADITIONAL AND NONTRADITIONAL FOOD DISHES

All meals start with rice, even on picnics. Japanese rice has its own texture and color, a bright fluffiness identifiable throughout Asia. In fact, most Asians can differentiate between their country's rice and that of other countries, and the Japanese are indeed proud of their sticky version, which has been a staple throughout the nation's history. Just about every household has its own rice cooker. Some companies provide rice cookers to their employees as part of their benefits packages. There are stores that specialize only in rice, and McDonalds in Japan offers rice. In addition, a fast food restaurant named Mos-Burger offers rice burgers with buns made of rice patties. Japanese rice, as an export that is a world staple commodity, has been discussed by governments during political diplomacy. Rice is eaten with chopsticks, but it is okay to bring the rice dish up to one's mouth, to make certain that no grains are dropped. When the rice is not being eaten, chopsticks are placed to the side of the dish. Chopsticks are only stuck in the rice during funerals.

Beyond rice, a few other basics adorn most Japanese meals. Miso soup, made with soybean paste, is a daily necessity and pickled vegetables such as daikon radishes and eggplants as well as *umeboshi* plums and dried seaweed show up at almost every meal. Other soybean products such as soy sauce, tofu, and fermented soybeans (*natto*) are favorite items on the Japanese table. Outside of rice, Japanese food is famous for its variety, its presentation, and its uniqueness. It is also known for having lots of side dishes. To many throughout the world, the Japanese cuisine can be culturally challenging. Raw fish (*sashimi*) is prepared carefully by chefs who know the art of cutting, while enhancing the taste and texture of the raw fish. Sashimi strapped with seaweed to a small ball of vinegared rice and served with green horseradish (*wasabi*), pickled ginger, and soy sauce is *sushi*. Sushi can also be eaten with the fingers, and some consider that to be the authentic manner to eat sushi. One of the most renowned fishes served in just a handful of restaurants is blowfish (*fugu*). Sashimi chefs must have a special license to serve fugu in that its veins, which contain a fatal poison, need to be removed. Accordingly, a fugu dinner runs around $100. Other raw meats may also be found in Japan, including beef, wild boar, and horse.

Not all meat and vegetables are served raw, though. *Tempura* is a means of frying lightly breaded vegetables and shrimp, later to be dipped in a light brown sauce (*ten-tsuyu*). Similarly, fish, meats, and vegetables can be put together into an omelet-like pizza known as *okonomiyaki*, which is topped with barbecue sauce and bonito fish flakes. Many restaurants will bring customers the ingredients so they can cook the okonomiyaki themselves on grills built into the tables. It is also easy to have skewered meats and vegetables. Chicken and onions are popular, and once in a while one may find barbecued sparrow. Teenagers love noodles, including instant ramen, as well as traditional thin brown buckwheat noodles (*soba*) and fat white wheat noodles (*udon*). With the noodles, it is okay to use chopsticks and slurp while eating. In the case of soba noodles, people intentionally add the slurping sound to increase the satisfaction of eating smooth noodles. Chicken and beef cutlets (*katsu*) are popular, as is eel. Often these are served on top of a bowl of rice. Katsu, a homophone of the Japanese word for "to win," is often served to children before a major exam by their mothers. Mothers will also prepare these dishes along with rice and pickles and place everything into partitioned boxes called *bento* boxes, which are taken to school for lunch.

Sometimes in the winter, families and friends will congregate around a communal clay pot called a *nabe* to eat food cooked in soy sauce and seaweed-seasoned soup. When thinly sliced beef, tofu, and vegetables from the nabe are dipped into raw egg for additional flavor, this is known as *sukiyaki*.

Although there are many differences between Japanese food and American food, many Americans who try Japanese food grow to love it. And while at first it may seem that Japanese food has no taboos, cats and dogs are not eaten, and many Japanese have been known to cringe at the sight, smell, or description of avocado salad, root beer, or licorice.

Fast food is an integral part of Japanese life. Hamburger, fried chicken, doughnut, and ice cream chains are found everywhere. In addition to the usual fare, teriyaki hamburgers, curry-flavored doughnuts, and green tea milkshakes are available. Pizza and spaghetti are also very popular; however, in addition to the regular toppings, choices may include shrimp, corn, umeboshi plums, seaweed, Korean gimchi, pineapples, and kiwi.

Japan is also known for its reverence for fresh fruit. Apples, Asian pears, strawberries, persimmons, chestnuts, and melons are very popular and can be extremely expensive. Only the highest quality of these fruits is permitted in stores. Melons may be given for holidays or as a get-well present, and they are considered quite lavish in that they may cost well over $100 apiece.

Often these fruits may be served as desserts, but other sweets are popular as well. Usually these are available at specialty stores and not in restaurants. Those of Japanese origin (*wagashi*) are often served with green tea for afternoon tea. Many wagashi consist of either a glutinous rice base called *mochi* and/or a sweet red bean filling called *anko*. Anko is often a surprise to newcomers to Japan in that it looks like chocolate but tastes nothing like it.

It is also easy to get snacks in convenience stores, but while the popcorn and chips may look the same at first (and some are indeed the same), they may be flavored with wasabi, soy sauce, or shrimp flavorings. An almost endless assortment of chocolates can be found, as well as spiced rice crackers and dried octopus or squid. Vending machines are found throughout the country, including on top of Mount Fuji, offering both hot and cold beverages. Drinks common in North America are available, but green tea, muskat juice with gelatin, and isotonic drinks called Pocari Sweat are also included. Vending machines also sell batteries, rice, train tickets, CDs, underwear, and even pornographic magazines. Cigarettes and whisky are also available, but teenagers tend to stay away from the items intended for adults as they are marked with a message asking those under age 20 to not use the machines. Most teenagers are happy to comply with this rule. People stand next to vending machines to drink their beverage, as it is considered bad manners to walk and drink at the same time.

SCHOOLING

The school year traditionally begins with the blooming of cherry blossoms in April.

School in Japan is mandatory through the third year of junior high. At that time, kids take exams in order to enter a particular high school. For each high school they apply for, they must take an individual exam. As a result, as one may expect, some schools accept students with a high standard score (*hensachi*). The same may also be said of college entrance exams.

Central to the students' scholastic life is their homeroom class (*kumi*). Kumis stay together for the entire school year and are given responsibilities throughout the school, which they work together on, taking care of the homeroom activities, including cleaning their own homeroom. (Japanese schools often do not have custodians.) Kumis tend to maintain their own rooms, with teachers visiting them rather than students rotating from room to room. Also, the seating is assigned to each student and may not be changed during the semester.

All subjects that students take are required, and there are no electives until they enter college. Some of the subjects that Japanese teenagers take include mathematics, science (biology, chemistry, physics), social studies (geography, Japanese history, and world history), and *kokugo* (reading, composition, and literature, which covers modern Japanese, classical language arts, and calligraphy), physical education, music, art (including woodblock print, oil painting, watercolors), ethics, and English.

When the school day is over and teenagers have finished dinner, they might return to a cram school (*juku*) to continue studying, with the principal goal of preparing for the standardized exams. Many students attend juku, some until 10 P.M. Presently, approximately a third of all elementary school students and around 60 percent of all junior and senior high students attend juku. High school students attend intensive sessions during their summer vacations, some going as long as five or six hours per day, Monday to Friday. During the school year, kids return home from school around 5 P.M., eat dinner, go to juku from 7 to 9, have a snack, and then study. Senior high school students preparing for a college entrance exam might study until 1 A.M.

During summer vacation, which begins in mid-July and lasts until the end of August (about 45 days), Japanese families take trips. However, with parents often taking only as many as three to five days off from work, families rarely take long vacations. Considering the limited time, they may go on a day trip to a nearby resort. During the summer, they may go hiking in the mountains, visit lakes, or pick fruits in the countryside. During the winter or spring break, they may go on a ski trip or visit a hot spring resort. Another popular destination is amusement parks such as Tokyo Disneyland and Universal Studios Japan, which opened in Osaka in 2001. Some families may take longer vacations, visiting the small islands within Japan or flying overseas. Hawaii and Guam are some of the most popular long-distance destinations for Japanese families. Some teenagers may choose to go on a solo trip, such as a bicycle trip to the mountains or to the northern island of Hokkaido, which is considered to be the frontiers of Japan. However, they usually wait until they graduate from high school to go on solo trips.

Japanese teenagers have similar dreams as those of their American counterparts. They may aspire to be athletes, businessmen, veterinarians, entertainers, flight attendants, teachers, and hair stylists. Until the economy worsened in the beginning of the 1990s, a degree from a good university meant a job at a good company and financial security for life. However, since the economic downturn, today's teenagers have had to change their mindset. As a result, there is more diversity in teenagers' goals. Some choose not to gear toward anything distinct at all. *Furiitaa*, from the English "free timer," has kids going from arubaito to arubaito, working on their hobbies, not worrying so much about traditional affiliations with established companies, particularly since these companies no longer can promise lifelong employment. Those who choose a career may seek to become archeologists, chefs, plumbers, United Nations officers, and so forth. Role models such as the baseball player Ichiro and animator Miyazaki, as well as musicians and actors, now give kids reasons to aspire to such positions, whereas even their older siblings might have suggested only that they work for a traditional Japanese company.

SOCIAL LIFE

As in Japanese families, social hierarchies based on age also exist in schools. Those with seniority and responsibility (*senpai*) are often addressed using formal Japanese grammar by their juniors. Younger people working their way up to senpai are known in the meantime as *kohai* and are addressed by the senpai using informal or plain Japanese. Such relationships exist throughout Japanese society, with the emperor, older people, teachers, city leaders, and doctors receiving the greatest amount of formality.

For Japanese teenagers, the bulk of their social life occurs in scholastic or club situations. However, kids often travel together as well. Class trips (*shugaku ryokou*) occur frequently. The teens go to famous cultural sites such as Kyoto or Hiroshima or to popular spots such as Tokyo Disneyland. Gifts (*omiyage*) are often bought on these trips. Kids are usually assigned an amount of money that they are allowed to spend on presents for their families and friends. Buying omiyage is vital in Japanese society, in that it is supposed to bring the memory back home to share. Gift giving is so highly prized in Japan that many people say they rely somewhat on the gifts they receive from their neighbors.

Fashion is certainly a critical part of a Japanese teenager's lifestyle. However, fashion is divided between what is acceptable at school and what one wears at other times. First of all, most of the junior high and senior high schools require the students to wear school uniforms. Many of the uniforms are designed after the British Marine sailor suit for girls and British Army for boys. Also, there are number of schools that require blazers and ties (or ribbons). On these uniforms, students must wear a school badge as well as name tag that indicates their name, grade, and kumi. Additionally, during physical education time, students will wear identical sportswear that is assigned by the school, usually color-coordinated by grade.

School regulations are generally rigid. Girls and boys must keep their hair rather short and manageable. Many schools require girls with long hair to either braid the hair or put it in a ponytail. Boys may be required to sport what is commonly called the *bozu* cut, named after the haircut of Buddhist monks, although this rule is becoming less and less common. Students are to bring their allotted schoolbags and must refrain from bringing any personal items to school. Naturally, accessories such as earrings, rings, bracelets, and necklaces are forbidden. However, these rules are violated from time to time by those who dare to go against the regulations as a means of self-expression or resistance. Kids may dye or bleach their hair, have perms, or wear light makeup, much to the consternation of school officials.

In addition to school uniforms, other aspects of school life are determined by gender. Classrooms often have seating orders in which there is a boy's row and then a girl's row. Until the beginning of the 1990s, many schools required only girls to take home economics and only boys to take engineering or physical education. However, recently all boys have been required to attend home economics as well in an effort to eliminate the gap between the genders.

Shoes are taken off at school (as they are at home, on gym mats, in department store changing rooms, and at some Japanese-style restaurants), and rubber school shoes kept at the school entrance are worn. Outside of school, students usually get out of their uniforms and wear something more casual and comfortable. They may wear school gym wear or get into jeans and T-shirts just like American teenagers. Sneakers are also popular: new Nike designs are quickly swept off the store shelves by teenage boys who admire Michael Jordan. Japanese teen fashions are influenced by what celebrities wear on TV and in magazines. However, the most recent trend is said to have been invented by the teenagers themselves: the notorious *ko-gyaru* fashions, including miniskirts, platform shoes, and loose socks. The phenomenon of *yamamba-meiku* (translated as "mountain witch makeup") has stunned the older generation, has girls bleaching their hair blond, tanning their skin dark at tanning salons, and wearing bright white lipstick and eye shadow. These girls, of course, do not represent the majority of the students, but they are certainly popular conversation topics. Many say that the *yamamba* look is a calculated antithesis of accepted norms. Girls with the platform shoes now are as tall as the boys and their black face with white makeup is the opposite to the geisha-inspired look, which is white face with red makeup. Coincidentally, the speech style of girls has become more and more masculine, with the girls using harsher expressions and dropping the characteristics of the traditional soft, polite feminine speech.

Kimono, literally meaning "thing to wear," is a traditional robe-style dress made of silk that has been worn by Japanese men and women for over a thousand years. Kimonos do not have zippers or buttons and are tied by a long and wide ornate belt (*obi*), sometimes as long as 10 feet, that is tied around the waist. However, with their expensive price and the modernization of everyday life, kimonos are worn less and less and only on special occasions. Teenagers seldom have an occasion to wear a kimono, although they may have worn them for the 3–5–7 holiday when attending a shrine at the age of 3 and 7 for girls and 5 for boys. They may also look forward to wearing kimonos in their adult years, namely for Coming of Age Day in January (a national holiday), when 20-year-old girls don colorful kimonos for a day. The kimono can be rented out from a beauty salon, or the parents may buy it to commemorate the special occasion.

Of particular interest to teenagers may be the topics of marriage and having children. The average number of kids per family in Japan is 1.3,

one of the lowest averages in the world. As a result, there are fewer children than there were a couple of generations ago. It is not uncommon to
be an only child. Many adults are choosing not to have children, principally because it can be so costly to raise a child. Women are also beginning to choose to marry later and later or even forgo marriage in favor of
a career. The average age of marriage for Japanese is one of the highest in
the world, with 27 for women and nearly 29 for men. Additionally, the
recent increase in the divorce rate may influence teenagers' ideas about
marriage and family.

In 1950, only about 20 percent of all marriages were between people
who had fallen in love. Today everyone wants this so-called love marriage, but not all people achieve this. People not married by age 30 may
experience a lot of pressure from family and friends to get married. Such
people may then be asked to attend an o-miai, a meeting for two people
who are in search of a spouse. The meeting often happens with a go-
between or set of friends and acquaintances who set up the meeting, much
like a friend setting up a blind date. Parents try to avoid being directly
involved in this process, even though they may overtly state that they
desire it. While the go-betweens do not get paid for putting a happy couple together, being asked to be a go-between is considered an honor, and
when it works, the go-between may incur thanks from the couple for the
rest of their lives. Regarding o-miai, many teenagers cringe and say,
"O-miai? No way!" However, nearly a third of all marriages begin with an
o-miai.

However, it is not too surprising that teenagers of the past had to rely
on arranged marriages. Certainly throughout the twentieth century it was
difficult for girls and boys to meet one another in social circumstances.
With school being the priority, and with many schools segregated by gender, it was difficult for girls and boys to meet and date. In some instances,
but certainly not all, so intense were the differences between girls' lives
and boys' lives that boys would dance with other boys and girls with other
girls at discotheques, each group being led by dancing cheerleaders. Only
the very bravest of boys and girls would get together to meet.

In the past five years or so, the dating scene has changed drastically,
principally due to the spread of cellular phones and the Internet as the
main method for communication. With cell phones (keitai denwa)
teenagers have been able to introduce each other and serve as pseudo "go-
betweens," simply by having their friends conveniently and immediately
talk to potential new friends. Also, many teenagers are constantly using
the cell phone to send short e-mails to their friends; they have gained the
nickname "thumb tribe" (oyayubi-zoku) from the way in which they type

messages using only their thumbs. Teenagers are also using an increasing number of Internet dating services. Twenty-two percent of junior high school girls have used Internet dating sites to arrange meetings with boys. Such sites are used innocently for making new friends as well as for arranging casual sexual encounters.

Families rarely discuss sex with their teenagers; health education courses at school provide the basic information. The greatest amount of information comes from magazines and manga (which display explicit sex and violence) and from TV programs. While families do not discuss sex openly, television presents nudity (female breasts may be shown occasionally) and discussions on sex regularly. A *rabu hoteru* (a Japanese term coming from the English "love hotel") caters to couples who seek privacy outside of their homes. Because privacy is so carefully guarded in love hotels, it is easy for teenagers to use them.

The legal drinking age is 20. However, many teenagers have their first taste of beer or other light liquor during the school years, secretly during the school trip or at club training camps. Drinking is a big source of entertainment in Japanese society, and being drunk in public is generally tolerated. However, teenagers usually avoid alcohol to stay out of trouble, even though it is readily available in neighborhood vending machines.

The same may be said of drugs, as they are discouraged not only by teachers and families but by teenagers themselves. Using drugs in Japan is looked down upon, even by young people. In the 1970s and 1980s, paint thinner was the main drug abused by teenagers. However, there has been a recent increase in drug use, principally use of hard drugs such as cocaine. In very rare instances, among teenagers associated with gangs (the most famous being a motorcycle gang called *Bousouzoku*), trafficking of cocaine and prescription medication has been recently noted. While the recent increase is observable, this behavior is still a rarity.

The most widely noted form of school trouble has been that of *ijime*, a form of bullying in which large groups of students pick out a weak student in the kumi and abuse this individual by physical and/or verbal violence. The situation has been serious enough that a number of teenagers suffering ijime have, in the most extreme circumstance, either committed suicide or died as a result of their injuries. Conversely, some ijime victims have retaliated against their attackers in the most brutal fashions.

Tamer types of trouble include smoking, violating school regulations (e.g., attending movies without chaperoning), and breaking curfew by playing at gaming centers and pinball-style *pachinko* gambling centers. Punishments at school include extra work around the school such as cleaning, corporal punishment (the most widely used being *seiza*, which has the student kneeling on a wooden floor for long periods of time), and in extreme cases suspension and expulsion.

RECREATION

While many students are busy with academics, many of them find recreation in their favorite sports and hobbies. Many watch sport programs on TV or go to games with their families. Professional baseball and soccer are the two most popular sports, with many teenagers having their favorite team and players to cheer for. The most popular baseball teams are the Yomiuri Giants, representing Tokyo, and the Hanshin Tigers, representing Osaka. Also, students watch the National Senior High School Baseball Tournament that gets broadcast for two weeks during the summer and spring. Literally all the baseball clubs in Japanese senior high schools enter this tournament with the dream of reaching the final championship game held at Koshien Stadium, which is the mecca for all ballplayers in Japan. Recently, with the spread of cable TV, many Japanese teenagers have been tuning in to American football and basketball as well as tennis matches. Compared to these Western sports, the national sport of sumo is not all that popular among teenagers. However, they are quite familiar with the Yokozuna champions such as Akebono (originally from Hawaii) and Takanohana.

Also popular are martial arts, such as judo, kendo, karate, and aikido. Some students practice these arts at school or in the neighborhood ashrams. Recently, more modern types of martial arts have gained popularity among the youth, such as professional wrestling and kick boxing. Both baseball and soccer are still mainly boys' sports in Japan, yet other sports such as swimming, gymnastics, figure skating, and track and field are enjoyed by both boys and girls. Notably, almost all schools in Japan are equipped with their own swimming pool (sometimes on the school's roof), and students learn to swim at a rather early age. Schools also hold annual sports festivals at which time the whole school, divided into the red kumi and white kumi, spends an entire day competing. The students may compete in tug-of-war contests, relay races, and centipede races (more than three students bind their feet together side-by-side and run as a group), as well as perform folk dances in the presence of teachers and guests.

Other forms of recreation for teens in Japan may include music and art. Many Japanese children take music lessons such as piano and violin (the Suzuki method is a world-renowned method for teaching violin to children) and keep practicing in their teen years as well. Some teens teach themselves to play the guitar and form bands consisting of a bassist, a drummer, and a lead singer. They may rent out a studio to practice and perform at the school cultural festivals or may opt to hold a small concert. Some talented groups debut professionally and gain popularity among the public. However, teenagers must refrain from these activities when they have to prepare for the entrance exams.

ENTERTAINMENT

Outside of school, teenagers may spend a lot of time with friends, just like American teenagers, but at different places doing different things. Instead of going to a mall, students may go shopping at department stores near the major train stations to window-shop and buy some small items. They also spend a lot of time at fast food restaurants and the so-called family restaurants for snacks and lunch. Other popular spots are game centers equipped with the latest games such as shooting games, virtual skiing games, and DDR, a game in which one must dance according to the steps suggested on the computer screen. A so-called karaoke box is another place for young people to spend some fun time with friends. In these places, people can rent a small room with a karaoke machine by the hour and take turns singing the latest hit charts while ordering some soft drinks and light snacks to enjoy. Many of the karaoke boxes operate until late at night, but teenagers generally stay away from karaoke boxes at those hours to avoid getting in trouble.

Music fans may also go to concerts at large auditoriums or at baseball stadiums. Their musical preferences can range from pop music to hard rock. Rock bands often sport the makeup, bleached hair, and tight pants of stars of heavy metal, much in the tradition of American bands such as Kiss. However, the fans of these rock bands, and the rock bands themselves, are equally familiar with and fond of soft bubble-gum rock.

A more quiet activity that teenagers may choose to do individually is to visit bookstores. There are many bookstores around train stations, and teenagers stop by to flip through their favorite magazines or purchase a volume of manga at the price of three dollars or more. For teenagers that are crazy for manga comic books but cannot afford to buy the volumes, they may use the service of the *manga-kissa*, a coffee shop filled with popular comic books. These are very popular places for students since with an order of a cup of coffee, they can read any manga on the shelves and stay as long as they please. Recently, there have been manga-kissas that furnish small sleeping areas for those who wish to take catnaps as well as coin-operated showers for those who end up staying overnight at those shops.

A rock concert in Yoyogi-koen Park in Tokyo, Japan. Photo © C. Rennie/
TRIP.

At home, many teenagers spend lots of time watching TV and playing
video games. There are many entertainment shows (called variety shows
in Japan), ranging from funny quiz shows to popular dramas, that cater to
teenage audiences. During the "golden hours" between 8 and 10 P.M.,
there may be many attractive programs that are popular among teens, but
they must balance their desire to watch TV against their need to finish
their homework. Evening soap operas are popular, as are quiz shows. Most
quiz shows have two hosts, a man and a woman, and questions often refer
to information presented in documentary-style film clips. Questions are
usually answered by guest singers or actors as well as the so-called *talento*
(originating from the English word "talent"), who are TV entertainment
personalities. Friends also visit each other's homes to play video games,
read each other's comics, and chat.

Watching movies is another favorite activity among the youth. However, movie tickets are quite expensive (often around $20 per ticket), so

attending the cinema is not tremendously popular. However, teenagers do rent videos. Foreign films are sought after, especially Hollywood movies. All Japanese are familiar with the name Steven Spielberg, and such U.S. megahits as *Jurassic Park* and *Titanic* were also big hits for Japanese audiences. Japan is also known for its appreciation of movies from all countries, enthusiastically importing movies from Europe and other places. Ghost story and kung fu movies from Hong Kong are extremely popular, and Korean films have recently gained an audience.

Japanese cinema is also vibrant. Akira Kurosawa, who directed such movies as *Rashomon, Ran,* and *The Seven Samurai,* is highly thought of among his peers. Popular especially among Japanese cinema fans in the United States is Juzo Itami, who directed many films that portrayed the dark side of Japanese society with a comical and cynical tone. Takeshi "Beat" Kitano is another well-known director; his often violent portrayal of Japanese mobs (*yakuza*) has captured many young hearts in Japan as well as international audiences.

Certainly, no country in the world is more famous for its animation. Many young Japanese grow up watching animation. This may be one common thread that teenagers may share with their parents' generation, since animation has been a popular source of entertainment in Japanese society for nearly half a century. If the father of Japanese manga comics is the late Osamu Tezuka—the creator of the Atomic Boy and Leo, the Jungle King—the father of animation is no doubt Hayao Miyazaki. Starting as a director of popular children's anime programs on TV, he later directed such motion picture animations as *Naucica, My Neighbor Totoro, Kiki's Delivery Service,* and *Princess Mononoke.* His 2001 *The Story of Sen and Chihiro* won best-film awards at international film festivals.

Japan is also known for more traditional types of entertainment, such as *Noh* and *Kabuki* theater, *Rakugo* comic storytelling, and *Joruri* puppet play. However, teenagers today do not associate themselves with these traditional forms of art and perhaps do not opt to go view these art performances. For them, these traditional art forms are archaic and not as exciting as what they see on TV or on the Internet. They may see traditional art forms on school field trips but not otherwise.

RELIGIOUS PRACTICES AND CULTURAL CEREMONIES

At first glance, one may wonder to what extent religion plays a part in Japan. All the major world religions may be found in Japan, but few teenagers claim any of them. And many older Japanese do not claim a certain religion. One of the reasons for this is because religious practices are a natural part of their everyday life. One religion, Shintoism, is native to Japan and is an integral part of Japanese everyday life, as many rituals are based on the Shinto tradition. Shinto is essentially based on animism and finds God throughout nature, from mountains (especially Mount Fuji) to trees. There is no idolatry involved in Shinto, and while there may be no particular icons of the Shinto religion, many houses hold a Shinto altar on which water and cooked rice are placed daily as offerings to God. New-born babies are taken to a Shinto shrine to ensure that their growth is healthy. New Year's Day is also a time when all Japanese pay homage at a shrine to pray for their year's luck. At Shinto shrines, one can buy fortune slips that tell one's fortune, ranging from great luck (*dai-kichi*) to great unluck (*dai-kyo*). Additionally, Japanese people will visit their neighborhood shrine frequently, praying for health, good luck for an upcoming exam, or prosperity.

Buddhism, which was introduced to Japan from China and Korea, is certainly a significant presence throughout Japan, with large and famous temples adorning all parts of the country. The first time Japanese visit a Buddhist temple may be when they play in the temple yards with friends as kids; there is limited open space in Japan, and temple grounds can serve as playgrounds. School excursions may take students to the ancient cities of Kyoto and Nara to visit famous temples. Japanese teens may experience Buddhist ritual more personally when they attend funerals. The majority of Japanese funerals are held in the Buddhist tradition: the corpse is cremated and the ashes buried in the ancestral graveyard.

Less than 2 percent of Japanese claim to be Christian. However, many of them choose to "act as Christians" once in their lives, at their wedding. With the image of the then-princess Michiko (the current Empress of Japan) adorned in a white American-style wedding dress on her wedding day, the Western wedding ceremony came to be the "romantic" way to wed among the Japanese after the war. Nowadays, young Japanese choose to walk down the aisle and say "I do" at a feigned church, clad in a wedding gown, even if their parents are Buddhists. As some people say, many Japanese are indeed "born a Shinto, marrying as Christian, and dying as Buddhist." Japanese also celebrate Christmas. Christmas is not a religious holiday for them but a time for couples and young families to celebrate romance and the fun of exchanging presents. Japanese confectionaries compete to sell their "Christmas cakes," which are eaten by friends and families after regular dinner on Christmas Eve or Christmas Day.

While there are few religious holidays in Japan, some holidays are related to Shinto and Buddhism. In addition to New Year's Eve and New

Year's Day, the *O-Bon* festival is the time when all Japanese go back to their hometowns to welcome back the ancestors' spirits in August. There are holidays for each member of the family throughout the year, such as Girls' Day or the Doll's Festival (March 3), Boys' Day or the Children's Day (May 5), Mother's Day, and Father's Day. Labor Day in October is the time to thank all the workers and individuals who contribute to and improve Japanese society. The Emperor's birthday is celebrated every year; the current Heisei Emperor's birthday falls on December 23. In the fall, there is also a Physical Education Day on October 10, commemorating the opening of the Tokyo Olympics in 1964.

Valentine's Day, celebrated on February 14, is also worth mentioning, as Japanese people altered this American tradition slightly to meet their cultural practices. In Japan, Valentine's Day is a day when girls and women give chocolates and/or gifts to boys and men and not vice-versa. While this seems like an unfair trade for women, men who receive gifts from women on Valentine's Day must give something back the following month when White Day is celebrated on March 14. Valentine's Day and White Day are commercialized events, but they are both good occasions for members of the younger generation to confess their feelings toward a special someone.

CONCLUSION

Today's Japanese teenagers face an interesting challenge. They have fewer guarantees than their parents, but they often take the initiative in creating new ways of contributing to society and establishing their own happiness. Today's teenagers take more risks than previous generations but have their grandparents as models of success through difficulty. They tend to have a sense of humor, be committed to study, and live in small families. Today's teenagers face a future in which the nature, tradition, and art of Japan will be maintained and transformed beneath the backdrop of metallic skyscrapers, bullet trains, and laser-beam lights.

RESOURCE GUIDE

Nonfiction

Feiler, S. B. (1991). *Learning to bow.* New York: Ticknor and Fields.
Hendry, J. (1987). *Understanding Japanese society.* New York: Routledge.
Kamachi, N. (1999). *Culture and customs of Japan.* Westport, CT: Greenwood Press.

Reishauer, O. E., & Jansen, M. B. (1995). *The Japanese today: Change and continuity.* Cambridge: Harvard University Press.

Rowthorn, C.; Ashburne, J.; Benson, S.; & Florence, M. (2000). *Japan: From asahi to zen.* Melbourne, Australia: Lonely Planet Publications.

White, M. (1993). *The material child: Coming of age in Japan and America.* Berkeley, CA: University of California Press.

Films

Emmerich, R. (Director). (1998). *Godzilla* [Motion Picture]. Columbia Tri Star.

Imamura, S. (Director). (1997). *Unagi* [Motion Picture].

Itami, J. (Director). (1984). *The Funeral* [Motion Picture].

Itami, J. (Director). (1986). *Tampopo* [Motion Picture].

Kurosawa, A. (Director). (1950). *Rashomon* [Motion Picture]. RKP Radio Pictures.

Kurosawa, A. (Director). (1954). *The Seven Samurai* [Motion Picture]. Kit Parker Films.

Kurosawa, A. (Director). (2003). *Ikiru* [Motion Picture]. Cowboy Booking International.

Teshigahara, H. (1964). *The Women of the Dunes* [Motion Picture].

Web Sites

http://jin.jcic.or.jp
http://jin.jcic.or.jp/access/index.html
http://www.cia.gov/cia/publications/factbook/geos/ja.html
http://www.isei.or.jp/books/75/Front.html
http://www.japan-guide.co
http://www.jinjapan.org

Japanese Culture, Pop Culture

http://jin.jcic.or.jp/kidsweb/virtual.html
http://www.geocities.com/EnchantedForest/3278/topher-zilla.html
Hayao Miyazaki animations: http://www.nausicaa.net/miyazaki

Japanese Language

Online Japanese-English dictionary server: http://www.csse.monash.edu.au/~jwb/wwwjdic.html

Japanese Fashion

http://web.mit.edu/jpnet/kimono

Japanese Folktales

http://mhtml.ulis.ac.jp/~myriam/deuxgb.html

Miscellaneous

Japanese Embassy in Canada: http://www.embassyjapancanada.org
Japanese Embassy in the United States: http://www.embjapan.org

Pen Pal/Chat

JPA Pen Pal Homepage. http://www.gakubun.co.jp/JPA
The Japan Page (the Pen Pal Depot). http://www.yorihuzi.net/japan.html

Chapter 7

MONGOLIA

Lilia C. DiBello

INTRODUCTION

Mongolia is a country nestled between Russia and China. It is divided into 18 different provinces and 3 independent cities. Ulaanbaatar, the capital of Mongolia, is the most populated city in the world's most sparsely populated country in persons per square kilometer. Mongolia is also one of the world's oldest countries. At the height of its power in the thirteenth century, the country was ruled by Genghis Khan. At this time, his influence was great and the land he ruled went west into what today we call Hungary and Poland. Inevitably, time and changes in government ultimately led to Mongolia becoming a province of China.

Government

Mongolia was long a province of China, and after winning independence in 1921 with the help of Russia, the country established a communist regime in 1924. This rich history has been retold in literature and film. The early 1990s brought much change in the political status of this country. The ex-communist Mongolian People's Revolutionary Party (MPRP) lost its monopoly of power to the Democratic Union Coalition for a time in the 1990s, when the DUC defeated the MPRP in a national election and attempted to reform and modernize the economy. The change was difficult in that many key positions were still held by members of the MPRP. Power recently shifted back to the MPRP with the election (1997) and reelection of President Nachagyn Bagabandy (May 2001).

Economy

Under the communist system, the state controlled all of the industry and commerce practices in Mongolia by either directly owning them or forming cooperatives. The only foreign trade that took place was typically with the Soviet Union and its allies. With the change in political climate in the early 1990s and the introduction of free market reforms, Mongolia had an immediate problem with respect to economic output and low foreign trade. This of course led to an increase in inflation and unemployment. However, by the mid-1990s the nation did begin to recover and livestock breeding and crop farming became important parts of the economy, with mining and manufacturing increasing in importance.

More than 25 percent of the labor force is engaged in agriculture. The Mongolians have a tradition of herding livestock, including sheep, goats, cattle, horses, and camels. Furthermore, the economy is supported by the farming of wheat, barley, potatoes, and forage crops. The country is also known to have extensive mineral deposits. Copper, coal, molybdenum, tin, tungsten, and gold account for a large percentage of the mining and industrial production. The economy is also helped by the local manufacturing, which typically includes building materials, processed food, alcoholic beverages, leather goods, woolen textiles, furs, and wood items.

The unemployment rate was at about 4.5 percent in the late 1990s, with approximately 40 percent of the population living below the poverty line. The exporting of materials traditionally takes place with China (30.1%), Switzerland (21.5%), Russia (12.1%), South Korea (9.7%), and the United States (8.1%). However, the import partners include Russia (30.6%), China (13.3%), Japan (11.7%), South Korea (7.5%), and the United States (6.9%). The government controls all foreign trade, and copper is typically the item most in demand.

The currency used in Mongolia is the tughrik (*tögrög*). There is a Mongolian law that states that all transactions must be made in tögrög and not in U.S. dollars, but occasionally Mongolians take illegal currency. Furthermore, in the countryside there is often a shortage of the smaller bills, so change is occasionally rendered in the form of sweets or sticks of chewing gum.

TYPICAL DAY

Urban Mongolia

Daily life in Mongolia is greatly affected by whether one lives near a city. Approximately 50 percent of the people in Mongolia now live in cities or towns. Life for them is typical of citizens in Third World or developing countries. In cities, children are required to attend school for the compulsory 10-year period and often the expectation is that the younger generation will continue further with schooling. Most teens living in cities live in apartments in large housing complexes. They typically have electricity, running water, and either central heat or a kerosene heater. The basic apartment is small and the older buildings have bathrooms and kitchens shared by two groups. City life requires people to shop for their food, and they often go to markets and pick up fresh items because many apartments do not have refrigerators.

Ulaanbaatar (the most heavily populated place in Mongolia) does have a typical rush hour where families get up and go off to work, because it is common for both wife and husband to earn wages in the city. Buses are used to transport a majority of city dwellers to their place of employment, but some ride bicycles when the weather permits. Teenagers either walk or ride buses to their school.

Rural Mongolia

In the country, life has been slower to catch up to modern times. The typical day of a teenager depends on the season. Teenagers are usually sent to study in neighboring cities if their township is not large enough to accommodate its own school site. But those remaining with their families would be expected to tend to their studies and to contribute to the family unit. In the spring, the Mongolian herders have their busiest season. The lambs and kids are born, and all family members help around the property. Every member of the family tends to all newborn animals, and older sheep must be shorn for the crop of wool they are to produce for that year. It is clearly the time of year when parents most need the help of their offspring. Hence, school typically lets out for summer break at the end of spring to accommodate parents' need for extra help.

The summer is the most relaxed season for Mongolians. The crops have been tended to and the herds are just put out to graze in the pasture.

Autumn in premodern Mongolia would find rural Mongolians preparing to migrate to their winter pastures. This has changed. Now autumn brings the establishment of herding cooperatives where neighbors combine their herds as the cold weather approaches, but there is no long migration for the families or herds. This is a time to check equipment, gather supplies, and prepare for the long winter months ahead.

Winter lasts for a long time in Mongolia. Temperatures hover well below freezing for many days and the winds can make the temperature feel even more treacherous. Students typically make their way home for at least a two-week break at this time of year. Coal stoves help keep them warm, and many dwellings have access to radio or TV to break some of the monotony of the long winter days. There are actually some rural families who move into temporary apartment housing for the winter and commute to their livestock by truck or horseback.

FAMILY LIFE

In a traditional nomadic society, women played a very important role. They were responsible for raising the children, preparing the food, and keeping the house. In the countryside their duties also included helping to tend to the herds. Clearly, though, the women in premodern Mongolia were subservient to men. Contemporary laws protect and guarantee the rights of women. This provides women the opportunity to have occupations typically associated with men, but their traditional duties still remain: cooking dinner, taking care of children, and doing housework. This is quite similar to the role of working women in Western societies.

Mongolia is said to have had a population of 2,616,000 in the year 2000. They are projected to be at 3,555,000 by the year 2025 and at 4,057,000 by the year 2050. In comparison, the United States in 2000 had a population of 275,563,000. Given that Mongolia is the most sparsely populated country, the government often provides incentives for larger families. Families who work within certain industries receive special bonuses for having large families. Furthermore, the government provides free or low-cost services, such as education, health care, and day care. It is uncommon to find advertisements for birth control or the use of contraception. The annual population growth rate is quite small in Mongolia (1.6%), with Mongolian women having an average of 3.1 children in 1998 ("Spotlight: Mongolia," 1998, p. 7) but 2.4 children by 2000. Given that children are welcome in this society and that family life is very important, it was recently reported by United Nations sources that "20% of Mongolian males experience sexual intercourse before reaching the age of 17 and 5% of females become pregnant before the age of 20" ("Large youth population in Mongolia," 2000, p. 2). Children are cared for in the home by elders, or day care is provided by neighborhood groups or the parental place of employment.

Mongolians living in the country typically live in white felt tents called *gers*, and many city dwellers still may choose this as their primary residence in the nonwinter months (particularly in the suburbs). Gers are seen all over the countryside of Mongolia. In the countryside the gers do not have electricity, but if a ger is located near a city it may have this touch of modern life. They are quite sturdy but are collapsible and can be moved quickly if necessary.

The internal layout of the ger is universal throughout Mongolia. The door always faces south. Once across the threshold, men move left (to the west, under the protection of the great sky god, Tengger), women to the right (east, under the protection of the sun). Toward the back, and a little to the west, is the place of honor set aside for guests.

The elders typically stay in the back as well, along with a wall or altar showing the family's most prized possessions. Family photos may be displayed on this back altar, along with their Buddhist symbols. On the male's side are the robes and saddles and instruments used for herding, and on the female side are all of the cooking utensils and water-gathering materials. Beds are typically placed low and against the walls, and clothing and children's toys are found about the ger wherever a space exists. All of the walls and the front door are always brightly painted.

TRADITIONAL AND NONTRADITIONAL FOOD DISHES

Urban Areas

In the capital city of Mongolia (Ulaanbaatar) the choices are vast and in many cases you can obtain food that is common in the Western world. This is the urban center of the country and the most widely populated section as well. Hence, it is not uncommon to see a variety of international food choices and supermarkets that are well stocked. This urban center is the place where most travelers stock up for excursions into the country. The markets (*zakh*) and shops (*delguur*) in Ulaanbaatar sell things as common as jam, salami, bread, noodles, chocolate spread, tinned fish, pickled vegetables, tea, coffee, rice, flour, and fruit and vegetables when they are in season. Most of the fresh food is much more expensive than in the West, because it is mostly imported from countries like Germany. It is not uncommon for shoppers to be asked to follow an old Russian custom— choose what they want by creating an itemized list, paying the cashier, and receiving the items on the way out the door. This system is slowly changing, and shoppers can now be found browsing and inspecting items. Teenagers in Ulaanbaatar can be found eating many of the same items that Western teenagers consume. The difference exists in the poverty level, in that local teenagers are not likely to be able to afford the luxury foods that might be around, such as smoked cheese, potato chips, pâté, nondairy creamer, muesli, and cornflakes (Mayhew, 2001).

Restaurants rarely provide menus in English. In fact, most menus are written by hand in Cyrillic and list mainly alcoholic beverages. Most restaurants in Mongolia are closed by 9 P.M. and sometimes even earlier. The most common food is mutton, which is often served with plenty of fat and flour. Steamed dumplings (*buuz*) are served with a mutton filling and the smaller boiled dumplings (*bansh*) are often served in soup or salty tea. A large pancake made with flour and mutton (*khuushuur*) is also very popular and traditionally served fried. Although in the West it is quite common to find Chinese restaurants that claim to serve Mongolian (barbeque) cuisine, these establishments serve very little traditionally Mongolian food.

Aside from mutton, Mongolians appreciate dairy products in their diet. These foods are known as "white foods" (*tssagaan idee*) and are similar to yogurt, milk, fresh cream, cheese, and fermented milk drinks, which are mostly available in the summer months. One of the most popular beverages is made from the milk of mares and yaks. In some regions, the milk of camels, goats, and sheep is also consumed. Also popular is tea, which in Mongolia is consumed at any time and is not sweet but salty. As previously mentioned, although these are the traditional foods found in Mongolia, the capital city does have a variety of foods that teenagers are exposed to.

There is a traditional Mongolian saying that goes like this: "Breakfast, keep for yourself; lunch, share with your friends; dinner, give to your enemies." Breakfast and lunch are traditionally the most important meals, which is one reason that restaurants typically close relatively early by Western standards.

Rural Areas

In the rural areas of Mongolia there is very little variety in food choice. Travelers are encouraged to bring their own canned food for long treks into the country, in that mutton with lots of fat and flour and maybe some dairy products or rice are the typical dish. The Kazaks found in western Mongolia are the exception, in that they do add some variety to their diet with horsemeat. When visiting Mongolians in their homes across the country, visitors are often offered snacks from a hospitality bowl and typically the salty tea. Snacks can be quite exotic— camel meat sausages, twists of deep-fried bread, an entire goat (*boodog*), or chopped sheep boiled in water and vodka (*khorkhog*). "When eating both boodog and khorkhog, it is customary to pass the hot greasy rocks from hand to hand, as this is thought to be good for your health" (May-hew, 2001, p. 99).

In the country, the canteen (*guanz*) is usually the only place to find food along the roads. Although the guanz looks like a ger, it has a table and chairs outside, and it may have a picture of a fork and knife outside to make it easier to spot. In the summer, Mongolian herdsmen typically live off of dairy products and the only animals killed are for guests. As previously mentioned, in the winter Mongolians eat mutton prepared many different ways with lots of fat and flour.

Nonalcoholic and Alcoholic Drinks

The Mongolians are big tea drinkers. The salty tea (*süütei tsai*) is the most common beverage. Men are encouraged to drink heavily, and there is much social pressure to drink. Very rarely do men refuse to drink vodka (*arkhi*), for fear of being considered a wimp. Their neighbors in Russia often drink Mongolian vodka, in that Mongolia has well over 200 distilleries and imports it north. Russian beer and Chinese beer are often available, and occasionally in larger towns you can find some expensive varieties of Western imported beer. Herders in the country make their own version of home brew (*airag*), which is made by fermenting horse's milk with an alcoholic content of about 3 percent. Mongolians often distill it further to produce *shimiin arkhi*. This version boosts the alcohol content to around 12 percent.

SCHOOLING

As was the case in early America, schooling in early Mongolia was traditionally reserved for the wealthy and was associated with religion. Education in Mongolia was largely controlled by the Buddhist monasteries and was limited to monks. In the early twentieth century, wealthy families hired tutors for their children, much like families living on large southern plantations in America. Education became more accessible in the 1920s under the influence of Russia. Educational development has always been regarded as important. The initial goals were to eradicate illiteracy, establish a free system of public education, and create a trained intelligentsia.

Contemporary education in Mongolia is mandatory for children between the ages of 6 and 16. The Mongolian model of schooling is heavily influenced by the Russian system. It follows the Russian model, in which the first four years are primary education and the second four are secondary education. While some students leave after eight years of compulsory schooling, others go on for two more years of general secondary education or attend specialized vocational schools. Vocational schools train skilled workers, such as machinists, heavy-equipment operators, and construction workers. They provide a terminal education to students who do not excel in the classroom. The specialized secondary schools, in contrast, offer two-year or three-year courses at the junior college level. These groups of students become primary school teachers, medical technicians, or bookkeepers, following the Soviet "technicum" (vocational school or special secondary school) model. It is the students who earn these specialized secondary school degrees who have the option of continuing on to earn admission to higher education.

Thanks to its focus on eradicating illiteracy, Mongolia boasts an illiteracy rate of only 8 percent for men and 7 percent for women. These are incredibly low figures, and more interesting is the fact that women have even lower illiteracy rates than men do. For a country that is so widespread, with very few major cities, achieving a literacy rate of approximately 90 percent is incredible. At least a fourth of the state budget is spent on education each year, and if students live in remote settlements with only a primary school then they are sent to a boarding school in order to complete the compulsory eight years of schooling. They have a two-week break during winter and a three-month holiday in summer. For the youngest of students there is a conscious effort to connect school with work and students are encouraged to put in some time each week to help with work around the community. Military training is included at times as well.

Women currently make up over 60 percent of all students in higher education, and girls constitute more than half of the students in specialized secondary schools. Women work as teachers in over 60 percent of all general schools, 50 percent of specialized secondary schools, and 33 percent of higher education institutions. Not surprisingly, a higher percentage of women than men hold professional positions in Mongolia (as doctors, lawyers, etc.). In 1999, over 70 percent of university students were female and around 77 percent of doctors and 60 percent of lawyers in Mongolia were women (Mayhew, 2001).

The Mongolian State University was first established in 1942 in Ulaanbaatar. For many years it was the only university in Mongolia. In the 1990s, however, many smaller, more specialized universities began springing up, with a focus on technology, medicine, and so forth (i.e., National University of Mongolia, http://www.num.edu.mn/pages/main.htm, and Mongolian Technical University). There are currently about 29 state and

40 private universities, mostly in Ulaanbaatar. This rapid introduction of new higher education institutions has had an adverse effect on educational standards in the past 10 years. Many Mongolians feel the need to travel to Russia or China in order to study at an institution that is respected internationally. Worthy of note is the fact that distance education has become quite popular in Mongolia and that nationwide educational radio programs supported by the United Nations Educational, Scientific, and Cultural Organization teach the nomads in the countryside many important skills.

SOCIAL LIFE

Teens living in the cities are exposed to many Western customs. They typically dress in Western clothing, although there are now more young people dressed in traditional clothing: a set of trousers and a long robe (*deel*) with two slits on each side to make bike riding easier. The clothing is typically made of silk or cotton cloth, but in the harsh winter they wear cloaks that are lined with fleece or fur. Both men and women wear boots, and they are often quite ornate. The hats worn by the men and women differ based on the tribe with which the individual is associated.

In the countryside, the Mongolian people still tend to wear traditional clothing, only occasionally opting for Western clothes. In the city, however, industrial workers typically wear work clothes made of heavy blue cotton. Even the government has been known to actively discourage urban Mongols from wearing traditional clothing. There was a hope that wearing more modern dress would encourage Mongolians to develop more Western patterns of thought and business habits. The dress now is typically modern in cities and traditional in townships, but there has been a resurgence of pride in traditional dress in the country as well as cities.

In Mongolia, children between the ages of 10 and 15 often belong to the Young Pioneer Organization. This is a group very similar to the scouting troops in America. It is a recreational group but does teach social service skills, sports, art appreciation, and good citizenship. Once they reach the age of 15, certain members of this organization are invited to join the Mongolian Young Revolutionary League. It is typically a handpicked group of the most promising teens, and an invitation is extended to children of well politically connected families. This new group is considered the training ground for future politicians and leaders.

In Mongolia it was often the custom for parents to arrange marriages for their children without consulting them. However, in contemporary times things have changed. Although it would be quite unusual for two young people to fall in love and marry without consulting their parents or elders, it is not unheard of. The vast majority of young people still rely on their families or close friends to introduce them to potential mates. Although this is the norm, it is still a much more personal process today than in years past.

For the younger generation to get a sense of the cultural aspects of living in Mongolia, a very beautiful exchange center was built in the 1970s for the purpose of introducing Mongolian youth to the outside world and the outside world to the wonders of Mongolia. The Nairamdal Zuslan International Children's Centre is located just outside of Ulaanbaatar in the Bayangol Valley. In the summer months it is filled with hundreds of children of all ages. Filatova, the wife of Russian leader Tsedenal, created it. She had a vision of enhancing Mongolia's prestige by allowing the country to host international summer youth exchange programs with both Eastern and Western countries. The center was constructed in styles from all over the world, and the hotel is the size of a palace. Summer is the busiest time of year, although the center is open year-round and parents are welcome to stay for a visit as well. This center gives outsiders an opportunity to experience first-hand the many social aspects associated with being a child or teenager in Mongolia.

RECREATION

Teens often meet at school and at festivals held in towns. The biggest event of the Mongolian year is the Naadam Festival. "Nadaam" means "holiday" or "festival," and in Mongolia this event is popularly called the People's Revolution Day because it is typically held in mid-July (11th or 12th) on the anniversary of the Mongolian Revolution of 1921. It is at this festival that citizens of Mongolia get to partake in "the three manly games": horse racing, archery, and wrestling.

Horse racing in Mongolia is similar to Western steeplechase races. They are held over land and not at racetracks. At all ages, females as well as males participate in horse racing. At the National Nadaam Festival, the most anticipated race is in the children's division (7–12 year olds). They dress in traditional costumes and ride their horses over a 20-mile cross-country course. Young children show great skill in horsemanship, and all children are expected to learn to ride very early on.

At the archery contests, both men and women square off in competition both on horseback and from the standing position. This contest features a short bow made locally by Mongolians that can shoot arrows as far

A Mongolian teen riding horse on one of the many steppes. Photo © M. Barlow/ TRIP.

as 200 yards. The archery contest is well attended, and this tradition attracts many of the young.

Wrestling is the only sport featured at the festival that does not include a women's division. Men approach the ring in colorful and traditional costumes consisting of tight-fitting briefs; a tight vest that covers the back, shoulders, and upper arms, leaving the chest bare; and heavy leather boots. The distinctive wrestling vest is a way of identifying the contestants as male. After a colorful entrance into the ring, once the referee engages the two men in a match, the first man to get the other to touch the ground with something other than his feet wins the match. At the completion of the match, the loser kneels so that the victor can place his victory sign over the head of the loser. Wrestling is the sport of passion in Mongolia, and the champion wrestlers (e.g., Titan, Lion, Elephant, Falcon) achieve great status. At the 2000 Naadam Festival the winning wrestler took home 1.5 million tögrög (roughly equivalent to U.S.$1,500).

A description of recreation in Mongolia would not be complete without mentioning the Holiday of the Ten Thousand Camels, which takes place at the infamous Gobi desert. The village of Mandal-Ovoo (also known as Sharkhulsan) hosts the event every January or February prior to the start of Tsagaan Sar (the lunar new year). This festival revolves around an 18-kilometer camel race across a nearby region called the Ongiin-Tal steppes. An average of 200 camels take part every year, and the winner typically takes under an hour to win the grand prize—another camel!

Another notable form of recreation in Mongolia is chess. Although some of the pieces are different from those found on a Western chessboard (e.g., a camel is used in place of a bishop), the rules are essentially the same. Children are taught at a young age to play this game of logic, and they play it well into adulthood. Many modern sports are now found in Mongolia as well. Basketball and soccer are played, and athletes are trained to participate in many Olympic sports. Olympic athletes have excelled in sports such as modern archery, gymnastics, weightlifting, and target shooting. Of course, in the winter, cross-country skiing and ice-skating are natural pastimes.

ENTERTAINMENT

Entertainment in Mongolia for teenagers is different from the Western tradition. There are very few movie theaters and no malls, bowling alleys, or other typically Western teenage hangouts. This does not mean that teenagers have nothing to do; there is plenty of nightlife in the cities. It has been noted that "Ulaan Baatar has a dozen or so discos and clubs that cater for students and the nouveaux riches. To make money—but more to put off the poorer Mongolians—there is often a hefty entrance fee of between T3000 and T5000, equivalent to a week's wage for some Mongolians" (Mayhew, 2001, p. 101). Mongolians are fond of music and dancing, so these establishments are quite popular with the older students. The countryside does not have these options, although occasionally in smaller cities you may find a Sports Palace (sports arena), and there are dances on weekends for locals and tourists. Bars in the cities can be hangouts as well, but most establishments are not open that late and a bar would be quite an uncommon sight out in the wide-open spaces.

Culturally speaking, the Mongols do have an active opera and theater schedule, and they have the Russian influence to thank for that. Typically, the most active times are summer months for tourists and winter months for locals who are looking for something to do indoors. Traditional music and dance performances are given year-round, with occasional puppet shows and the state circus in Ulaanbaatar being popular draws. Ulaanbaatar has several movie theaters to choose from, but most of the other city theaters are closed and there are none in the country. The most common films shown in theaters are produced in Russia, although it is not uncommon to spot some action films or soft-porn films brought in from India, Korea, Japan, or the United States. Most of the films are not dubbed because of the cost involved and the lack of technology, yet dubbing is becoming more readily available.

Music and dance are very popular in Mongolia. The most popular form of music is vocal music usually accompanied by the few basic types of instruments available in Mongolia: the fiddle (*morin khuur*), a banjo-like instrument (*tovshuur*), and a variety of flutes, drums, cymbals, gongs, and tambourines. The traditional folk music is often a form of Mongolian poetry that centers on themes of herding and work. A majority of the more traditional songs are sung by herders who are known to sing to their animals in order to control them. The unique style of vocals involving the use of the throat is what makes traditional Mongolian music unique. Teenagers are still drawn to this form of traditional singing, particularly while in the countryside in that the songs typically reflect their thoughts about nature and herding. Throat singing (*khoomi*) is one of the oldest arts in Mongolia: "The style of singing produces a whole harmonic range from deep in the larynx, throat, stomach and palate, and has the remarkable effect of producing two notes and melodies simultaneously—one a low growl, the other an ethereal whistling" (Mayhew, 2001, p. 37).

Nevertheless, there has been a Western influence on the music and youth of Mongolia. Videos of Western music are now available for the youth of Mongolia to watch on satellite TV. This has led many locals in Ulaanbaatar to develop their own version of Western music in Mongolian. Teenagers like groups like Kharanga and Niciton (heavy metal), Chinggis Khaan (pop), Ariunna and Saraa (female vocalists), and Hurd (rock with local instruments). Mongolian music can be downloaded courtesy of Infosystem Mongolei at http://userpage.fu-berlin.de/~corff/im/Musik/overview.Music.html. The younger generation is often found listening to music and dancing to all styles of music, particularly during the traditional festivals held across the country.

Spectator sports are rarely found in Mongolia, and although Mongolians do engage in many sports it is uncommon for them to pay to see a team play. There is a local soccer league with teams in Ulaanbaatar, Erdenet, and Darkhan, but the sport has not caught on in Mongolia. They do occasionally view basketball games on TV, but there is no place to catch a game live, although there are hoops in some of the major cities. Boxing does occasionally appear in the cities, but it is not regularly scheduled. As mentioned previously, the three big sports are wrestling, archery, and horse racing—and citizens prefer to participate in all three.

Shopping in the Western sense is nonexistent in Mongolia. Souvenir and antique shops in Ulaanbaatar cater to tourists. There are also some small shops near the Erdene Zuu monastery or in the south Gobi Desert. Tourists are often cautioned that they may not leave the country with antique relics. Almost all of the crafts sold are intended for tourists and in Mongolian terms are expensive. A local teenager will never be found hanging out with friends at a local mall.

In essence, TV does play a big role in connecting Mongolian teenagers to the outside world. Not all teenagers have a television at home, though. If they live in the country, they definitely will not have one in their ger, but if they live in the city chances are that they will meet someone in their building or at school who has access to a TV. Technology is becoming a very important part of Mongolian culture, and as is the case in most cultures, it is the younger generation that gravitates toward it. In Mongolia there are 60.7 TV sets per 1,000 people and 74 radios per 1,000 people, so although technology is effecting change there has not been a revolution yet.

RELIGIOUS PRACTICES AND CULTURAL CEREMONIES

Mongolians are predominantly Tibetan Buddhists. There is a long history between Tibet and Mongolia, and devout Buddhist Mongolians try to take at least one trip to the holy city of Lhasa in their lifetime. In the early 1920s, the communist takeover abolished over 110,000 monks living in over 700 monasteries. All of the monasteries were closed and ransacked and all religious worship and ceremonies were outlawed. It was not until 1990, with the collapse of Soviet rule in Mongolia, that freedom of religion was restored.

Close to 150 monasteries have reopened, although an entire generation of Mongolians has been raised without religion and there are some issues with the Tibetan texts and the lack of trained monks in Mongolia. Although many of the old temples have been destroyed, there are still three monasteries that the Mongolians consider important for visitors to view: the Gandan Khiid in Ullan Baatar (which also contains a Buddhist university), the Erdene Zuu Khiid built in Övörkhangai aimag, and the remote Amarbayasgalant Khiid near Darkhan. Visitors are welcome at the monasteries, but they need to be careful not to step in front of the monks; rather, they must work their way clockwise around the back of the temple. Visitors can make small cash offerings and bow in front of the altars, but they are prohibited from taking pictures.

There are many common Buddhist symbols, but in Mongolia there are eight Auspicious Symbols (*naimin takhel*) that are associated with the gifts given to Buddha in order to receive protection and good luck. The precious parasol, the banner of victory, the white conch shell, the two golden fishes, the vase of great treasures, the knot of eternity, the eight-spoked golden wheel, and the lotus flower are the eight most popular Buddhist symbols found in Mongolia.

Although Tibetan Buddhism is the religion practiced by the vast majority of Mongolians, it is important to note that there are other religions practiced in the country. There is a small percentage of Muslims (6%) who live in the western sections of Mongolia, and a small group of Mormon and Christian missionaries have come to Mongolia to teach English and spread their religious beliefs. In Ulaanbaatar, there are now more than 30 non-Buddhist places of worship. The new Catholic Church found in the capital is known to locals because it cost more than $1 million to construct. Shamanism is the last religion of note in Mongolia, and it is not uncommon to view *ovoos* (pyramid-shaped collections of stones, wood, and so forth prepared as an altar of offerings to bring good luck) all about the countryside.

Due to the fact that religion is new again to this country, teenagers do not typically spend much time in temples or places of worship. There is no religious ceremony attached to a rite of passage into adulthood in Mongolia.

CONCLUSION

Contemporary life in Mongolia is a unique mix of tradition and change. Politically speaking, the country has adjusted to living without the full support of Russia, and there have even been shifts in political power. The youth of Mongolia will play a major role in steering their country into the future. As things currently stand, if teenagers live in a city or move to a city for education it is paid for by the state and attendance is compulsory. Many teenagers recognize the need for education and the opportunities that are afforded to them if they complete this track.

This is a country that is rich in tradition, and the elders are still accorded a level of respect, often sought for their guidance and advice. The Mongolian way of life has been characterized as "laid-back, patient, tolerant of hardship and intimately connected with the ways of animals. Despite urbanization, the traditions of the steppes live on" (Mayhew, 2001, p. 39). This is one of the most intriguing aspects of Mongolia—the residents feel no need or desire to rapidly develop their beautiful country. Although there have been some environmental problems in the cities, the countryside remains pristine. Western teenagers have less access to unspoiled land than Mongolian teenagers do.

This connection to the outdoors makes Mongolia a unique nation. In general, a teenager's life truly depends on what section of Mongolia he or she lives in. The farther away from the cities, the more traditional and nomadic the lifestyle. Technology will most certainly have a major impact on this country in the generations to come; even now the concept of distance learning exists. Time and the political climate in the surrounding countries (Russia and China) are going to provide some interesting scenarios for this quiet little section of the earth.

RESOURCE GUIDE

Large youth population in Mongolia. (2000). *Popline, 22,* 2.
Mayhew, B. (2001). *Mongolia: Discover a land without fences.* Victoria, Australia: Lonely Planet Publications.
Spotlight: Mongolia. (1998). *Population Today, 26,* 7.

Nonfiction

Bawden, A.R., & Bawden, C.R. (1989). *The Modern History of Mongolia.* London: Routledge.
Bawden, C.R. (1968). *The history of Mongolia.* New York: Praeger.
Reynolds, J. (1994). *Mongolia: Vanishing cultures.*Orlando, FL: Harcourt.
The secret history of the Mongols. (2003). (I. de Rachewiltz, Ed.). Boston: Brill Academic Publishers.

Films

Mikhalkov, N. (Director). (1992). *Close to Eden* [Motion picture]. Paramount Home Entertainment.
Wise, R. (Director). (1953). *Destination Gobi* [Motion picture]. 20th Century Fox.

Web Sites

CIA—The World Factbook 2000—Mongolia: www.odci.gov/cia/publications/factbook/geos/mg.html

United Nations in Mongolia: www.un-mongolia.mn
www.eurasianet.org/
www.indiana.edu/~mongsoc
www.mol.mn
www.mongoliatoday.com
www.mongoliatourism.gov.mn

Newspapers

Mongolianews: http://www.mongolianews.com
MONTSAME News Agency: http://www.montsame.mn
Mongolia This Week: http://www.mongoliathisweek.mn/
Mongol Messenger: http://www.mongolnet.mn/mglmsg/index.html
UB Post: http://www.ulaanbaatar.net/news

More Information

Embassy of Mongolia in the United States of America
2833 Main Street NW
Washington, DC 20007
Web site: http://members.aol.com/monemb
E-mail: monemb@aol.com
Telephone: (202) 333-7117
Fax: (202) 298-9227

Friends of Mongolia
PO Box 1269
New York, NY 10276
E-mail: friendsofmongolia@worldnet.att.net

Mongol-American Cultural Association
50 Louis Street
New Brunswick, NJ 08901
Fax: (908) 297-1140

Mongolia Society
322 Goodbody Hall
Indiana University
Bloomington, IN 47405
Web site: http://www.indiana.edu/~mongsoc/index.html
E-mail: monsoc@indiana.edu
Telephone: (812) 855-4078
Fax: (812) 855-7500

Permanent Mission of Mongol to the United Nations
6 East 77th Street
New York, NY 10021
E-mail: mongolia@un.int
Telephone: (212) 861-9460
Fax: (212) 861-9464

Consulate and UN Representative
E-mail: mngun@un.int
Telephone: (212) 472-6517
Fax: (212) 861-9464

Each year in New York City, the mission sponsors a festival of Mongolian music, art, dance, and sports.

Chapter 8

NEPAL

Laura Bullock

INTRODUCTION

The landlocked kingdom of Nepal lies on the continent of Asia sandwiched between two giants, India and China. The extent of Nepal's physical diversity ranges from the flat Terai Plain (60–300 meters above sea level) to the looming Himalayas, which include the world's tallest mountain, Mount Everest, at 8,848 meters above sea level.

Nepal is one of the poorest countries in the world, with nearly half of its population living below the poverty line. Around 70 percent of Nepal's children suffer from malnutrition, and only 37 percent of the population has access to safe drinking water. The average Nepali earns $200 a year. In 1999, the estimated population was a little over 24 million, and in 1992, there were only an estimated 45,000 televisions in the country (*The world factbook 1999—Nepal*, 2000). Nepal's 2000 unemployment rate was less than 2 percent for the country generally but 7 percent in urban areas. In contrast, the U.S. unemployment rate was 4.2 percent in 1999 with a 275,562,673 population estimate in July 2000. More than 90 percent of Nepal's population exists by subsistence farming of jute, sugarcane, tobacco, and grain. The farmers are able to grow only what they need to survive. They cannot afford to farm for profit. Even if they have a successful year, if they do not own the land they farm, up to 50 percent of the crops will go to the owner as payment for rent. Sometimes, animals are raised for food, but this is uncommon as the animals are unhealthy owing to lack of fodder (crops such as corn and hay used to feed the livestock).

This problem leads to another serious situation. Nepal's remaining forests are being used increasingly for animal fodder, leading to deforestation. This has had a great impact on the country's ecosystem, which is directly related to world ecology. Because of these problems, the government has been especially encouraging trade and foreign investment, and the country has economic growth potential with its knowledge of hydropower and its tourism industry. Still, Nepal's prospects for economic growth are considered bleak for several reasons. Its landlocked, remote location prevents its economy from flourishing, and this prevents important technological advancements that need money to become reality. Additionally, because Nepal is surrounded by the Great Himalaya Range to the north and the Indo-Gangetic Plain to the south, it is quite susceptible to natural disasters. Researchers conclude that Nepal must address the following concerns in order to move forward and become more prosperous: economic policy, international debt, low labor productivity, income distribution, and population growth. Additionally, it is believed that Nepal must work toward a restructuring of its political and social views, values, behavior, and attitudes toward women, as they play an often overlooked yet paramount role in the development of the country (Basnet-Thapa, 1999).

The government of Nepal is a constitutional monarchy/parliamentary democracy. This means that the executive powers are exercised by not only a king but a prime minister and other ministers as needed. Even though there are executive, judicial, and legislative branches of the government and a multiparty system that includes the Nepal Communist Party—United Marxist Leninist, the Nepali Congress, the National Democratic Party, and the Nepal Workers and Peasants Party, the king still retains much of his power and prestige and is considered "the symbol of the nation and the unity of its people" (Savada, 1991, p. 155). The change from an absolute monarchy to a constitutional monarchy/ parliamentary democracy occurred after 1990 and owes itself to the Nepalese People's Movement, the Nepali Congress, and communist forces that convinced the king to lift the ban on political parties and give more sovereignty to the people of Nepal rather than continue his rule as an absolute monarch. King Birendra was respected and well liked by many since he helped Nepal move toward a more democratic form of government and way of life. He was also considered a reincarnation of the Hindu god Vishnu. Sadly, on June 1, 2001, King Birendra Bir Bikham Shah Dev, his wife Queen Aishwarya Rajya Laxmi Devi Rana, their children Princess Sruti Rajya Laxmi Devi Rana and Prince Nirajan Bir Bikram Shah, and seven other relatives were killed or injured by the king and queen's eldest son, the Crown Prince Dipendra Bir Bikram Shah Dev. Prince Dipendra opened fire on the family and guests during a dinner party and then shot himself. He was appointed king as he lay on life support; however, he died and late King Birendra's brother, Gyanendra Bir Bikram Shah, was made king. The country experienced riots and unrest during the mourning period; Hindu men shaved their heads and shops closed out of respect for the royal family. There is speculation that a weakened royal family could pave the way for Maoist groups to infiltrate the government and usurp power.

The Nepalese desire for a democracy has led to some unrest within the country. Since mid-1991, when there was a move toward a more democratically elected government, there have been a number of nationwide strikes called for by domestic political parties. Most of these strikes involved minimal injuries and disrupted commerce and transportation for only a couple of days. However, over 100 people have died in isolated Western districts of Nepal in violent Maoist insurgencies since 1996. The communist groups responsible for such outbreaks of violence appeal to the poor and their communities, and violent coercion is used when necessary. Other instances of unrest come from Nepal's position between India and China. It is frequently referred to as a Sino-Indian buffer zone since India and China have never really been on friendly terms and Nepal is situated in between these two large countries. Nepal sees China as a potential communist threat; however, a highway linking the Tibetan and Nepali border was constructed in the 1960s and Nepal purchased Chinese air defense weapons in 1988. These activities strained relations between Nepal and India. When India imposed trade restrictions on Nepal, it took 15 months for Nepal to agree not to purchase defense items abroad (in China, for instance) without consulting New Delhi, India's capital. This coercion by India only served to further Nepal's opinion that India refuses to fully recognize it as an independent nation and will also bully Nepal until India is able to meet its foreign policy objectives. Nepal is 5 hours and 45 minutes ahead of Greenwich Mean Time, and India is 5 hours and 30 minutes ahead. Some say this is Nepal's way of distinguishing itself from India.

Nepal's population comprises Indo-Aryans from India and Tibeto-Burmans from the Himalayas, but there are many ethnic groups within these general groups. There is no easy way to divide these groups up and say one is exclusively Hindu while the other is exclusively Buddhist. The two religions are often intertwined within a culture and sometimes are combined with other religions such as the pre-Buddhist religion of Bon or shamanism. There are the Khas and Bhotya of the Himalayan region. These peoples include the Sherpa, Manangpa, Lopa, Thakalis, and Tamangs. Most are farmers, and the Sherpas are nomadic herders. Most are Buddhist, but some sects such as the Thakalis have adopted Hinduism, and the Tamangs practice Bon. The Magar, Gurung, Newar, Rai, and Limbu hail from the midlands region, and these groups are composed of farmers, with the exception of the Magars, who are also soldiers. These tribes practice everything from the shamanistic religion of the Gurungs to the synthesis of Hinduism and Buddhism of the Newars to the Rai and Limbu's shamanistic religion with a strong influence of Hinduism. The Tharu, Abadhi, Danuwar, Bhojpuri, and Mithila are from the Terai region. The Tharu follow an animist religion that is strong influenced by Hinduism.

Unique to Nepal and a few other predominantly Asian countries is the existence of the Hindu caste system. This is a way of determining social class and was modeled after the Brahmanic system of the Indian plains. It came into existence around 300 C.E. because of the Indo-Aryan invasion and the restructuring of the country into a feudalistic economy. The higher-caste Hindus were able to appropriate, sometimes from local tribes, the more fertile and accessible lowlands, and they soon thereafter introduced the concept of individual ownership so they could maintain their hold over the prime areas of land. There are four caste divisions, with the untouchables residing beneath the caste system and designated as "casteless" or outcasts of society. The four in descending order are Brahman (priests and scholars), Kshatriya or Chhetri (rulers and warriors), Vasiya (merchants and traders), and Sudra (farmers, artisans, and laborers). The Newars, inhabitants of the central midland zone of the Kathmandu Valley, have their own caste system and among them, intercaste marriage is rare and the untouchables are still oppressed. Hindu theory does not recognize a relationship between caste and ethnicity, but sometimes these two traits become confused and intertwined with each other, as in the case of the Khas. When Parbatiyas (Hindus of varying caste and ethnicity) arrived in the western midlands from the Indian plains after the Muslim invasion of India in the twelfth century, most were Brahman or Kshatriya. The Khas were lower caste, but the Parbatiyas of these higher castes upgraded many of the members of the Khas to the caste of Kshatriya, thereby raising the Khas' status in the caste system. This is unusual since Nepalese are born into a caste and membership is permanent unless a Nepali has migrated to a new area and/or married into a new caste. These activities can lead to an upgrading or downgrading of caste, and marriage between castes was not common years ago since there was more of a social stigma attached to intercaste relations. Caste can determine wealth, political power, and occupation, but with the approach of a more modern society, this very rigid system has been in decline. Today, there are more intercaste marriages, and more contact with the West has given the Nepalese a new perspective on the caste system. In 1962, the government made it illegal to discriminate against the untouchables, and the legal system now treats all castes equally, including free education for everyone. Still, even today, some young men or women will consider only those of the same caste for marriage. Other young men and women do not mind considering those of a different caste. There is still caste discrimination, mostly in rural areas, but this ancient system of class distinction has definitely weakened considerably.

TYPICAL DAY

Nothing is more important to the future of a country than its children. Children under 18 years of age account for approximately 52 percent of Nepal's total population. So what is a typical day in the life of a Nepalese teenager? Where do teenagers live? Some houses may be constructed of brick and stone with a mud finish washed in lime or red ochre and a thatched roof. In the Terai, homes might be made from bamboo and timber and built high up on woodpiles. Two-story rectangular or square homes covered in red clay are common among the Magars. Additionally, some houses may have a porch or courtyard, and many homes in rural areas use the ground floor as a stable for animals, with pumpkin and cucumber vines growing on the roofs. When a teenager first awakens in the morning, he or she may "go to the river." This is the bathroom, as many homes do not have indoor facilities. If a teenager is attending school, he or she may have to awaken very early since the walk may take several hours and there may be homework to complete prior to the long walk. Homework time is often in the mornings since teenagers usually help with household tasks once they return home from school in the evenings. If teenagers are working at home for their family, they will begin their chores early. Sometimes a teenager is a servant for a wealthy family in an urban area or a factory worker and he or she works outside of the home and brings the money home. Preceding work or school in the mornings will be prayer, either at home or in a temple with the entire family. So, most of the day is taken up with attending school, working, or doing both.

Chores around the household and on the family's farmland vary according to the seasons. There are certain activities that can be accomplished only in spring, just as there are certain jobs that will not need to be performed in winter. Much of a Nepali's life is taken up with survival and the basic necessities. The concept of time differs greatly from the Western notion. A native Nepali commented on this saying, "Nepalese people are very careless in this matter. Time is not so important in Nepal."[1] Translated, this means that meeting a friend at 3 P.M. here might mean meeting a friend sometime in the afternoon in Nepal. More than likely, there would be no agreed-upon time. Life is more relaxed and runs at an unhurried pace. Every activity, with the exception of work for sustenance, is done at an almost leisurely pace. This, however, does not suggest laziness. It does express the Eastern appreciation of time as something not to be rushed, measured, or confined. Time is to be spent mindfully; if one measures it, one is more concerned with this rather than the actual activity or purpose.

Whether a teenager attends school or works, clothing is a concern. In the more urban areas such as Kathmandu, teenagers dress in more Western clothing. Especially among the small affluent population in Kathmandu, teenagers will emulate teens in the West in terms of dress and taste for American pop music. Chances are a family living in a rural environment, who are probably of a lower caste, will not be able to afford the jeans, pants, and popular T-shirts worn by more urbanized Nepalese. Some Nepalese claim that television, even though not prevalent in Nepal, has had a big impact on the increasing popularity of Western clothing. The more rural tribes stick to their traditional garb, and most of their clothing is handmade. Most teenagers attending school wear uniforms. Wearing a *sari*, traditional women's clothing, is common among women and girls, especially in Kathmandu. The sari consists of a large expanse of cloth, often in a silky material with vivid patterns, draped artfully over a simple cloth skirt and shirt, both of which usually match some color appearing in the sari's pattern. Amongst the Tamangs, influenced by the Newars, women and girls wear colorful wraparound skirts, blouses, jackets, and scarves. Gold or brass earrings and nose rings set with semiprecious stones are commonly worn on important occasions. Tamang men and boys may wear loincloths or traditional Newari pants, short-sleeved jackets, and traditional hats (*topis*). Even the males may wear cloth wrapped around the waist. A Newari woman or girl will wear a sari and blouse with a shawl. The men or boys wear baggy trousers similar to jodhpurs, a long untucked double-breasted shirt, a vest or coat, and a *topi*. Females of the Newari Jyapu caste wear black saris with a red border, and the males belonging to this caste, mostly farmers, wear the traditional clothing and also wrap a long piece of cloth around their waists.

FAMILY LIFE

Family life in Nepal contains two types of systems. One is the large extended family. This is the norm among the wealthier and higher-caste families, who tend not to share living quarters, as well as the Newar and some Terai inhabitants. In the more impoverished families, parents live with their married sons' families. A smaller, nuclear family unit is becom-

An extended family in Chobar Heights, Nepal. Courtesy of Laura Bullock.

ing increasingly common since landholdings are not as massive and smaller units of land will support only so many family members. Also, in this society, the eldest male of the family has the most control, and women perform an excessive share of household tasks, including almost total care of the children.

Work by household members in Nepal is very different from work in developed countries. In Nepal, only a few women work outside of the home. Women are usually the housewives and homemakers in this patriarchal, male-dominated society. In addition to keeping house, women often spin and wind wool for knitting and process the crops farmed by the men of the family. One such job may involve separating the millet flower pods from the stems, separating the outer husks from the seeds, and grinding the seeds to make flour for bread. Young boys are usually prepared for the world of work and positions of authority and young women are trained to become housewives and mothers. Women are taught to provide for their family first and then after marriage for their husband's family. Men learn traditional jobs and crafts as boys and usually continue their learned trades well into adulthood. Examples of work are various handicrafts, *thangkas* (painted religious icons on a silk background), papermaking, and agriculture.

Many children do work, especially in the agricultural sector. Since agriculture is the mainstay for many families, intensive labor is required. Many Nepalese families have many children since their value as laborers and supporters in their parents' old age is more valuable than the cost of feeding and clothing them. Children fetch water, collect firewood, graze cattle, care for younger children, and help their families in the fields. Some are even sent to work as domestics for the wealthy. A Nepalese child between the ages of six and nine will work three hours a day on average. Those between the ages of 10 and 14 will work as many as five to six hours a day. Girls work twice as many hours as boys (Evans, 1992). In fact, among the Magars of Banyan Hill in central Nepal, girls are more important as a source of hard farm labor than boys are. Girls here will cook, weave, and carry manure. Boys plow the fields, butcher livestock, make religious sacrifices, and weave baskets, nets, ropes, and thatched roofs. Both sexes spin textiles; operate oil mills, rice hullers, and grindstones; carry water and milk; make rice and straw mats; harvest fodder; and catch fish. Children in other areas of Nepal may take part in these activities and may also help their fathers in the fields or make traditional handicrafts such as puppets, clay figures, or pots. Many children work outside the home in brick factories where the bricks are made by hand. A small factory can make more than a million bricks a year. Most common is work in carpet factories and stone quarries where rocks are broken by hand. One example is a 13-year-old boy who has worked in a carpet factory for two years from 5 A.M. until midnight every day. Even though he is a bonded worker working to pay back his parents' debt, his parents never even received the loan. A middleman stole it. He eats two meals a day of rice and lentils. Three fingers of his left hand have been cut to the bone as a result of his work. Children work for primarily one reason, because their parents need the money. Some adults feel it is better for their children to learn a trade such as carpet weaving or working the quarries since it is unlikely they will be able to afford an education for them. Also, once a formal education is completed, jobs are still hard to come by for the well educated since Nepal is not a country of industry and technological advancement. Most work is agricultural or trade oriented. The only groups exempt from hard work seem to be the very wealthy and the elderly, especially older men. Many will sit around talking, smoking pipes, and wearing topis.

TRADITIONAL AND NONTRADITIONAL FOOD DISHES

Mealtimes are different in various parts of Nepal. A rich family is more likely to partake of a meal together. In most families, the majority of which are poor, the males eat first, having been served by the women of the household. Then the females are allowed to finish what is left. Mornings usually begin with little more than tea. Utensils are not widely used, and people often eat with their right hand since the left hand is considered unclean, used for the toilet. Bringing freshly prepared food into contact with a used utensil or plate, even if that plate is just placed on a table with food that has yet to be served, is believed to pollute and contaminate the untouched food and make it inedible. Also, Nepalis drink from cups or bottles without letting the container touch their lips. When food is offered to a person, the container is held with both hands. In some areas, broad green leaves are used as plates and whole-wheat pancakes (*chatmaries*) and hot chili pickles are popular. Cooked rice and lentils (*daal bhat*) is usually eaten for lunch and dinner and is one of the most common foods in the country. Other foods include dumplings (*momos*), mushroom chicken, chicken chop, tomato chicken, grilled meat or seafood (*sekuwa*), fried potatoes (*aloo tareko*), mushrooms with gravy (*chyau ko tarkari*), chicken with gravy (*kukhura ko ledo*), smoked mutton (*khasi ko chwela*), curried peanuts (*badam sandheko*), and fried wild boar or pork (*bandhel tareko*). Special-occasion foods include *yomari*, a kind of dumpling made in many different animal shapes (e.g., dogs, cats, lambs, and fish) and filled with a sugary sesame substance. *Yomari* is prepared during *Yomari Purnima*, a holiday observed during the full moons between November and January.

Mainly the women are in charge of cooking, but some men enjoy the culinary arts as well. Girls especially, around the ages of 10 to 14, enjoy helping their mothers cook. Most of the time, the Nepalese will kill their own animals (e.g., goats, chickens, pigs, buffalo) for food, having raised the animals for this purpose, rather than purchasing already prepared food at the market. However, many Nepalese who are of a higher caste, especially Brahmans, are vegetarians. In fact, for all Hindus, the cow is considered to be a holy animal and killing a cow is prohibited. Therefore, one will not find beef in Nepalese restaurants unless the restaurant caters to foreigners and has imported the beef. While the Nepalese subsist mainly on grains such as rice, they love oily and fatty foods. Even though there are long-standing traditional dishes and foods, teenagers still love to eat in restaurants and hotels that cater to foreigners. They enjoy roast chicken, pizza, hot dogs, and burgers. With food comes drink, and the drinking age in Nepal is 21. There does not appear to be a big problem with teenagers and alcohol, especially since many Hindus do not drink alcohol.

SCHOOLING

Since work is the mainstay of the family and even the children engage in it, schooling is less important in this country, like many third-world

countries. Also, before the 1950s and during Rana rule, an educated public was feared and the ruling elite was the only group allowed access to
education. Public schooling was opposed and the Rana rulers allowed formal instruction for only their own children. They believed that this would
secure their domination of the country's government and keep the general
public out. Although the Ranas have been gone for a while, the effects of
this approach linger: still today, only 27.5 percent of the country's population, age 15 and older, can read and write. A 1995 estimate concludes
that 40.9 percent of this literate group are males and 14 percent are
females (*Facts and figures on Nepal*, 1999). Prem Magar, an 11-year-old
carpet weaver in Kathmandu, lives on a small farm and did attend school
for a while. Now he works 16-hour days with his parents. "I did not mind
looking after cattle before and after school and working as a farm laborer
during the holidays," he says. "I did not mind going hungry now and then
as long as I could go to school" (Parker, 1998, p. 72). Most families cannot afford the fees for their children to attend school and prefer that their
children be kept at home to work. In 1975, primary schooling was made
free and attendance became compulsory for children from ages 6 to 11.
However, once the child completes the primary level and is ready to move
on to the secondary level, lasting five more years, the parents must assume
all costs. Additionally, in many rural areas, girls are sent to school as long
as household and farm help is sufficient. Once the girl is needed to work
in the home and fields, she is taken out of school. The parents feel justi-
fied in doing this since they believe it would be difficult for them to find a
husband for an educated girl. In more urban areas, though, girls' education
is considered more important.

For those children lucky enough to attend school, a typical school day
runs from around 9:30 A.M. until 4:30 P.M. There are schools for handicapped children and the blind, but these tend to cost a lot, as they are
usually private institutions. There are also schools that offer one-year
scholarships to gifted children since education is so costly. The children of
wealthy parents attend private schools, sometimes overseas, especially for
higher education, and the majority of the children attend government
schools at least until age 11, if they go at all. The government schools can
be likened to the West's public school system. Trade schools such as the
vocational schools in the West are uncommon since trades are usually
learned from parents or other relatives. There appears to be an over-
crowding problem in the government-run schools, and they seem to
emphasize quantity rather than quality. Most government schools are
coed; however, there are private schools such as the British-run St.
Xavier's for boys and St. Mary's for girls. The children study English and

Nepali and subjects such as social studies, math, science, geography, grammar, and general knowledge. The lunch break is usually around noon, but this differs from school to school. Grade levels are similar to those in the West, running from first through twelfth. Not unlike the West, there is lecturing at most secondary levels and there are books with practice lessons for everyone. The private schools appear to give more homework since there is fierce competition between them to draw students in from wealthy families, and since the wealthier parents are able to invest more time and money in their children's education, they therefore push for more homework from the teachers.

Once a school year is at its end, all students must take a final term exam that determines whether they will pass to the next grade. After completing the higher-secondary level (similar to grades 10, 11, and 12), students must pass a government exam known as the School Leaving Certificate Exam before they will be allowed to pursue further academics such as college. The dropout rate is low in primary schools since education is free and most children in Nepal view attending school as a privilege. They would rather sit in a classroom than plow a field. However, when children reach the secondary level and their families must pay for their education, there is a high dropout rate since most families cannot afford to send their children to school.

SOCIAL LIFE

There is a fine line between a woman and a girl in Nepali culture. Because many females are married off at such a young age and have adult responsibilities, the designation of teen or woman is not clear.

With taboos still in place regarding male and female interactions, how do boys and girls meet in Nepal? Is there dating? Usually not. Even though boys and girls do spend recreational time together, some Nepalese teens hold fast to their parents' traditions and refrain from interactions, still sometimes considered taboo, between the opposite sexes. The parents are concerned that interactions between their son or daughter and members of the opposite sex could lead to sexual situations. A girl is expected to wait until she marries before she has sexual intercourse since intercourse and pregnancy outside of marriage are highly taboo, but there is still a high teenage pregnancy rate, partly because most females marry and have children when they are still in their teens. Teen pregnancy appears highest in rural areas and among those who are more materially destitute or impoverished. Among the Tamangs and Magars, rural tribes, a much more liberal stance is taken regarding interactions between boys and girls.

Many teens, no matter their parents' views, still feel comfortable interacting with their peers, male or female, on most occasions and even engage in sports with the opposite sex, but usually this is away from the home so as not to show disrespect for their parents. And if there is any casual interaction between the opposite sexes, it may be only within the same caste or socioeconomic class even though caste appears to be not as important as it once was to the Hindus of Nepalese society. Still, the ancient rules of caste appear to be followed the most closely by Brahmans, possibly because they would like to maintain their position at the top of the hierarchy. Even though laws forbid girls from marrying before they are 16, child marriage is a common practice dating back to ancient Hindu scriptures sanctioning such an event, and actual dating between boys and girls is by no means commonplace unless teenagers seek it out. Strict moral Hindu laws dating from before Christ state the importance of marrying off a daughter between the ages of 8 and 10 or before the girl reaches puberty. Even with these laws, open discussions on menstruation, sex, and pregnancy are not common between young girls and their mothers in Hindu households. Most teenagers, especially girls, learn the facts of life from their peers. Great importance is placed on the virginity of the bride and fidelity of the wife toward the husband, so sexual relations outside of marriage for women are definitely taboo. Additionally, a young girl can be married off to a very old man, and men can have more than one wife for pleasure and child-rearing. A girl, however, even if she becomes a widow, can have only one husband. The custom of *sati*, where the girl or woman was burned alive on the funeral pyre of her husband, was outlawed in the nineteenth century, but it is still taboo for a widow or a divorced woman to remarry. However, in the Rai culture, there is a special process called *Laasaa Watmaa* when a divorced female can marry again after her family and other relatives meet to discuss the issue. Rais also have a more relaxed attitude toward widows remarrying, and there appears to be more sexual and marital freedom within their culture as well. In fact, the Rais have several types of marriages. One is *Dotma Khatma,* the traditional arranged marriage. The boy's family asks the girl's for consent to the marriage. Once this is given, a Hindu priest is consulted for the wedding date. Another type of marriage is *Khama Khatma* or the "stealing" of the girl by the boy but with her consent as well as her family's. *Fungma Khatma* is similar to the West's version of eloping, when the boy and girl, in love, run away from home. Unlike in the West, though, the families look for the couple and agree to declare them as a couple.

Still, discrimination toward females in most sectors of Nepalese society is prevalent and relates to the fact that their worth is seen as restricted to their roles as daughters, wives, and mothers only. No value is placed on the female's individuality or anything separate from her identity as first a child, then wife, and finally mother. According to Hindu scriptures, a wife must look upon her husband as if he were a god. Girls get less medical care, less education, and less food than their brothers. In fact, Nepal is one of the few countries in the world where a female's average life expectancy is shorter than a male's. Girls are viewed as a commodity, someone else's wealth, and because of this, investments in their education, health care, and future are lacking. A popular saying in rural areas is, "Raising a girl is like watering a neighbor's tree. You have the trouble and expense of nurturing the plant but the profit goes to somebody else" (*Children and women of Nepal—A situation analysis*, 1996). Therefore, money is not spent on females since there will come a time when they are no longer an asset to the family. A dowry (*tilak*) from the bride's family to the groom's is really the only major expense the bride's family is willing to incur in relation to their daughter. The *tilak* is based on the groom's education, qualifications, and social standing so the girl is encouraged to marry young so that the groom does not require more of a dowry as he advances in age, social standing, and education. Also, another factor influencing early marriage is the maintenance of caste purity. Even though inroads are being made to place less importance on caste, engagement between infants (*magani*) is still in effect in some parts of Nepal. This ancient practice reserves a groom or bride, sometimes even before birth. With the exception of the Mongolian or Tibeto-Burman culture where females are allowed to choose their partners and where they hold a higher status than in other Nepalese tribes, females are told to obey their fathers when they are daughters, obey their husbands when they are wives, and obey their sons when they are mothers. Still, even though the Tibeto-Burmans are from another culture very different from the Nepalese, the females still struggle under this ancient precept if they live in Nepal. Even with relaxed standards in today's Nepal, parents still prefer arranged marriages and teenagers hold firm with their ideal of love marriages or marrying for love rather than marrying the person their parents have told them to marry.

RECREATION

Teenagers sometimes have free time on Saturdays to visit the public swimming pool or play and watch football and cricket. Sporting events at the Eighth South Asian Games Federation included tae kwon do, volleyball, swimming, boxing, table tennis, football (soccer), target shooting, weightlifting, wrestling, and kabaddi, similar to the West's version of hide and seek (*Games*, 2001). Boating and hunting, sports that teens in the West may enjoy, are virtually unheard of as pastimes in Nepal. Even though Nepal has a women's national football (soccer) team and Nepalese teens are enthusiastic sports fans, only some secondary schools have sports teams. The majority of schools, government run, do not since it is too costly. Teenagers still have their national sports heroes in Hari Kadka (football), Raju Shakya (football), Sangeeta Rajbhandai (tae kwon do), and Tika Bogati (running). When not playing sports, Nepalese teens may be found watching television—if their family has a television. Going into the woods to graze their family's cattle or visiting relatives may be a big part of a Nepali teen's recreation.

ENTERTAINMENT

Leisure time and time to mingle with friends is not as prevalent in Nepal as in the West, and transportation is a major factor. Most Nepalese teens, even if they are of the legal 16-year-old driving age, do not have cars. In fact, many families may not even own a car. Only the children of wealthy business tycoons, a minority, have their own vehicles. In fact, some impoverished people in rural locations, adults and children alike, have never seen a car or bus.

Despite the economic limitations, the new generation of teenagers and young adults in Kathmandu is very Americanized, partly because of the media: television, movies, radio, magazines, and newspapers. Tourism has an even larger influence on teenagers. Teens see Westerners with the latest hair and clothing styles and covet these things. They equate these popular mores with the West and believe that the West means money, success, and happiness. Additionally, the impact of Hollywood on Indian productions has led to a newly coined term: Bollywood (from India, specifically Bombay or Mumbai as it is now known, and Hollywood). The influence of Hollywood on Bollywood is great in terms of dress and music appearing in Indian productions, and teenagers, when able, flock to these movies and programs. Western influence has led to Nepalese tastes for pool, football, cricket, badminton, and table tennis; heavy metal, rap, and soft rock; and clubs and discos. Still, such clubs and discos are uncommon and dancing usually takes place in a casual environment without flashy lights but plenty of music and fun. Often, there will be no lights at all, not because of preference but because of "load sharing"—planned blackouts to conserve energy. If the monsoon season has been drier than usual and there is not enough hydropower, the blackouts occur more often. Blackouts usually last an hour or two in the morning and at night. People, no matter where they are or what they are doing, are usually indoors in their homes at 10 P.M. Everything shuts down, and night visiting is often thought of negatively. Another popular pastime between teenagers is singing to each other. Devotional songs with folk and classical elements are important parts of religious ceremonies and family get-togethers.

RELIGIOUS PRACTICES AND CULTURAL CEREMONIES

Nepal is primarily a Hindu country. However, Buddhism was introduced first. Even though Hinduism is the religion of the majority, the two religions often blend together so one religion's traditions may be indistinguishable from the other's. For example, both religions have a complex pantheon of gods and goddesses such as Hinduism's Hanuman the monkey god; Ganesh the elephant god; and Shiva, one of the most important gods, considered to be the creator and destroyer of the universe. Avalokiteshvara, a major Bodhisattva or "enlightened one" of Buddhism, can be compared easily to Lokesvara, the Hindu manifestation of the god Shiva. Both religions have teachings (*dharma*), involve worship ceremonies (*puja*), and share the concept of the law of cause and effect (*karma*). Religious tolerance appears to be strong, and there is tacit acceptance and respect by both religious groups of each other's religion and beliefs. An interesting perspective can be garnered from a walking tour from Pashupatinath to Bodhnath. The former is considered to be the god Lord Shiva's temple and one of the most important Hindu temples on the subcontinent, and the latter is an important center for Nepal's Tibetan Buddhist population. The holy Bagmati River and cremation *ghats* (broad flights of steps leading down to the bank of a river, used especially for bathers), a statue of Shiva's bull Nandi, and other Hindu statues in Pashupatinath gradually give way to colorful Buddhist prayer flags and the great stupa (summit) of Bodhnath, where devout Buddhists circumambulate and spin their prayer wheels. Somewhere in between these two great religious centers, it is hard to tell where one religion ends and one begins. There are small Christian and Islamic populations in Nepal as well.

There are many festivals associated with Hinduism and its numerous gods and goddesses. One of the most important, which usually occurs in October, is Dasain. Dasain is the time of harvest, when the rice and millet are ripe and ready. New clothes are traditionally worn and houses painted in water, cow dung, and orange mud are a common sight during this festival. Dasain is celebrated for 10 days ("das" meaning 10 in English), and many Nepalese abroad return home to Nepal to celebrate with their families. Another festival is Tika Day, when shotguns are fired and a *tika* (a dab of rice, curd, and red coloring) is placed by an elder on a young person's forehead. This holiday places importance on lineage and the respect due old age. Diwali or Tihar celebrates the return of the god Rama to Ayodhya, where he was crowned king after a 14-year war. It occurs in October or sometimes November. Diwali is sometimes called the festival of lights with its preponderance of earthen and paper lanterns. During Diwali, brothers receive a secret, holy thread from their sisters to mark the festival. Holi celebrates Lord Krishna's defeat of the winter demon Holika and takes place in February or March. After observing a bonfire that symbolically represents the burning of the demon, people spray brightly colored paints on each other and dance joyously. On Naga Panchami, snakes are honored on the fifth day after the new moon in the month of Saaun (July–August). Pictures of snakes are hung over doorways, and food is placed out for the reptiles. Gaijatra (meaning "cow procession") is another important festival in which teens actively participate. Families who have lost a loved one during the past year take part in this ritualistic holiday. During Gaijatra, Yama Raj, the god of death, is believed to decide the level on which the deceased will be reincarnated. Hindus believe the reincarnation process is particularly difficult and fraught with obstacles, especially if bad deeds were done in the former life. So, they pray for a sacred cow to guide their loved ones by allowing the person to cling to the cow's tail. Cows, bedecked in flowers, and their owners parade through the streets. If a family cannot afford cows, young boys in the family will often dress as cows. Other young boys or men may dress as yogis or holy men, women, clowns, and devils to try and scare away the spirits. Many people wear comical hats with pictures of cows on them, and there is a carnival-like atmosphere. The parade files past important Hindu temples where rituals are performed and money and food are given to grieving families. Drums and cymbals, kitchen utensils, and metal pots and pans add music to the procession. The belief is that noise will drive away evil spirits or the ghosts of ancestors still haunting their former homes while they are between death and rebirth.

Aside from all of these nationwide holidays, there are many more that take place in specific regions of Nepal. Daily religious observances involving worship (*puja*) offerings to different gods in the form of rice, tea, and flowers left inside and outside temples are commonplace. *Mha Puja* is a special tradition unique to the Newars. It is devoted solely to physical and spiritual enrichment of every family member and involves a mandala and offerings of light, yogurt, and flowers. The Newars believe *Mha Puja* offers a definition of life and that by first understanding themselves and their role in the world, people can better understand others. All of the festivals, closely related to the Hindu religion, serve to remind the Hindus of the importance of their religion and the need to honor their gods and goddesses. Religion is part of everyday life in Nepal since there is a significant festival or holiday almost every day of the year. Still, the wealthier and those of a higher caste are able to spend more time in worship compared to those who must rise early and work the fields until late. Teenagers often willingly attend temple and take part in the festivals and prayer offerings since to not do so would leave them out of a lot of events. Even with the popularization of Western culture in the East, teenagers still feel a natural instinct to preserve the cultural traditions of Hinduism and Nepalese society.

Buddhism, even in its minority position, has its own set of festivals. Losar, or the Tibetan New Year, is celebrated in February. Many celebrate the New Year by circumambulating the great stupas of Bodhnath and Swayambhunath. The walk around the stupa is done three times or more and always in a clockwise fashion. Buddha's birthday, celebrated in April or May, is also a source of joy for Buddhists residing in Nepal. Again, peak celebrations usually take place at Buddhist sites such as the aforementioned stupas and the area of Patan. Gunla falls in August or September and is a time of atonement and fasting complete with ceremonies to mark this 15-day period. Finally, the Sherpa people of the Solo Khumbu region of Nepal, near Mount Everest, celebrate Mani Rimdu. This festival takes place at Thyangboche Monastery and is three days of masked dances and dramas performed by the monastery's monks. This holiday celebrates Buddhism's triumph over the older Bon religion that preceded Buddhism.

Rituals are as important as the holidays and often signify passing from one stage of development to the next. Certain tribes within Nepalese society have rituals and ceremonies specific to their lineage. The Magars have specific rites that mark the passage from a toddler to a young child. A girl receives a new shirt on the day she turns three years old. A three year old boy gets a haircut, but not in the way children in the West might. He is tied to a stool by a cow's rope. Facing the boy east, the uncle in charge of this ceremony knots a lock of the boy's hair at the crown and the rest of his hair is cut. The knot always stays and is never cut in the Hindu tradition of this tribe. The uncle then places the cut hair in the rafters of his own house, never to be removed. The boy receives a blessing of mustard oil, a new shirt, and two caps, and a tika, signifying hope and respect, is placed on his forehead. The boy is also given money to give to all unmarried girls in his family as well as a plate of curds to share with everyone in the family. During a Magar girl's first menstruation, there is a

15-day restrictive period when she is to stay away from all males in the family, avoid the kitchen, and not touch any food or water. Additionally, she is not allowed outside for five days from the onset of her menstruation. She is deemed unclean until day 15, when she washes in a spring and dons clean clothes. Other girls, specifically Brahmans in the Kathmandu Valley, experience *gupha*, when they must sit inside a room for more than a week and cannot see the sun or any male during this time. However, this latter practice has become less and less frequent today. At age seven, a Newari boy's head is shaved, except for a topknot of hair much like the Magar ritual. At this time also, a Newari girl is married symbolically to the soul of her future husband. The ceremony of the clipping of the hair (*kesanta*) is done for Hindu males of all castes except for the Sudra and "casteless" untouchables. All men of the three highest castes, those considered "twice born," also receive *janai*, meaning sacred thread, as boys. The receipt of this thread, which is actually three threads representing Brahma the creator, Vishnu the preserver, and Shiva the destroyer, gives the child a second birth and makes the guru or spiritual teacher the child's symbolic father. From then on, the child is allowed to study the Vedas— the main scriptures of Hinduism. The *janai* (a yellow cotton string) is looped over the left shoulder and tied under the right arm and is worn throughout the man's lifetime and changed once a year during the festival of Janai Purnima. Some Hindus also believe there are gods and goddesses who demand living animal sacrifices. The live sacrifice, they believe, helps appease the god or goddess's wrath and encourages prosperity and good health in the years to come. The entire family, children included, often visit the temple at Dakshinkali to participate in this ancient, animist-influenced ceremony. After the animal is killed, it is cooked and eaten by the family, and a portion is shared with the god or goddess whom the family hopes to influence positively.

Other customs nonspecific to particular regions and practiced throughout Nepal include removing shoes before entering a house and refraining from throwing garbage into fire since fire is viewed as being sacred. Buddhists are required to walk clockwise around Buddhist stupas and other religious sites or buildings. Sometimes leather articles of clothing and always shoes, leather or not, must be removed before entering a Buddhist or Hindu temple. Also traditional is the bestowment of a white blessing scarf called a *khata* upon a Buddhist lama or *rinpoche* (meaning "precious one") when meeting him. Sometimes the lama or rinpoche will return the blessing or give his own by placing the scarf around the visitor's neck. Other customs and cultural differences, not necessarily ritualistic, are the reluctance to show public displays of affection and the avoidance of using the feet to touch or point, as they are the lowest part of the body. It is also inappropriate to touch anyone's head, as this is the highest and most spiritual part of the body. Raising voices or shouting is considered unacceptable behavior, and it is taboo to inquire about a person's caste. Even handshakes are not commonplace, and saying thank you (*dhanyabad*) is not as common as in the West. Finally, *namaste* (meaning "I salute the god within you") is a common greeting. Often, people will clasp their hands together in a prayerlike gesture and greet strangers on the street with this form of "hello."

Closely related to customs and cultural traditions are the attitudes of adults toward children and the way in which children are treated by adults. Also important are the children's attitudes and behavior toward their parents. According to a 2000 estimate, youth (ages 15–24) make up 20.1 percent of Nepal's population (*Nepal: People and Society*, 2000). Especially among the Magars, children are much desired and loved. They are born into homes with little tension. In other Nepalese tribes and in a predominantly Hindu society such as Nepal's, boys are more desired than girls, and when a boy is born to a wealthy family, a feast is given for the family and neighbors. Even though daughters are highly regarded in Magar society, there is still the troubling female infanticide, sometimes voluntary, in which the baby girl is neglected and left to die in tribes other than the Magars. Especially in Magar society, gifts to unmarried girls have high ritual value and religious merit. Also common in Nepalese society is the tacit respect between parents and children or adults and young people. Berating or beating children in private or public is extremely rare. Often, a boy will place his forehead on his parents' feet when he returns home after a lengthy time away. A daughter will cover her head and bow from the waist to show her respect for her parents. There is also a strong bond between brothers and sisters in Nepalese society. A brother may visit his sister and touch his head to her feet in the same gesture, as he would offer his parents. A girl may rely on her brother more than her father. Sometimes a brother will even provide land and a home for one or all of his sisters.

CONCLUSION

Even though there are differences between the teenagers of Nepal and the teenagers of the West, both groups have similar hopes and dreams. Most teenagers in Nepal, even if they do not attend school, desire to better themselves through education, as do the teenagers of the West. Since most Western teenagers have more material possessions than the teens of Nepal, they possibly take more for granted and do not realize how lucky they are to have a free public education. Both teenagers in Nepal and teenagers in the West participate in their family's household activities, whether these are chores, meals, or special occasions. There are many teenagers in the West who are forced to work for their family's necessities; however, most Western teens do not experience the hard, physical labor a Nepali teen must often endure. Teenagers in both the West and Nepal love Western food, styles, and entertainment, and both groups seek to fit in with their peers. Often this means having "the latest" in terms of style and material accoutrements. Still, Nepalese teenagers appear to be more spiritually influenced and in touch with their religion and traditional beliefs, whereas teens in the West appear to be more influenced by materialism and its corresponding culture. Perhaps this is because material luxuries are not usually as accessible in Nepal: a bored teenager in the West can usually find something to watch on television, and a bored teenager in Nepal may not have a television or even a radio. There is a stigma attached to premarital sex in both areas of the world, and the topic concerns parents in Nepal as much as it does parents in the West. Parents in both areas of the world put restraints on their teenagers' interactions with members of the opposite sex. Finally, marriage or finding that special someone with whom to share life is important to teenagers in both countries. Many parents in the West have high expectations as to whom their children date. This can be likened to the importance of arranged marriages in Nepal. Both Nepalese teens and teens in the West must struggle on a daily basis to meet their parents' and families' expectations as well as society's.

NOTE

1. Pujan Malla, personal communication, 31 October 2000.

REFERENCES

Basnet-Thapa, S. (1999, July). Women and environment: A symbiotic relationship. *Nepal Digest.* http://library.wustl.edu/~listmgr/tnd/0311.html.

Children and women of Nepal—Chapter 3: Survival. (1999, June 7). http://www.panasia.org.sg/nepalnet/socio/children/ch3.htm#intro.

Evans, J. L. (1992, September). *Nepal from entry point to consolidation: An assessment of early childhood provision in Nepal with recommendations for Unicef's involvement.* Retrieved October 24, 2003, from http://www.ecdgroup.com/archive/nepalf.html.

Facts and figures on Nepal. (1999, June 7). http://www.panasia.org.sg/nepalnet/facts_fig.htm.

Games. (2001, January 17). http://cs.art.rmit.edu.au/projects/media/elephants/dr.../gamesdat.htm.

Nepal: People and society. (2000, June 28).http://www.nepalhomepage.com/general/people.html.

Parker, D. L. (with Engfer, L. & Conrow, R.). (1998). *Stolen dreams: Portraits of working children*. Minneapolis: Lerner Publications Company.

Savada, A. M. (Ed.). (1993). *Nepal and Bhutan: A country study*. 3rd ed. Washington, D.C.: U.S. Government Printing Office.

The world factbook 1999—Nepal. (2000, June 28). http://www.cia.gov/cia/publications/factbook/np.html.

RESOURCE GUIDE

Nonfiction

Anderson, M. (1977). *Festivals of Nepal*. New Delhi, India: Rupa & Co.

Ayer, V.A.K. (2001, January 18). *Investiture of sacred thread*. http://www.hinduism.co.za/sacramen.htm.

Bista, D. B. (1987) *People of Nepal*. 5th ed. Kathmandu, Nepal: Ratna Pustak Bhandar.

Children and women of Nepal—A situation analysis, 1996. (1999, June 7). http://www.panasia.org.sg/nepalnet/socio/children_main.htm.

Children in Nepal. (2000, October 26). www.cwinnepal.org/childrennepal.html.

Country assistance plans—Nepal: I. Country performance assessment. (2001, September 18). http://www.adb.org/Documents/CAPs/NEP/0101.asp.

Cultural life. (2001, January 11). http://www.geocities.com/SunsetStrip/Villa/7371/.../nepal_detail_profile_geo.htm.

Cultural practice of Kirant Rai. (1999, July 15). http://www.geocities.com/Tokyo/Fuji/5187/rai.htm.

Daniel, A. (2001, January 18). *The religious form of caste system in India*. http://adaniel.tripod.com/religious.htm.

Dhaubhadel, M. N. (1993, November). Mha Puja—A unique Newa tradition. *Nepal Digest*. Retrieved October 24, 2003, from http://library.wustl.edu/~listmgr/tnd/0010.html.

Dhital, R. (2000, October 26). *Child marriage in Nepal*. http://www.cwinnepal.org/childmarriage.html.

Dobrin, A. (1972). *To Kathmandu: A story of Nepal*. New York: Thomas Y. Crowell Company.

Education under Rana rule. (1991, September). http://memory.loc.gov/cgi-bin/query/r?frd/cstdy:@field(DOCID+np0058.

Everist, R., Finlay, H., & Wheeler, T. (1997). *Lonely planet travel survival kit: Nepal*. Oakland, CA: Lonely Planet Publications.

Freeman, D. (2001, January 12). *Kathmandu, Nepal-Gaijatra*. http://www.whatsgoingon.com/coolest/place/19990827/.

Games for South Asian federation '99. (2000, June 28). http://www.safgames99.org/games.html.

Hagen, T. (1961) *Nepal—the kingdom in the Himalaya*. Bern, Switzerland: Kummerly and Frey.

Hitchcock, J. T. (1980). *A mountain village in Nepal*. Dallas: Holt, Rinehart and Winston.

Kellner, D. (2000, September). Rana Tharu women. *National Geographic*, 82–99.

Krakauer, J. (1999). *Into thin air*. New York: Anchor Books.

Margolies, B. A. (1992). *Kanu of Kathmandu: A journey in Nepal*. New York: Four Winds Press.

Pradhan, G. (1999, June 7). *Challenging child labour*. http://www.cwin-nepal. org/childlabour.html.

Schubert, A. (1999, June 7). *Disabled children in Nepal* http://www.angelfire.com/ az/Anisha/DisKids.html.

Shah, V. (2001, June 7). *Festivals of Nepal: Janai Purnima and Raksha Bandhan*. http://www.nepalhomepage.com/society/festivals/janaipurnima.html.

U.S. Embassy, Kathmandu. (1999, July 15). *Nepal country commercial guide—FY 1998*. http://www.state.gov/www/about_state/business/com_guides/1997/ southeast_asia/nepal98.html.

Fiction

Mantinband, G. (1993) *Three clever mice: Folktales*. New York: Greenwillow.

Web Sites

Himal: http://www.south-asia.com/himal.html
Independent: http://www.south-asia.com/news-indep.html
Kathmandu Post: http://www.south-asia.com/news-ktmpost.html
http://www.catmando.com/wwwvlnp.htm
http://www.info-nepal.com/firstpage/
http://www.travel-nepal.com/ayo-gorkhali

More Information

Embassies/Nepali diplomatic offices:
2131 Leroy Place NW
Washington, DC 20008
Telephone: (202) 667-4550

Pen Pal/Chat

http://www.agirlsworld.com/geri/penpal/
http://www.epals.com
http://www.ks-connection.org/penpal/penpal.html
http://www.mightymedia.com/keypals

Chapter 9

NORTH KOREA

Myung Sook Hyun

INTRODUCTION

North Korea, or the Democratic People's Republic of Korea (DPRK), is one of the most heavily militarized countries, with over 1 million military personnel out of its population of 23 million. According to the International Institute for Strategic Studies in London, DPRK's military budget is around U.S.$5.4 billion a year, and it has the world's fifth-largest army. North Korea is one of the world's leading suppliers of ballistic missiles and missile technology, and has developed, produced, deployed, and exported a broad range of missiles. North Korea is selling complete missile systems, components, and missile technologies to Iran, Syria, Egypt, and Pakistan. North Korea's long-term commitment to a massive force-improvement program does not seem to change despite the country's economic hardships. According to estimates by South Korea's central bank, North Korea's economy, which remains under tight state control, grew by 6.2 percent from 1990 to 1999 after a sustained reduction since 1990. Yet the people of North Korea suffer from hunger.

Land and History

Korea is a peninsula off the coast of eastern China. Its total area is 85,288 square miles: 47,077 in the north (about the size of Mississippi), and 38,211 in the south. Eighty percent of the land area is moderately high mountains separated by deep, narrow valleys and small, cultivated plains. The remainder is lowland plains covering small, scattered areas.

Korea was colonized by Japan in 1910 and was under its rule until 1945, when World War II ended and Japan gave up all rights to Korea to the Allied Forces. Japan had used Korea as a factory to create many goods needed to sustain Japan during the war.

After World War II, Korea was separated into North and South Korea. It was decided that Korea would rule itself, with the United States helping South Korea and the Soviet Union doing the same thing for North Korea. North Korea was modernized and industrially centered, while South Korea was more farming and agriculturally oriented. When the United States decided that it had completed its mission and made sure that Japan did not try to regain the country, it pulled out all its forces. North Korea then attacked the capital city of South Korea, Seoul, on June 25, 1950.

The United Nations, finding out that North Koreans violated the treaty, asked the North Koreans to halt their attack. But the North Koreans were intent in their conquest. The United Nations rallied allies to send aid to the South Koreans. The conflict was settled for the time being in 1953 by reaching a cease-fire agreement between the North and South. The 38th parallel, the center point of Korea, serves as the military demarcation line dividing Korea into two countries, with North Korea occupying the northern part of the peninsula and South Korea the southern part of the peninsula. North and South Korea maintain a ceasefire, with the Neutral Nations Supervisory Commission for Armistice stationed at the 38th parallel.

People and Language

Koreans are an ethnically homogenous, Mongoloid people who have shared a common history, language, and culture since at least the seventh century, when the peninsula was first unified. The official language of both North and South is Korean. The Korean alphabet, called Hangul, was developed and introduced in 1446.

Climate

Located between 38 and 43 north latitude, North Korea has a continental climate with four distinct seasons. It has long, cold, dry winters as a result of northern and northwestern winds that blow from Siberia. The daily average high and low temperatures for P'yongyang, the capital, in winter are −3°C and −13°C. Summer tends to be short, hot, humid, and rainy because of the southern and southeastern monsoon winds that bring moist air from the Pacific Ocean. The daily average high and low temperatures for P'yongyang in summer are 29°C and 20°C. Approximately 60 percent of all precipitation occurs during the summer. Spring and autumn are transitional seasons marked by mild temperatures and variable winds that bring the most pleasant weather.

Government

The 1972 revised constitution states that the DPRK is a socialist state representing the interests of all the Korean people. The North Korean government consists of three branches: administrative, legislative, and judicial. However, they are not independent of each other.

Administrative Branch

The Korean Worker's Party (KWP), the ruling party, takes the reins of government through the Central People's Committee (CPC). Many KWP members hold key positions in the government. The constitution proclaims the establishment of the positions of president and vice-president and a supercabinet called the CPC. The president is the head of state and the head of government in his capacity as chairman of the CPC. The president of state is elected by the Supreme People's Assembly (parliament) for a five-year term, with no limitation on the president's reelection. The president chairs the CPC, the top administrative body supervising the activities of the Administration Council (cabinet).

Legislative Branch

In the DPRK, the Supreme People's Assembly (SPA) is the unicameral legislative body. By constitution, the SPA is the highest organ of state power. The SPA has the right to elect or recall the key members of the state, including the president, the vice-president, and the president of the Central Court. It also has the right to approve economic development plans and the state budget. Yet it has always acted on the instructions of the KWP. SPA has never initiated legislation independently, and it has never modified or rejected a bill or measure proposed by the government.

Judicial Branch

North Korea has a three-level judicial system patterned after the Soviet model. The system is set up on the basis of the socialist concept of law and justice. It consists of the Central Court, under which are the court of the province or of the municipality and the People's Court. Judges are elected by the organs of state power at their corresponding levels, those of the Central Court by the SPA's Standing Committee, and those of the lower courts by the provincial and county-level people's assemblies. The prosecutor-general of the Supreme Public Prosecutor's Office is appointed by the SPA, and he or she, in turn, appoints all other prosecutors.

Political Ideology

The cornerstone of party construction is *juch'e:* "the independent stance of rejecting dependence on others and using one's own powers, believing in one's own strength and displaying the revolutionary spirit of self-reliance" (Savada, 1994, p. 183). Juch'e was presented by Kim Il Sung while North Korea attempted to cope with the challenging task of applying Marxism-Leninism in the North Korean environment. It emphasized the need for self-reliance: the need to rely on domestic resources, heighten vigilance against possible external challenges, and strengthen domestic political solidarity. Sacrifice, austerity, unity, and patriotism are dominant themes in the party's efforts to instill in the people the importance of juch'e and collective discipline.

Relationship between the Government and the KWP

The KWP formulates national purpose, priorities, and administrative hierarchy. It is the central coordinator of administrative and economic activities at the national and local levels. The party members hold positions in government and economic agencies, oversee administrative operation, and enforce state discipline. Government organs are expected to implement the policies and directives of the party by mobilizing the masses.

Economy and Social Strife

The North Korean government stopped publishing economic statistics in the mid-1960s. However, according to the Bank of Korea's estimate, per capita gross national product (GNP) in DPRK was $957 in 1995. The economic statistics by outsiders indicated a significant decline in its GNP in 1998. The GNP decreased by 55 percent from 1990 to 1998. Foreign trade dropped by 70 percent in the same period as its socialist economy weakened. In 1998, the country's foreign debt, in default since the 1980s, amounted to almost $12 billion, equaling 96 percent of the country's GNP. The same year, United Nations officials indicated that 23 million North Koreans were eating only one meal a day, consisting of about 100 to 150 grams of food, far below what is minimally adequate. Today's worsened food situation is attributed to adverse weather conditions since

1995, years of economic mismanagement, and a decline in economic assistance from socialist trading partners, including Russia and the People's Republic of China.

Unemployment

In North Korea, the rate of unemployment is not indicative of the health of the nation's economy as it is in nonsocialist countries. Although the nation's economy is in bad shape, the unemployment rate of North Korea is zero. The Socialist Labor Law states that it is the law that all people must work and be paid equally for equal work. Everyone who is 16 and older must work. This has an effect on teens. In 1992, the workforce consisted of 15,238,000, or 62 percent of the population age 16 and older. Jobs are classified by four categories: worker, farmer, official, and industrial cooperative worker. As in other socialist countries, the means of production are owned by state and cooperative organizations.

TYPICAL DAY

As in many socialist countries, in North Korea the government rigidly controls the population. Individual rights are subordinate to the rights of the state and party. Young people are not an exception. When there are no party instructions for the day, the daily routines of school-age children are set. On weekdays, students get up at around 6 A.M. and help parents with cleaning the house and getting ready for school. They eat breakfast and leave home between 7:00 and 7:30, as schools begin at 8 A.M. The distance between school and home is no more than a one-hour walk. A few students in cities commute by bus, but most of the students in cities and in the countryside walk to school. In principle, students are expected to walk to school. They are to meet at a designated place near their neighborhood and form a group and march in rows to school. Individual arrival at school is not permitted and is subject to a punishment. The idea is part of the ongoing process of fostering collectivism. When students arrive at the entrance of the school, Hak Seng Kyu Chal Dae (members of student government body) inspect their dress and hair, which must both be tidy, and check to see that they are wearing a Kim Il Sung pin (a pin that has a picture of the late president on it).

In the morning, there are 50-minute classes and 10-minute breaks. After the second class, 30 minutes are designated for an in-between class exercise. Lunch is from 1 P.M. to 2 P.M. Students bring their own lunch boxes. Classes resume at 2 P.M. and continue until between 3 and 4 P.M.

Following the afternoon classes, students participate in various extra-curricular activities until 6 P.M.; these are planned and taught by the authority (Kim Il Sung Socialist Youth League). The extracurricular activities consist of political lectures and seminars; debating contests; poetry recitals; scientific forums; visits to museums, monuments, and historical sites of the Korean Revolution; physical training; and military education and training. Students come home after the extracurricular activities are over and at about the same time as their parents are coming home from work. Dinner at home is around 8 P.M. On evenings when there are party instructions, students need to go to a learning/study group of 7 to 10 members (Hak Seup Ban) to follow up on the instructions. Hak Seup Ban is a work group that is government organized. When there are no party instructions, they can play with their friends or do homework or help parents at home. The family generally retires at around 10 P.M.

FAMILY LIFE

As stated above, the workforce in North Korea is 62 percent of its population, or 15,238,000 who are age 16 and older. Women consist of 49 percent of the overall workforce due to the fact that 12 percent of men (6 percent of the population) are enlisted in military services and women are needed to fill in the labor market. In principle, North Korea strongly supports sexual equality. On July 39, 1946, authorities in North Korea passed the Sex Equality Law. The 1972 constitution asserts that "women hold equal social status and right with men." Also, the 1990 constitution stipulates that the state must create various conditions for the advancement of women in society. Women are paid as much as men for equal work. Nevertheless, the roles of the majority of women at home remain much the same. Women do most if not all of the housework, including preparing a morning and evening meal, in addition to working outside the home; much of the responsibility of child rearing is in the hands of nurseries (t'agaso) and the school system. A great number of women work in light industry or in secretarial or clerical jobs in office settings.

Both men and women work. Most people report to work by 7:30 A.M., in time for the 30-minute morning exercises. After following up on party instructions people receive the day's assignment. Lunch is eaten from 1 to 2 P.M., following the afternoon work period of 2 to 6 P.M. Political and job-related classes meet until 7 to 8 P.M. Most families eat at the same time when they can get together in the evening.

In North Korea, those who are 17 and older are regarded as adults. They are eligible to vote, drink, and drive a car. There are about 3,000 cars in

North Korea owned by individuals, with 2,000 cars registered in P'yongyang. A very few privileged teenagers own a car. Usually, these teens' parents are top KWP officials or sports heroes or movie stars.

The living standards of people in P'yongyang and those of other areas are markedly different. Only qualified people can reside in P'yongyang. The authorities periodically weed out those who are politically and physically unqualified for residence in the capital—those not following the Marxist-Leninist political order by not working positively for the collective or appearing to disobey the rules. These individuals are banished to the countryside.

TRADITIONAL AND NONTRADITIONAL FOOD DISHES

Rice, the staple food of the Korean diet, is eaten at most meals. Millet, wheat, barley, corn, and sorghum are also eaten. The vegetables Koreans eat include potatoes, Chinese cabbage, turnips, and onions. Garlic and red peppers are used as seasonings. Pickled vegetables (*kimchi*) is a favorite dish. Fish and other seafood are the usual sources of protein. Eggs have also become popular. Rice cake (*ttog*) is a popular confection.

Family members share household chores, but women do most if not all of the housework, including preparing a morning and evening meal, in addition to working outside the home. Before severe food shortages hit the country in the mid-1990s (or earlier in some outlying areas), biweekly food rations were distributed to each family, including grains and supplemental food items such as soy sauce, bean paste, and salt. Each household has a ration card indicating the amount and mixture of grain to which it is entitled. The distribution is supposed to be based on one's age and occupation, but in practice, political position and connections play an important role.

With a worsening food situation, the government's food ration system broke down. In 2000, the World Food Programme helped to feed 5.4 million people, more than one-fifth of the population (23 million). The country depends almost entirely on foreign supplies as the food shortages remain severe. The signs of malnutrition are evident throughout the country. Almost everyone is thin. Malnourished children exhibit stunted growth. Diseases such as tuberculosis are widespread. Digestive system problems result from eating indigestible foods. The energy level of workers is predictably low. And most tragically, the death rate from hunger and diseases has risen dramatically since 1995, with estimates ranging from several hundred thousand to 3 million malnutrition-related deaths.

SCHOOLING

There is not much difference between teens' typical days and teens' typical school days, as their primary responsibility is learning. They are to study during school and after school following the plan organized by the authority (both KWP and Sarochung). The constitution stipulates that the state must support a mandatory 11-year education system, comprising two years of kindergarten, four years of primary school, and five years of senior middle school. In 1959 "state-financed universal education" was introduced and was implemented fully in 1978 in all schools: Not only instruction and educational facilities but also textbooks, uniforms, and room and board are provided to students without charge.

Education is directly controlled by KWP and serves as a process of indoctrination in communist ideology. School curricula emphasize nurturing the students to become faithful communist revolutionaries who are loyal to the party and its leader. Kim Il Sung's 1977 Thesis on Socialist Education set forth four guiding principles: inculcation of party and working-class consciousness; establishment of juch'e in education; combination of education and revolutionary practice; and government responsibility for education. Kim stipulated that the educational curriculum should consist of political education in juch'e and communism, general education, physical education, and military education and training.

School classes are 60 percent instruction, 10 percent presentation, and 30 percent practical training/on-the-job training. Homework is given for 4 to 6 subjects. Teachers assume that students have done the homework, because it is unusual for students not to. Students are evaluated for their level of achievement both in academic performance and social education. There are two exams a year—one at the end of a term and another at the end of a school year—in August and December, respectively. Teachers of various subjects also give unscheduled exams throughout the year. Exams are both written and oral and the type is primarily essay. Students are expected to discuss the subjects given in the questions. Grades range from 1 to 5, 1 being the lowest and 5 being the highest. Students must have 3 points to pass and advance to the next level. When students have three or more subjects lower than 3 points, they are left back to repeat the grade. Those who fail to advance three times are expelled from the school.

Boys and girls receive essentially the same education in coeducational institutions through senior middle school. Upon completion of this 11-year compulsory program, at the age of 16 or 17, most girls in the cities go to work, either on farms or in local factories. Most males begin their eight years of obligatory military service after middle school. Approximately 30 percent of all privileged male students, usually the sons of high-ranking government and military officials, however, are exempted from military service to continue their education through college or, possibly, university. Among those who complete their military duty, about 5 percent enter a one-year preparatory course for college or university after the service. The army decides which of its "graduates" will go on to college and which will be placed in construction jobs. There seems to be a tendency among unprivileged teens to favor a school-to-army-to-college career progression (Hunter, 1999).

There are also schools for those who have special talent in the arts. They are schools of dance, music, the formative arts, industrial arts, physical education, science, and foreign languages. Dancing, music, and the formative arts are for children who are talented. They are admitted to the schools starting in upper kindergarten and continue through the 11-year compulsory education. Industrial arts and physical education are a part of the higher education system. Senior middle school graduates who have special talent are selected and receive a 4-year special education. Also, there are institutions that produce professional athletes. Choong Ang Academy of Physical Education, for example, focuses on preparing athletes who will represent the country in international games. Graduates of primary school are selected and trained through 8-year courses. There are 12 science academies in North Korea, and they offer a 6-year course. Primary school graduates with excellent academic records in science are

Music class, P'yongyang, North Korea. Photo © J. Sweeney/TRIP.

selected for the program. The curriculum focuses on science-related courses such as mathematics and physics. The schools are equipped with state-of-the-art laboratories and facilities, including a student dormitory, a swimming pool, and a gymnasium.

The academies of foreign languages select primary school graduates and provide 7-year courses. Admission decisions are made according to the following priorities: one-third for family background, one-third for academic score on the entrance examination, and one-third for cooperative spirit in group activities.

Teachers are the graduates of four-year teachers' training colleges and are prepared to teach various levels of students. Most parents have great confidence in compulsory education and believe that success at school is important in preparing their children to get ahead in the world.

There are no trade schools in North Korea, but there are institutions that provide job-related training as part of continuous education for workers. Also, there are three-year senior middle schools and four-year technical high schools for young people in the worker category.

The principal qualifications for admission to institutions of higher learning are political reliability and personal connections. Senior middle school graduates who wish to continue their study at a higher level must take the national qualifying examination for college and be designated as successful candidates in order to apply for the school they would like to attend.

Parents think education is important as skills and knowledge will help their children to get ahead in the workplace. The literacy rate of the nation reached 90 percent in 1996.

SOCIAL LIFE

Although socialism promises a society of equals, the North Korean government established a social classification based on family background reaching back for several generations. In terms of political and ideological criteria, family background is extremely relevant to one's social status and standard of living. In a report delivered to the Fifth Korean Workers' Party Congress in 1970, Kim Il Sung, the late general secretary of KWP and president of the state, outlined a classification system consisting of three loyalty groups and 51 subgroups. The population was divided into a core class, the basic masses, and the "impure class." The core class, which includes those with revolution... lineage, makes up approximately 20 to 25 percent of the population. The basic masses—primarily workers and peasants—account for around 50 percent. The impure class consists of descendants of pro-Japanese collaborators, landowners, or those with relatives who have defected to South Korea.

Sons and daughters of revolutionaries and those who died in the Korean War are favored for educational opportunities and advancement, while the children and descendants of "exploiting-class" parents—those who collaborated with the Japanese during the colonial era, opposed agricultural collectivization in the 1950s, or were associated with those who had fled to South Korea—are discriminated against. Persons with unfavorable political backgrounds are often denied admission to institutions of higher education, despite their intellectual qualifications. Basically, people associate with those of their own class, with rare exception. The same is true with young people. Most teenagers brought up under Confucian ideas follow their parents' wishes.

The primary and secondary education in this country is coeducational. Basically, teens meet other teens in the same school or in the neighborhood. However, boys and girls are discouraged from mingling in social settings outside of school. Unlike American schools, North Korean schools do not have socials. Students are expected to dress and behave like students. Schools have very specific guidelines about how to behave at school and outside of school. Students who do not conform to the rules and regulations of the school are subject to punishment, depending on the nature and degree of the violation. Students are to wear school uniforms all times. College boys wear white dress shirts and black pants, while college girls wear typical Korean costumes with white tops and black skirts. In 1989, when the Thirteenth World Festival of Youth and Students was held in P'yongyang, Western hairstyles and clothes were introduced to North Korea and became popular. In the early 1990s, long hair, jeans, and T-shirts with foreign languages on them were in vogue among young people. However, Kim Jong Il, general secretary of the KWP, labeled these symbols of capitalism and banned the trend in 1993. Those who wore jeans were caught and sent to jail for 10 days.

In the past, marriages were arranged by parents or by go-betweens called *chungmae*. Today, however, young people, particularly those living in cities, more often choose their own mates. Nevertheless, children still seek their parents' permission before getting married. The legal age for males to marry is 18; for females, it is 17, but marrying in one's late twenties or early thirties is common because of work and military service obligations. Men usually marry at about age 30; women, at about 26. City dwellers tend to marry at a somewhat later age. Kim Jong Il once stated that it is appropriate for women to get married at 26. The taking of second wives is prohibited.

Traditional clothing called *hanbok*, made of cotton or synthetic materials, is worn only by some people in the rural areas and by others on special occasions. Nearly all men in the cities and most of the farmers have adopted Western-style clothing: shirts, trousers, suits, and shoes.

The Confucian ethical system has greatly influenced Korean culture. Young people are discouraged from engaging in premarital sex. Girls in particular are taught to be virgins until they get married. However, there have been instances of teenage pregnancy. When this happens, most parents force their daughter to abort the child.

RECREATION

School sports teams are organized in schools as part of military drills and to build group consciousness and physical fitness. Great emphasis is given to team games such as soccer, basketball, volleyball, and mass gymnastic exercises. All students, both boys and girls, are expected to participate in physical training focusing on basic training, including racing, long jump, pole vault, and javelin.

Soccer is the most popular game among people of all ages. Young people like to play the game because it does not require state-of-the-art facilities or equipment. They can play anywhere in the field without technical knowledge or skills. Aside from authority-organized physical exercise, most young people like to take a stroll to relieve the stress from school.

The North Korean government has been promoting professional sports since the 1980s to improve the country's international reputation. A professional athlete like Choi Chul Soo who won an Olympic gold medal in Barcelona is praised as a national sports hero and is an object of envy among young people. There are a number of sports heroes who have won international competitions. They include Lee Myung Hoon, who once was approached by the National Basketball Association to play on a major U.S. team.

ENTERTAINMENT

The population of North Korea is rigidly controlled. Individual rights are subordinate to the rights of the state and the party. Almost all activities, including entertainment, are planned and organized by the authorities (KWP and Sarochung). Literature and music are used for the political education of young people. Wednesday is designated as a day for culture. Teenagers go to concerts, movies, or plays as the authorities see fit for educational purposes. However, they like to spend their own leisure time by doing things they like. As they cannot afford expensive entertainment, they do simple things for fun. They like to watch TV, listen to music, go to movies, play electronic or computer games, go for a walk, and read books of their choice. In North Korea, there are households that cannot afford to have a TV, and students whose family does not own a TV often flock to their friends' houses to watch movies or shows on weekends or holidays. Movies are well attended. One of the most influential films, *An Chung-gun Shoots Ito Hirobumi*, tells of the assassin who killed the Japanese resident-general in Korea in 1909. An is depicted as a courageous patriot whose efforts to liberate Korea were frustrated because the masses had not been united under "an outstanding leader who enunciates a correct guiding thought and scientific strategy and tactics." In addition, teenagers like to play electronic games and computer games. Since the first electronic game room was introduced in Man'gyongdae students' and schoolchildren's halls and palaces in 1991, the number of electronic game rooms has multiplied.

A very few privileged teens in cities own personal computers and like to play computer games on them. The North Korean government encourages production of computer games and distributes them among students. Unlike those in the United States, most of these computer games are educational games, providing instruction in sciences, languages, or other subjects.

RELIGIOUS PRACTICES AND CULTURAL CEREMONIES

Article 54 of the 1972 constitution states that "citizens have religious liberty and the freedom to oppose religions" (also translated as "the freedom of anti-religious propaganda"). Yet the North Korean government discourages religion, and religious activities have been virtually nonexistent since 1960. Religious services are performed after permission for them is granted and in accordance with the instructions given by the party.

Religious organizations such as the Korean Buddhists' Federation, the Christian Federation, and the Chondogyo Youth Party are state sponsored. They exist not to provide religious activities for believers but to show the world that North Koreans have religious freedom. Most North Koreans do not belong to an organized religion. All traditional religion in North Korea is regarded as an expression of "feudal mentality," an obsolete force opposing political revolution, social liberation, economic development, and independence.

By the end of World War II, some 50,000 Catholics, 300,000 Protestants, and millions of Buddhists and Chondoists, members of the ethnic

Korean religion, were active in North Korea. However, all the activities of these religions ended in the 1960s, when the government policy turned against all religions. All foreign missionaries were expelled from the country while many Buddhist temples and Christian churches were taken possession by the government and converted to other uses. Some important Buddhist temples and shrines still exist, mostly in rural or mountainous areas; most of them function only as tourist sites or museums. Showcase Christian churches have also been exhibited to foreign visitors in the past in an effort to claim that North Koreans enjoy religious freedom, but they are all state-sponsored religious organizations and are just showcases.

Religion is discouraged by the North Korean government, and young people are not permitted to participate in religious ceremonies. North Korean students do not understand what religion is. On the other hand, the party encourages young people to participate in traditional Korean cultural ceremonies, including memorial services for their ancestors.

CONCLUSION

In socialist North Korea, teenagers are considered a part of a system and an organization and have to perform their part as is instructed by the government. They are expected to participate in political and social activities while providing labor during and after school hours. The purpose of education is to produce faithful communist revolutionaries who are loyal to the party and its leader. The authority of North Korea states that "school education is not enough to turn the rising generation into men of knowledge, virtue, and physical fitness. After school, our children have many spare hours. So it's important to efficiently organize their after school education." Daily routines of students are planned and organized in detail by the government. Education is directly controlled by the ruling KWP. Students are at school from 7:30 A.M. to 6:00 P.M. attending classes and extracurricular activities.

Students must comply with the authorities' rules and regulations. Otherwise, their family may be punished. When students cause trouble at school, a party authority at the child's school reports the incident to his or her counterpart at the child's parents' work unit and the supervisor of the parents. Then the parents are criticized for failing to carry out the revolution at home. Moreover, in cases when a student is absent once without notice or leaves school early three times a month, one day's food ration of the student is taken away as a penalty. Students are penalized by being deprived of their food.

REFERENCES

Hunter, H. (1999). *Kim Il-Song's North Korea*. Westport, CT: Praeger Publishers.
Savada, A.M. (Ed.). (1994). *North Korea: A country study*. 4th ed. Washington, DC: Federal Research Division.

RESOURCE GUIDE

Nonfiction

Kang, S.J. (1997). A proposed North and South Korean education system consolidation plan for a reunified Korean peninsula. *Dissertation Abstracts International, 58*, no. 09A. (University Microfilms No. 3381).
Oh, K.D., & Hassig, R.C. (2000). *North Korea: Through the looking glass*. Washington, DC: Brookings Institution.
Wehrfritz, G., & Takayama, H. (2001, March 5). Riding the Seoul train. *Newsweek, 20–27*.

Web Sites

http://cns.miis.edu/pubs/dprkrprt/97janfeb.htm
http://newfirstsearch.altip.oclc.org/WebZ/FTFETCH?sessionid=:entityemailftfrom
=SIRS_F
http://www.asianinfo.org/asianinfo/north%20korea/north_korea.htm
http://www.apcc.com.tw/NorthKorea.html
http://www.asd.k12.ak.us/schools/romig/asia/History/Unification%20of%20Kore
a/index2.html
http://www.asianinfo.org/asianinfo/north%20korea/pro-education.htm
http://www.guardian.co.uk/korea/article/0,2763,489062,00.html
http://www.house.gov/international_relations/nkag/report.htm
http://www.lonelyplanet.lycos.com/north_east_asia/north_korea/culture.html
http://www.stat.ualberta.ca/people/schmu/kitc.html
http://www.state.gov/www/background_notes/north_korea_0696_bgn.html
http://www.tang-soo-do.org.uk/korea.html
http://www1.worldbank.org/education/tertiary/news_archive/1123b69.html

More Information

The United States does not maintain any diplomatic, consular, or trade relations with North Korea. Moreover, it includes North Korea on the list of states supporting international terrorism since January 1988, after North Korean agents bombed a South Korean airliner—KAL flight 858—on November 29, 1987, causing the death of 115 people.

U.S. law prohibits almost all financial and commercial transactions with North Korea by persons or firms subject to U.S. jurisdiction.

The U.S. Department of State's Consular Information Program provides Travel Warnings and Consular Information Sheets to those who travel to North Korea, as the State Department recommends that Americans avoid travel to this country. However, there are no U.S. government restrictions on travel by private U.S. citizens to North Korea.

Travel bureau: there is one state travel company, called Korea International Travel Company (KITC), and its branch offices are in Beijing and Dandong in China. For those who wish to travel in this country, a tourist card is issued instead of a visa in the Beijing office or in the DPRK embassy or consulate.

Pen Pal/Chat

North Koreans live in the most closed society on Earth. The government controls information flow. The masses receive no foreign newspapers, radio, or television broadcasts, and they meet few foreign visitors. In addition, overlapping security organizations monitor North Korean people, including neighborhood surveillance. A person entitled chief is appointed by the ward people's committee to keep track of everything that occurs in the neighborhood of 15 to 20 families and report unusual, suspicious, illegal, or antiregime behavior to the authority. The only way to find a pen pal in North Korea is probably to arrange it through the government.

Chapter 10

PHILIPPINES

Deborah Hasson

INTRODUCTION

The Republic of the Philippines is an archipelago made up of more than 7,100 islands in the Pacific Ocean between mainland Asia and Australia. A part of the Malay Archipelago that extends 1,150 miles north to south from Borneo to Taiwan and 700 miles east to west, the country is approximately 750 miles east of Vietnam. The islands, approximately 4,000 of which have been named and 1,000 inhabited, comprise a land area of almost 116,000 square miles, close to the size of Arizona. The three major island groups are Luzon in the north and west, consisting of Luzon, Mindoro, and Palawan; Visayas in the center, made up of Bohol, Cebu, Leyte, Masbate, Negros, Panay, and Samar; and Mindanao in the south. The majority of the population of 81.1 million people—called Filipinos—live on the 11 islands with the largest land mass.

Because of their volcanic origins, the Philippine islands have high mountains, active and dormant volcanoes, and many valleys, plateaus, and rivers. The Philippines has a tropical climate, with an average temperature of 80°F to 82°F and an annual rainfall of 160 to 200 inches. Monsoons mark the beginning of the wet and dry seasons. The rainy season lasts from May or June to November, while the dry season, with cool and hot spells, occurs from December to April. Due to its geographic location, the country is prone to many different types of natural disasters. From June to October is the typhoon season. Since the archipelago is situated in one of the most active typhoon areas in the Pacific, each season can bring up to 20 typhoons. Winds from the most dangerous typhoons during the last 30 years were clocked at up to 172 miles per hour, killed many thousands of people, and destroyed homes, crops, and much of the infra-structure of the populated areas. Numerous earthquakes are also part of the Philippines experience, with some of the strongest ones measuring up to 7.9 on the Richter scale. The islands even have tidal waves upon occasion, and flooding is common.

The Philippines has an extraordinary animal and plant life due to the volume of rain it receives. Important crops include rice, corn, coconuts, and sugar. The country is one of the world's largest exporters of the latter two as well as timber and veneer products. A variety of different minerals are found on the islands of the Philippines, including iron ore, copper, and zinc, and the country is one of the largest producers of gold in the world. The main industrial export items include electronics, garments and textiles, and metal products. Despite the richness of these resources, however, the country experienced an unemployment rate of 13.3 percent as of April 2001, down from 13.9 percent the previous year, and the inflation rate jumped from 3.9 percent in June 2000 to 6.7 percent in June 2001. It is important to note that the labor force in the Philippines numbers approximately 26 million individuals between the ages of 15 and 64.

People and Languages

As of July 2001, the population of the Republic of the Philippines was 81.1 million, with approximately half a million more males than females. The life expectancy for Filipino women is 71.9 years, while for men it is 66.6 years. The infant mortality rate in 1998 was 35 percent, which improved from 49 percent in 1995, and presently, the projected population growth rate is estimated at 1.99 percent. Filipinos are a relatively young people, with 50 percent of the population below the age of 22, and they are highly educated, reflecting a literacy rate of 93.9 percent. However, there exists a large disparity between rich and poor. In 1997, approximately 32 percent of the total number of families in the Philippines lived in poverty, and the middle class currently composes only about 25 percent of the population.

Ethnically, Filipinos have Malay roots to which were added Chinese, Arabic/Muslim, Spanish, and American blood. This is a reflection of a rich and varied history of colonialism and occupation throughout the last few centuries. With the indigenous populations and the infusion of colonial blood, there are more than 75 ethnic and linguistic groups on the islands. These are also influenced by geographic location, elevation, regional characteristics, and social boundaries. For example, the culture of mountain inhabitants is different from that of people who live on the

coast, even on the same island. The Muslims, also called Moros, of Mindanao and the Sulu islands are the largest cultural minority in the Philippines, and the Visayans, who live in the central portion of the country, are
another important group. Other ethnic groups include the Tagalogs from
central Luzon, the Negritos of the mountain jungles, the Tagbanua of
Palawan, the Mangyan hut dwellers of Mindoro, and mountain people
such as the Ifuago, the Benguet, and the Bontoc. In 1971, a Stone Age
tribe called the Tasaday was discovered; some anthropologists consider it
to be a hoax, but others have studied the tribe's habits to understand how
Stone Age people lived on a daily basis.

The Republic of the Philippines is the only country in that region of the
world that is considered to be Christian. The majority of Filipinos (84%)
are Roman Catholic, and about 10 percent follow different denomina-
tions of Protestantism, including Presbyterians and Methodists. Catholicism was brought to the islands by the Spaniards in the sixteenth century,
and Protestantism was introduced by the Americans at the end of the
nineteenth century. Included in these are also members of the Philippine
Independent Church, the Aglipayans, and of the Iglesia Ni Kristo
(Church of Christ), which were founded in the early twentieth century.
Additionally, there is a significant Muslim population (4%), mainly in the
south, in Mindanao. Islam in the Philippines dates back to the fourteenth
century, when Arab traders began commercial relations with the island
natives. A minimal number of Filipinos observe Buddhism. It should be
noted that many Filipinos follow local folk customs and beliefs in addition
to their religious affiliations. For example, trust in faith healing and con-
sultation with herb doctors are not believed to conflict with more traditional religious practices. It is also not unusual for Filipinos to worship and
pray to their ancestors.

The national language of the Philippines is Filipino, formerly known as
Pilipino. Not everyone in the country speaks this language since it was
only decided in the 1930s that a national language was necessary to unite
the Filipino people. Historically, there were large numbers of ethnic
groups who spoke over one hundred different languages throughout the
islands of the Philippines. The eight major languages were Ilocano, Pan-
gasinan, Pampango, Tagalog, Bicol, Cebuano, Hiligaynon, and Waray-
Samarnon. While these languages belong to the same Malay-Polynesian
language group, they are mutually incomprehensible. Even through the
1980s, one of these eight languages was the native language for approximately 90 percent of the population.

Spanish and English were official languages of the Philippines due
to the history of Spanish colonialism (see next section) and American

political and economic hegemony. With the 1935 constitution, it was decided that the country needed a national language based on one of the indigenous languages. A committee of linguists representing each of the major language groups met and recommended that the national language be based on Tagalog. The Pilipino language was introduced as a subject of study in the 1940s and later became a medium of instruction in schools and of communication in the mass media and official channels. In 1973, it was recommended that the national language be renamed Filipino and be based on more of the indigenous languages. The 1987 constitution makes this official, and Filipino is now used as one of the languages of instruction in schools, as well as in government and the media. English is still considered to be an official language, and it is also used as a medium of instruction in schools and in business dealings. A combination of Filipino and English words and phrases called Taglish is also widely used in informal settings. Due to the widespread use of both Filipino and English, language barriers among the different ethnic groups in the Philippines are starting to decline.

Historical Overview

The islands of the Philippines have been inhabited for many thousands of years. The ancestors of present-day Filipinos were the aboriginal Negritos, who were present some 25,000 to 30,000 years ago. They were followed by the Indonesians and later, the Malays from Eastern India, around 200 B.C.E. The Malays established the lowland peasant culture that is reflected in folk literature and song. There was an early history of trade with the Chinese that predated trade with any other group, and this trade would resume throughout the history of the developing nation as some Chinese settled in the area and became important and powerful members of Philippine society. Islam was brought to the Sulu islands and Mindanao between the fourteenth and fifteenth centuries by missionaries from Borneo, so there was an Arabic influence as well. This community continues to flourish in the nation today.

The early people of the Philippine lowlands lived in kinship groups called *barangay*, which were led by a *datu*, or a chieftain. There were three classes of people: the nobility, the freeholders, and the servants or slaves. The religion they followed was animism, which included a mixture of monotheistic and polytheistic beliefs. There were, for example, rituals for evil spirits. It was a fairly fluid society, and while the barangays formed confederations after the introduction of Islam, they never had any form of centralized government.

Perhaps the most influential event in the early history of the Philippines was the arrival of Ferdinand Magellan on the island of Cebu in 1521 under the Spanish flag. In the sixteenth century, European countries were in an expansionist mode as they set out to find new worlds and conquer new territories. The routes to the Far East were charted in an attempt to claim spices and riches for each country's crown. For Spain's King Philip II, for whom the republic is named, there was the additional element of converting native pagans and the people they called Indians to Christianity in the form of Roman Catholicism. The first permanent Spanish settlement in Cebu was established by Miguel Lopez Legazpi in 1565, and the city of Manila, now the capital of the Philippines, was founded in 1571.

The Spanish dominated the islands until the nineteenth century. Trade was set up between the Philippines and Mexico, with exchanges of Chinese silk for silver from the New World. By the end of the sixteenth century, the Spanish controlled all of the Philippines except for southern Mindanao and the Sulu islands, which were populated by Muslims who did not convert to Catholicism. The focus of missionary work in the provinces was to bring Christianity and the Spanish culture to the indigenous tribes on different parts of the islands.

By the seventeenth and eighteenth centuries, the Roman Catholic Church had acquired much political power, land, and wealth, and it had established a network of schools and hospitals. Public education through the church, with a controlled curriculum in Spanish, became available in 1863. By the 1880s, the wealthy began to send their sons to Europe to study. This new class of educated Filipinos formed a movement toward Philippine nationalism and reform that would alter the course of the country's history.

The Philippine revolution against Spanish domination began in 1896. When Philippine independence was declared on June 12, 1898, it was the first time an Asian country had been able to rid itself of European colonialism. The first president of the Philippines was Emilio Aguinaldo. However, while the independent movements were taking place, the country was affected by the Spanish-American War of 1898 when American troops landed in Manila to overpower the Spanish naval forces. The United States supported the Philippine independence movement, but when Spain was finally ousted from the islands, the Americans did not allow the Filipinos to claim sovereignty over their country. As part of the Treaty of Paris between the United States and Spain, which took place on December 10, 1898, the Philippine archipelago was ceded to the United States, and American military rule was established.

The second part of the Philippine revolution began in 1899 with war declared against the Americans. The Filipinos did not recognize American rule, and the Americans overlooked Filipino claims of independence. The hostilities lasted until President Aguinaldo was captured in 1901 and swore allegiance to the United States. The Americans established a civil government throughout the country by 1902. It was not until the 1930s that the U.S. government granted, through legislation in Congress, that Filipinos would have independence by 1946 after 10 years of commonwealth status supervised by the Americans. The Philippine Constitution of 1935 was approved by President Franklin D. Roosevelt, and Manuel Quezon became president of the commonwealth.

In 1941, the Japanese bombed Pearl Harbor and invaded the Philippines. Japanese control over the Philippines lasted until 1944. The civil government was restored by the United States, and finally, in 1946, the Republic of the Philippines attained its full independence, with Manuel Roxas as its first president. A free trade agreement was established with the United States to help the country begin the process of recovery. The Americans were also given a 99-year lease on military and naval bases.

Rebel forces, political opposition, and civil unrest, along with corruption and crime, characterized the first two decades of the independent Philippine republic as it tried to establish itself. The economy had been completely destroyed, and there was much internal strife. The Hukbalahap (Huk) Rebellion that began in 1946 as tenant farmers protested the social injustice that they had suffered was finally suppressed in the early 1950s, but other insurgent groups surfaced. The election of Ramon Magsaysay as president in 1953 gave hope to a people waiting for economic and social reform, but his early death in 1957 led to the continuation of social unrest and instability.

Ferdinand Marcos became president of the Philippines in 1965 and was reelected in 1969, the first Philippine president to serve more than one term. Under the guise of stopping violent student demonstrations, Marcos declared martial law in 1972 and immediately had key enemies and opposition leaders arrested. A new constitution in 1973 helped to consolidate his power, both politically and economically, throughout the 1970s. Muslim rebel groups in the south and communist insurgents around the country increased their activities in protest of Marcos and his corrupt government.

Martial law ended officially in 1981, but Marcos was elected to another six-year term. When opposition leader Benigno Aquino returned to the Philippines from exile in the United States and was assassinated upon his arrival, Filipinos protested even more and increased their opposition to the Marcos regime. Aquino's widow, Corazon, ran against Marcos in the 1986 elections. While he was declared the winner, it was evident that the elections had been manipulated, and Corazon Aquino assumed the presidency.

A new constitution was ratified in 1987 to restore democratic institutions, such as the bicameral legislature that existed prior to 1973 and the separation of power among the branches of government. The 1987 constitution also guaranteed freedom of speech, religion, assembly, and press, and equality under the law. Under Aquino's presidency, however, needed economic and social reforms did not materialize right away. It was not until the early 1990s, under her successor, Fidel Ramos, that the economy began to improve somewhat. The economy has been affected by global market events of the past few years, much like the economies of other countries in the region. The current president, Gloria Arroyo, began her term in January 2001. She replaced Joseph Estrada, a former actor who was charged with corruption and impeached in 2000.

Government

Administratively, the Republic of the Philippines is divided into provinces, cities, municipalities, and rural villages. Any Filipino who is at least 18 years old may vote in Philippine elections at any level. The country is a constitutional democracy, and like the United States, its government is made up of three branches: executive, legislative, and judicial. The executive branch has the president as the head of state. Presidents and vice-presidents are elected by popular vote for six-year terms. A president may not be reelected, although a vice-president may serve for two successive terms. The legislative branch of government is the Philippine Congress. It has a House of Representatives, whose 254 members are elected from particular provinces and districts, and a Senate, whose 24 members are elected from the nation at large. The president may appoint up to 50 representatives based on lists provided by the political parties. This is done to ensure appropriate representation of women, minorities, and economic and labor groups. Representatives may serve up to a maximum of three three-year terms, while senators have a limit of two six-year terms. The judicial branch is made up of a chief justice and 14 associate justices who are appointed to the Supreme Court by the president.

TYPICAL DAY

A typical day in the life of Filipino teenagers depends on where they live. The most obvious distinction would be the difference between rural and urban youth, but socioeconomic class plays a large role, as does geographic location. Common to all Filipino children and young adults, though, is the closeness of family ties and weekly religious observance, whether the families are Christian or Muslim.

There are no particular morning rituals. Most teens get up in the morning, eat breakfast, and go to school or work. They wear clothing that is similar to what American teenagers wear. Boys wear jeans and T-shirts, while girls wear skirts and tops. Traditional clothing is used for only special occasions or holidays. The majority of teens use some form of public transportation to get to high school or college, either buses or jeepneys, reconverted World War II jeeps that carry up to 17 people and are very colorful, with elaborate decorations and loud, blaring music. There are no afternoon breaks, although the *merienda*, or snack, is an important meal in the afternoon.

Teenagers in urban areas typically go to school and do not work, except in summer. However, younger city children who are at or below the poverty level help to support their families by working on the streets selling candy, washing cars, carrying groceries or shopping bags, and doing other assorted small jobs. Teenagers in very poor families may not go to school at all and may work at different types of jobs to help support their family. Children in rural areas may not finish primary schooling because they have to help their parents on farms, whether it is helping with crops or raising animals and livestock. In some villages, teenagers work from sunrise to sunset transporting children to school on motorized tricycles that carry up to 12 people. Others work on pedicabs, which are bicycles with carriages attached to them. Some teenage girls even work as midwives. Teens who do continue their schooling after the elementary level may attend a vocational or trade school, and some even go on to college.

After school or work, teens socialize with their friends. In urban areas, there are fast food restaurants, malls, movies, sporting events, museums, and other amenities found in Western countries. Rural teens help their families in the rice fields and play basketball with their friends or catch spiders for spider fights after dinner. All teens have access to radios and televisions, even Nintendo. Even if a family cannot afford a computer, computers are usually available at schools or community centers. Schools also have playgrounds and fields for sports. Basketball is a national passion for Filipinos, and much time is spent playing and watching it. Thus, as for U.S. teenagers, there is time for work and time for play for Philippine teenagers.

FAMILY LIFE

The family is the most important social unit in the Philippines. The family unit includes parents, children, and grandparents who are very close, and there are strong ties to other relatives and godparents, who are named at different religious ceremonies throughout the life of a child. Men are regarded as the head of the household, responsible for the welfare of the family and decision making. While it is not uncommon for educated women to work outside of the home, caring for the family and the house is still considered to be their primary role. They are the emotional center of the family and in some circumstances, women may have a dual role because they also have to act as the breadwinner. It is also not unusual to have three generations living together in one house. Respect for elders is paramount, as are good manners in all social situations. Children are also taught to respect their teachers as if they were parents.

There are specific gender roles played by men and women in the Philippine society. Fathers are the primary breadwinners in Philippine homes. Women who work outside of the home engage in a variety of jobs and have entered different professions on an equal basis with their male counterparts, but they are still responsible for doing most household chores or for supervising a servant who performs them. Women do most of the cooking, cleaning, laundry, and general home organization and maintenance. Philippine society is male dominated in other ways. For example, a Filipina cannot sign a contract without her husband's consent. Adultery on the part of a woman is punished more severely than for men. Also, a separated wife may have a different tax exemption than her husband. Separated couples face great difficulties because there is no divorce in the Philippines. While couples may separate legally, they may not remarry legally.

Child rearing is a communal activity in the Philippines, especially in the more rural areas. Children are the center of a Filipino family and are never alone. There are always siblings or cousins and other extended family members for company. Independence is not a primary value in Philippine homes because individuals are part of a family and community. Filipino boys are taught from a very early age that the family will provide for their basic needs and that they have an obligation to respect older family members and friends, assist in caring for their younger siblings, do chores around the house, and behave in an honorable fashion that will not bring shame to the family. Children are not really thought of as adults until they are married and have their own children. Once grown, however, adults retain an obligation to their parents and families in addition to caring for their own spouses and children.

Increasingly in the larger cities, traditional customs regarding gender roles and family customs are thought to be changing. This is due, in large part, to urbanization and Western influences, particularly from the United

States. The Philippines has always been more Westernized than many Southeast Asian countries because of the North American occupation and economic power. Nevertheless, even with modernization, Filipino values regarding the family and the roles within it appear to have remained intact. Meals, for example, are shared by the whole family, and while there is no separation between men and women while eating, the meals are prepared by the women. Filipinos generally eat five times a day: breakfast, morning snack, lunch, merienda, and dinner. This tends to bring families together, at least for the main meals.

The extent to which women work outside of the home may be determined by the family's economic status and circumstances. As noted previously, one-third of Filipinos live in poverty. There are large disparities between the rich and the poor in the Philippines. There is also a sharp distinction between rural and urban populations. For example, many Filipino families cannot afford cars or trucks, so it would be very unusual for a teenager to own a car, unless the family was extremely wealthy. In very affluent families, there are usually maids that do much of the household work.

TRADITIONAL AND NONTRADITIONAL FOOD DISHES

Food in the Philippines is as varied as its people. In addition to its Malaysian origins, Filipino cooking has influences from Chinese, Spanish, Mexican, and American cuisine. Because of the Philippine characteristics of hospitality and generosity, it is customary to share anything that is opened or eaten in front of another person. If someone happens to make a visit during a meal, it is considered rude not to invite him or her to partake of the meal, although the guest is not actually expected to accept the invitation.

For the majority of the population, rice is a staple food, accompanied by fish and seafood as the main sources of protein. It is estimated that Filipinos consume 70 pounds of seafood per person on an annual basis and that 80 percent of all fish caught on the islands is eaten fresh. For up to one-fifth of the population, corn is a staple, particularly on the Visayan islands and in northern Mindanao, where it is largely produced. For people who cannot afford rice or corn, root crops such as yams, sweet potatoes, cassava, and taro are staples.

Philippine food is not as spicy as the foods found in other countries in that region. In cities, most food is purchased in grocery stores, much like in the United States. In rural areas, seafood is readily available, and most families have vegetable plots next to their homes. Throughout the coun-

try, women are primarily involved in food preparation. Children sometimes help with the cooking; indeed, the first thing Filipino children learn
how to cook is rice. Modern conveniences like microwave ovens and
other appliances are helpful, but many women rely on traditional utensils
for cooking. In Manila and other large cities, fast food is readily available
through chains like McDonalds, Burger King, and Pizza Hut, and there are
numerous fine restaurants offering foods from all ethnic groups. There are
also roadside restaurants for laborers and jeepney drivers. Teenagers enjoy
fast food, which sometimes may lead to conflict with their parents.

A typical Filipino meal might consist of boiled rice or rice noodles;
some type of fish, chicken, or meat; stewed vegetables; and fruit. Rice is
served at all meals, even breakfast and snacks (*meriendas*). Seafood and
fish are prepared simply, over coals or uncooked in a vinaigrette. A popular tangy soup, *sinigang*, includes fish and seafood along with some type of
fruit, like tamarind or guava, to give it a distinctive flavor. Another popular national dish is *adobo*, which is a chicken and pork stew with soy sauce
and plenty of garlic. Special occasions, *fiestas*, call for *lechon*, a whole roast
pig stuffed with rice or banana leaves that is cooked on a bamboo spit for
hours and served with an apple in its mouth. Dessert usually consists of
tropical fruits such as bananas, papayas, watermelon, jackfruit, mangoes,
pineapples, guava, and native oranges. A popular dessert, *halo-halo*, is a
mixture of shaved ice with dried fruit and custard, and a special baked
Christmas dessert, *bibingka*, is made of rice with coconut, eggs, and milk.

SCHOOLING

Education is very important in the Philippine culture since it provides
a means of improving one's economic situation and social standing. At
almost 94 percent, the literacy rate in the Philippines is among the highest in the world, with equal numbers for males and females. While school
networks were begun through the Catholic Church during the Spanish
colonial period, education was also very important during the years of
U.S. influence. Teachers were brought in from the United States to train
Filipino teachers in the early part of the twentieth century, and with the
immense educational opportunities offered to Filipino children, the literacy rate doubled to 50 percent by the 1930s. As is the case in many countries, education led to increased social mobility within Philippine society.
Because schooling was conducted in English, a larger percentage of Filipinos spoke English than any of the native languages by the 1940s.
Today, schooling is provided in a bilingual format at the elementary level,
with Filipino and English used for different subjects. Usually mathematics

and science are taught in English, while Filipino is used for the rest of the subjects. Arabic is also used for instruction in some areas of the country.

Education begins at age six and is free and compulsory through the sixth grade. In 1987, 96.4 percent of school-age children were enrolled in elementary schools throughout the country; 56 percent were enrolled in high schools during the same year. There are elementary schools in all cities and towns and almost every village. School is in session from June to March, with vacation during the hottest months of April and May. Elementary school children in the Philippines study the same subjects that American elementary school children study, only they have classes in two languages. In addition to core subjects, some students may also study cooking and sewing in home economics classes. The typical school day lasts about seven or eight hours, somewhat longer than American schools, and there is a great deal of homework. Most children wear school uniforms, and many ride private buses to school. Traffic is so heavy in some of the larger cities that it sometimes takes 40 minutes to an hour to get to school. In rural areas, some children may ride on motorized tricycles, which are really motorcycles with sidecars and a roof, or else they walk to school.

Public schools are not highly regarded, especially in the poorer rural areas. They are generally thought to be for low-income families. Classes can be very large, with up to 40 students with one teacher. There is also a shortage of books and materials, which makes it difficult for both teachers and students. There are sharp distinctions between schools, for example, in Luzon and Southern Mindanao, that are linked to economic factors. Many poor families cannot afford to educate their children beyond elementary school. The quality of education in private schools is much better, but it is very expensive. There are both religious, mostly Catholic, and nonreligious private schools. Sometimes parents will make many sacrifices to have their children attend these schools. Approximately 6 percent of elementary school children go to a private school.

Many children go to work once they complete elementary school. In urban areas they may be hired by private companies or government agencies, or they may work in family-owned businesses. Rural children generally work on the family farm. For those who do not go to work, additional schooling at the secondary level is available. High school in the Philippines consists of four years, starting when students are 13 years old. It is not usually free, although the government may subsidize secondary education in some areas. The first two years are devoted to general studies; then in the second two years, students go through either a college preparatory program or a vocational education track. Private high schools are considered to be of higher quality than public schools. Most of the private high schools are run by Catholic religious orders, and they are very expensive. Approximately 63 percent of students enrolled at the secondary level are in a private school. Still, few teenagers finish high school, usually due to economic constraints and family obligations.

Entrance examinations, for example, the National College Entrance Exam, are required for students who wish to continue through college and university. There are 63 universities and over one thousand colleges throughout the country. The largest public institution is the University of the Philippines in Manila. The best-known private institution is also the country's oldest: the University of Santo Tomas was founded in 1611. Students may remain in college for four to nine years, depending on the degree they wish to attain. Only half of the students who graduate from high school go on to college. There are also vocational schools beyond the secondary level that provide training in a trade for an additional one to two years.

SOCIAL LIFE

Filipinos tend to be very hospitable and social, and Filipino teenagers are no different. Teens have opportunities to meet other teens at school, in the neighborhood, at parties and dances, and in discos or bars. Some coeducational schools sponsor parties and dances, while single-sex schools may team up to provide similar social activities for their students. Courtship rituals in the Philippines have been influenced by Hispanic values and morality. Boys usually ask girls out, and they are expected to pay for all the activities related to the date. Many girls still have to ask their families for permission to go out with a boy, and the observance of curfews is important. Chaperones, who may be a sister or another female relative, are common on dates where the couple is not with a larger group. While dates are not arranged, Filipinos enjoy playing matchmaker and setting up blind dates for their relatives and friends.

A person's appearance is an essential aspect of portraying the pride and self-esteem for which Filipinos are known. Cleanliness and personal hygiene are very important, as is being well-groomed and fashionably dressed. Especially on a date, young ladies are expected to behave in a manner that reflects modesty and decorum. A boy may woo a girl with flowers and candy, which she may choose to ignore or reject to test his seriousness. In rural areas, a boy may even serenade a girl under her window. Similar to American teenagers, Filipinos may go on group dates. Whether solo or in groups, most dates include dinner and going to a rock concert or a disco. It is not appropriate to kiss on the first date, and pre-marital sex is out of the question. While marriages are not arranged in the Philippines, a family must give its approval. This will be discussed more in the section on religious practices and cultural ceremonies.

RECREATION

Sports are an important part of Philippine life. Basketball is the major national sport in the Philippines. Every school and park has a basketball court, and there are also courts in every town plaza. The game is probably the main after-school activity for the majority of Filipino boys, even those who work. Robert Jaworski is one of the best-known and greatest basketball players in the Philippine Basketball Association. School sports that are played in teams are basketball, baseball, volleyball, and soccer. While girls and boys play together in informal settings, organized team sports are not usually coeducational.

These sports are also included in a vast array of spectator sports, to which boxing, *jai alai, sipa,* and *arnis de mano* can be added. Jai alai is similar to handball, except that wicker basket scoops are used to maneuver the ball. This sport has its origins in Spain. Sipa is like tennis, only instead of a racquet, players use their knees and feet. Arnis de mano is a unique Philippine form of martial arts, reminiscent of fencing with sticks, that is used for self-defense.

Gamecock fights, called *tupada,* are a very popular form of recreation in most villages, towns, and cities. In rural areas, spider fighting is common among children, and much time is spent collecting spiders for this activity. In addition, chess matches are held in both urban and rural areas. A source of national pride is Eugene Torre, who is Asia's first world grand master of chess. The Philippine National Games are held on a yearly basis and are also well received by the public.

ENTERTAINMENT

Teenagers in the Philippines are like teenagers all around the world. In general, they like to spend time hanging out with their friends, watching television and movies, listening to music, going to dances, reading comic books, and going to the mall. There are differences between the types of activities that are available to teens in urban and rural areas. Large cities like Manila and Cebu City are much like Western cities in what they have to offer. There are sporting events, concerts, dances, malls, fast food restaurants, and museums. Teens go to discos and karaoke lounges, discuss fashion, watch television variety shows and soap operas, and participate in other aspects of popular culture. In rural areas, entertainment is more seasonal, with picnics and dances in the summer and storytelling and listening to the radio during the rains.

Listening to and playing music is a favorite pastime of teens in the Philippines. American popular music dominates the airwaves, although radio stations are obligated to play Filipino songs every hour. Many Philippine popular music stars sing American songs in Filipino or Taglish. Sometimes they blend Philippine folk instruments with modern ones to create distinctive sounds. Latin American music also has a strong influence on the sound, rhythm, and language of Philippine popular music. A well-known figure from the Philippine music scene is Bobby Enrique, who is known as the king of Filipino jazz.

Dances are a popular form of entertainment in the Philippines. Traditional dances that tell stories are reserved for special occasions or *fiestas*. Many of these folk dances, which have Muslim and Spanish influences, are taught in the public schools. Teenagers, especially in the cities, are more interested in dancing to popular music, preferably American music. To dance, teens go to parties at friends' homes or to discos or music lounges. Boys and girls can dance together in public, as they can in most Western cities. Some girls have a debut, a large party or *cotillon*, on or near their 18th birthday to mark their passage to adulthood. This formal occasion also provides an opportunity for teens to socialize and dance.

Teenagers enjoy watching American and Filipino movies. Some Filipino and Filipino American stars have had much commercial success in the United States and may be familiar to American audiences. Included in this group are Phoebe Cates, who starred in the films *Anniversary Party*, *Princess Caraboo*, and *Gremlins*, and Lou Diamond Phillips, who starred in films such as *La Bamba* and *Dark Wind* and also on Broadway's *The King and I*. Lea Salonga is a singer and actress who was in *Miss Saigon* on Broadway and who was also the voice of Jasmine in Disney's *Aladdin* and Mulan in *The Legend of Mulan*.

An increase in the number of paved roads and the widespread use of radio, television, cable, and satellite in the islands is leading to the mainstreaming of minority groups. It is estimated that 45 percent of all Philippine households have television sets and that more than half of the population over the age of 10 is exposed to television. Most of what is televised is aimed at the urban sector, which has a strong influence on the culture and behavior of rural Filipinos. Despite the fact that most Filipinos obtain their information and entertainment from the radio, it is television that has had the most profound impact on Philippine youth. A

1993 study on Filipino youth found that television and the pop idols it portrays often act as a surrogate parent, teaching what is important and what is correct. Because of these influences, young people are more interested in current trends and changes that are based on Western culture than in the old traditions. This often leads to conflict with their parents and the older generations.

RELIGIOUS PRACTICES AND CULTURAL CEREMONIES

Religion and ceremonial ritual are an essential part of Philippine life. Weekly observance and attendance to services, whether at church or at the mosque, are expected. The majority of Filipinos are Roman Catholic. Many of the ceremonies of this faith, including baptism, confirmation, first communion, and marriage, are rites of passage as children grow into adulthood. Going to morning mass, praying before meals, and saying family rosaries are also common daily or weekly occurrences in Philippine Catholic homes. Muslims who live in the southern part of the country

Partaking in one of the Catholic festivals of the Philippines. Photo © A. Tovy/TRIP.

pray five times a day in Arabic and observe their own traditions. Some religious observances have become part of the national fabric of the Philippines.

Holidays

Many Christian holidays are celebrated as national holidays, including Holy Thursday, Good Friday, Easter Sunday, All Saints Day (November 1), and Christmas (December 25). Each town also has an elaborate *fiesta* to celebrate its patron saint, and it is not uncommon for people to request blessings for new homes, cars, and businesses. Other nonreligious national holidays observed in the Philippines are New Year's Day (January 1), Freedom Day (February 25), Bataan Day (April 9), Labor Day (May 1), Independence Day (June 12), Filipino-American Friendship Day (July 4), National Heroes' Day (August 27), Barangay Day (September 11), Bonifacio Day (November 30), and Rizal Day (December 30). Some of these honor important figures in the country's history and struggle for independence.

Rites of Passage

Godparents and the idea of godparenthood (*compadrazco*) are an extremely important part of the Filipino family. A set of godparents is carefully selected for each child at the time of baptism. These godparents act as a second set of parents and are supposed to care for the child if something should happen to the parents. It is typical for godparents to give their godchildren gifts for birthdays and Christmas. As the child matures, it is expected that the godparent will provide him or her with some type of assistance in procuring a job or help in some way to establish a secure future for the child. There are also godparents who sponsor children at their confirmations, and all couples who marry have godparents at their wedding ceremony. These kinship relationships beyond blood ties are an essential part of Filipino culture. They are observed more stringently in rural areas than in cities.

In the Philippines, puberty is marked by circumcision in males and the onset of menstruation in females. There is no official ceremony to mark this time. In the country, boys go to an herb doctor or a barber and prove their manhood by not having anesthesia during the procedure. In the city, the process is more clinical and less painful. Girls are taught proper hygiene and modesty. Appropriate behavior on the part of girls is believed to be very important so that they do not bring shame and dishonor to the family.

Marriage is a sacrament in Filipino culture; divorce does not exist. A boy's parents ask a girl's parents for her hand in marriage in a formal ceremony called *pamanhikan*. The groom's family pays for the wedding, which usually involves a church ceremony and a reception. Some wedding-related customs include a prohibition from leaving the house the night before the ceremony for both the bride and the groom and the bride not trying on her dress until the morning of the wedding. During the reception after the wedding, there is a dance during which money is pinned to the couple's clothing.

Death is viewed as the beginning of a life beyond life on Earth. It is traditional for dying Catholics to receive last rites from their priest. Burials usually occur from one to three days after a person dies. Family and friends gather to console each other. Family members who are away or overseas are expected to return home. Wakes are not at all solemn, and the bereaved family is accompanied during night vigils. Wreaths or monetary donations are sent, and mourners wear black clothing. Nightly prayers are said for nine nights after the burial, and a mass is offered by the family in the local church to mark the first anniversary of a person's death. Visits to a deceased relative's grave are made on the person's birthday and on All Saints Day. As with other aspects of Philippine life, modernity has made inroads on religious tradition as young people are influenced by media and begin to abandon the rituals and practices that have been the customs of their parents and ancestors for generations.

CONCLUSION

In general, teen life in the Philippines mirrors that of teens all over the world. There are clear distinctions made between rural and urban living. Education and globalization are starting to diminish these differences, however. There are many similarities between Filipino teens and American teens, especially those living in urban centers. Teenagers in Philippine cities have the same amenities and activities available to them that American teenagers have, while rural teens tend to live a more traditional lifestyle. The long-standing American influence in the Philippines continues through commercial dealings and the popular media. American music, clothing, films, pop idols, and fast food heavily influence the attitudes and opinions of Filipino teens, even in rural areas. For a people who revere custom and tradition, this poses a challenge for Philippine parents.

A large difference, though, between Filipino and American youth is the extent to which socioeconomic status plays a role in how they live. The contrasts between rich and poor families in the Philippines are striking.

The fact that many children and teenagers of poverty cannot go to school because they have to work to help support their families is something that many American teenagers may not be able to relate to. The stark living conditions for these families and their dependence on agriculture as a means of subsistence is something that is most likely unfamiliar to teens in Philippine urban centers as well. Still, in terms of their tastes and interests, Filipino and American teenagers, despite their cultural differences, would probably get along rather well.

RESOURCE GUIDE

Nonfiction

Articles

Belvez, P. M. (2000). *Development of Filipino, the national language of the Philippines.* National Commission for Culture and the Arts. Retrieved October 24, 2003, from http://www.ncca.gov.ph/ phil._culture/other_cultural_info/language/language_development.htm.

Catacataca, P. D. (2000). *The Commission on the Filipino Language.* National Commission for Culture and the Arts. Retrieved October 24, 2003, from http://www.ncca.gov.ph/phil._culture/other_cultural_info/language/language_cfl.htm.

Churchill, B. R. (2000). History of the Philippine revolution. Retrieved October 24, 2003, from http://www.ncca.gov.ph/phil._culture/cultural_heritage/historical/historical_history.htm.

Churchill, B. R. (2000). The Philippine-American war (1899–1902). Retrieved October 24, 2003, from http://www.ncca.gov.ph/phil._culture/cultural_heritage/historical/historical_philamerican. htm.

Cruz, A. C. (2000). *Language and culture.* National Commission for Culture and the Arts. Retrieved October 24, 2003, from http://www.ncca.gov.ph/phil._culture/other_cultural_info/language/lang-&culture.htm.

Espiritu, C. (2000). *Filipino language in the curriculum.* National Commission for Culture and the Arts. Retrieved October 24, 2003, from http://www.ncca.gov.ph/phil._culture/other_cultural_info/language/language_lang-curriculum.htm.

Peralta, J. T. (1994). *Glimpses: Peoples of the Philippines.* National Commission for Culture and the Arts. Retrieved October 24, 2003, from http://www.ncca.gov.ph/phil._culture/traditional_arts/glimpses/peoples_glimpses.htm.

Tuazon, R. R. (2000). *Radio as a way of life.* National Commission for Culture and the Arts. Retrieved October 24, 2003, from http://www.ncca.gov.ph/phil._culture/other_cultural_info/communic.../communication_radio.htm.

Books

Aquino, B. S. (1988). *Testament from a prison cell*. Los Angeles: Philippines Journal.
Brittan, D. (1997). *The people of the Philippines*. New York: PowerKids Press.
Davis, L. (1999). *The Philippines*. Mankato, MN: Bridgestone Books.
Dolan, R. E. (1993). *Philippines: A country study*. Washington, DC: Federal Research Division, Library of Congress.
Kinkade, S. (1996). *Children of the Philippines*. Minneapolis: Carolrhoda Books.
Mendoza, L. (1999). *Philippines*. Milwaukee: Gareth Stevens.
Olesky, W. (2000). *The Philippines: Enchantment of the world*. New York: Children's Press.
Ramos-Shahani, L. V. (1989). *Philippines . . . in pictures*. Visual Geography Series. Minneapolis, MN: Lerner Publications.
Roces, A., & Roces, G. (1994). *Culture shock! Philippines. A guide to customs and etiquette*. Portland, OR: Graphic Arts Publishing Company.
Rodell, P. *Culture and customs of the Philippines*. Westport, CT: Greenwood Press, 2001.
Steiner, D. J. (2000). *The Philippines: A singular and a plural place*. 4th edition. Boulder, CO: Westview Press.
Timberman, D. G. (1991). *A changeless land: Continuity and change in Philippine politics*. New York: Institute of Southeast Asian Studies & M. E. Sharpe Inc.
Tope, L. R. (1991). *Cultures of the world. Philippines*. New York: Marshall Cavendish.
Williams, B. (1998). *Insight guides: Philippines*. Hong Kong: APA Publications.

Fiction

Brown river, white ocean: An anthology of twentieth-century Philippine literature in English. (1993). New Brunswick, NJ: Rutgers University Press.
Hamilton-Paterson, J. (1994). *Ghosts of Manila*. New York: Farrar, Strauss & Giroux.

Videos

Asian treasure bag of folk tales [Motion picture]. (1994). Churchill Media.
Come join our multicultural band. Volume 2: Mexico and the Philippines [Motion picture]. (1995). Wagner's World of Music.
The Philippines: Pearl of the Pacific [Motion picture]. (1996). International Video Network.

Web Sites

http://www.asianinfo.org/asianinfo/philippines
http://www.asianjournal.com
http://www.dlsu.edu.ph/gen/

http://embassyworld.com/embassy/Philippines
http://www.filipino.com
http://www.filipino-americans.com
http://www.filipinorecipeslink.com
http://www.geocities.com/diariofilipino/
http://www.globalserve.net/~studiopi/Flip/civics.htm
http://www.ldb.org/phillipi.htm
http://www.ncaa.gov.ph
http://www.nscb.gov.ph
http://www.pcgchicago.com
http://www.philippines.com
http://www.philonrise.com
http://www.philstar.com
http://www.pinoyzone.com
http://www.portalinc.com/~anton/toks.html

More Information

Embassy of the Philippines
1600 Massachusetts Avenue NW
Washington, DC 20036
Telephone: (202) 467–9432

Pen Pal/Chat

http://asia.yahoo.com/Social_Science/Communications/Writing/Correspondence/
    Pen_Pals/Children

Chapter 11

SINGAPORE

Oneyda Paneque

INTRODUCTION

Singapore is an island nation in Southeast Asia consisting of the main island of Singapore and some 63 offshore islands. Its official name is the Republic of Singapore. It is situated in the tropics only a little more than 85 miles, or one degree north, of the equator. The main island of Singapore is about 584.8 square kilometers (240 square miles) in area and has a coastline approximately 150.5 kilometers long. It is so small that it takes only an hour to drive from one end of the island to the other.

The country is an urban area surrounded by suburbs. Its population is multiethnic with a rich, diverse cultural, religious, and linguistic heritage. The capital of the Republic of Singapore is Singapore, also known as the Lion City because the lion symbolizes courage, strength, and excellence; or the Garden City because of its many beautiful gardens and parks. Singapore is the largest port in Southeast Asia and one of the world's greatest commercial centers.

Singapore is important because of its strategic location on the sea route between two large trading markets, India and China. The port of Singapore is one of the busiest in the world. Its closest neighbors are Malaysia, Brunei, and Indonesia. Singapore is linked to the Malay Peninsula by a causeway that stretches two-thirds of a mile and carries a road, a railway, and a water pipeline. The three largest offshore islands are Pulau Tekong, Pulau Ubin, and Sentosa. Two of the offshore islands, Sentosa and Pulau Brani, are connected to the main island by a causeway. Sentosa Island, a popular tourist attraction, can be reached by cable cars from Singapore's highest hills. Passenger ferries can also reach the smaller islands. A third causeway links Singapore to the smaller island of Pulau Damar Laut.

Singapore has two seasons, the wet Northeast monsoon season that lasts from December to March, and the drier Southwest monsoon season that lasts from June to September. The monsoon seasons are separated by two brief intermonsoon periods during which there are frequent afternoon showers and thunderstorms. Thunderstorms occur during 40 percent of the days of the year. December is the coolest month and the temperature is around 77°F (25°C). May is the warmest month of the year, and the temperature is around 81°F (27°C). Singapore has plenty of rain and humidity year-round, and temperatures remain relatively uniform. During the heavy rain season, floods are quite common in certain areas. In general, the climate is hot and humid.

Singapore is one of the most densely populated countries in the world. In 2000, the population of Singapore was 4.02 million people, including foreign residents. It was the first Asian country to implement population control measures because the number of people living there grew so rapidly. Presently, the rate of population growth is low. Usually there is only one child per family.

Singapore has a varied linguistic, cultural, and religious heritage. Several different ethnic groups live in Singapore: 77 percent are Chinese, 14 percent Malay, 8 percent Indian, and 1 percent members of other ethnic groups. The official languages are Malay, Chinese (Mandarin), Tamil, and English. Mandarin is spoken by most people of Chinese descent, which is the largest group, Malay by those of Malaysian descent, and Tamil by those of Indian descent. English is the language that is mostly used in government, professions, businesses, and schools. Approximately half of the population is literate in more than one language.

Although Singapore's history dates from the eleventh century, the island was little known to the West until the nineteenth century. In 1819 while en route to China, Sir Stamford Raffles landed in Singapore and decided it would be a free port. Later in 1824, the British purchased Singapore Island, and the following year the city of Singapore became a major port. In 1942, the island was captured by Japan and remained under its control until 1945, when the British returned. In 1946, Singapore became a separate British Crown Colony. Then, in 1959, it became self-governing. Later, in 1963, it joined the newly independent Federation of Malaya, Sabah, and Sarawak to form Malaysia. Singapore became an independent republic on August 9, 1965, when it separated from Malaysia. Every year August 9 is celebrated as a national holiday.

Singaporeans enjoy a high standard of living. Some compare it to the standard of living in Switzerland. It is one of the most prosperous countries in the world. According to the World Bank, it is classified as an upper-middle-income country. Its people are the primary natural resource. The people of Singapore are committed to the welfare of the society, and they are known to be hard workers.

Since 1959, the prime minister of Singapore has been Lee Kuan Yew, who formed the People's Action Party. This group has been in charge of Singapore since then, although there have been a few members elected to Parliament from other groups. The government controls the cultural, economic, political, and social lives of its people. For most Singaporeans, there is no problem with this governmental control because their needs are met.

The development of Singapore has been marked by three major periods. The first was the colonization by the English from 1819 to World War II. The second period, from after World War II until the early 1960s, was a time of transition to a self-governed country. The third period, still in effect today, is one of independence marked by rapid industrialization and modernization. In the past, especially during the transition period, teenagers and young adults were very involved in political issues and concerned about the welfare of the country. Now since Singapore is enjoying a period of stability and economic prosperity, the youth are not as politically involved, although there are some who are not in favor of so much government control and are becoming more and more politically involved.

The core values of Singaporeans stem from Confucian beliefs. They believe in consensus, harmony, reverence for those in power, and stability. Rulers are bound to honesty and caring for those whom they rule. Duty to the group is more important than personal liberty. Creativity and talent are rewarded with better and special privileges.

Overall, Singapore is a stable, safe place to live. It is a modern society where teenagers can enjoy growing up knowing that they are expected to become responsible adults who will make positive contributions to their families and the community.

TYPICAL DAY

On a typical day, a teenager in Singapore gets up early. After eating a quick breakfast, the teen dresses and goes to school. There the teen is expected to study hard and do well. In fact, a teenager's primary responsibility is to do well in school. Most do not have jobs until they complete their education.

If the teenagers have free time during the week after completing homework, many use the Internet to communicate with friends. Others relax by watching movies or television, while others enjoy listening to music. Many teenagers also play sports and are involved in extracurricular activities at school.

FAMILY LIFE

Most families in Singapore are small, usually comprising the parents and one or two children maximum. The adults in the family work very hard to support the family. The government does provide many services such as good health care. Families understand the value of hard work and believe that the group is more important than the individual. They pass down these beliefs to their children.

In many Singaporean families, both parents work outside of the home. As in many modern urban societies, having working parents and smaller extended families leads to a breakdown in communication and support for the youth. In spite of occasional conflicts, parents are very concerned about their teenage children, give their children the best, and expect the best from them. Parents also depend on the schools to be responsible for socializing their children.

Although the type of rapid modernization that has happened in Singapore sometimes leads to family instability and conflicts between generations or males and females, families there are relatively stable. There is a low divorce rate in Singapore and much concern for the care of the elderly.

The government has built around 85 percent of the housing in Singapore. Housing is scarce because there are many people in Singapore and there is little land. Approximately 90 percent of Singaporeans live in apartments. Residence committees are quite common in the government housing. These committees ensure that there is harmony and order in the area. Therefore, teens are accustomed to living close to their neighbors and being respectful of them.

Cars are very expensive, so most people travel by public buses and subways. Rarely does a teenager own a car, and rarely do teens have the opportunity to drive one.

Most teens do not marry young. The average age for a female at marriage is 23. Among the three major ethnic groups there is variation in that

Chinese women tend to marry later than their Malay and Indian counterparts.

TRADITIONAL AND NONTRADITIONAL FOOD DISHES

The foods eaten in Singapore depend on the family's origins. Many Singaporeans are of Chinese descent, and they eat typically Chinese food
that includes pork, rice, spicy sauce, and tea. Some who are of Malaysian
origin will add their own ingredients such as coconut to the traditional
Chinese dishes. The Indians in Singapore add their own spices to create
delicious dishes. The diversity of the cultural groups in Singapore can be
seen in the food they eat.

Many families eat out quite often because of their busy lives, especially
since both parents frequently work outside of the home. Home cooking
usually takes place on the weekends. Food centers can be found throughout the country. They are called hawker centers because many years ago
food hawkers would take food to the mostly male workers who were too
busy to cook for themselves. These centers are in open and covered markets, as well as in air-conditioned food courts. There are also many fine
dining restaurants, although many Singaporeans would say that the
hawker centers are better.

Students often stop by coffee shops known as *kopi tiam* either on their
way to school, if they attend the afternoon session, or after school, if they
attend the morning session. In the mornings, breakfast is served: black
coffee (*kopi*) or coffee with condensed milk and toast, jam, eggs, or noodles. Many adults eat dinner at these coffee shops, which stay open until
late in the night.

As in many places throughout the world, the youth enjoy burgers, hot
dogs, sandwiches, and pizza. Many also eat foods that are typical of Singapore, especially when they are with their families.

Chinese Singaporeans eat with health in mind. They try to establish a
balance between certain foods that are "cooling" (*yin*) and others that are
"heating" (*yang*); other foods are neutral. The concept of yin and yang is
thousands of years old. Yin and yang are the two forces present everywhere
that complement each other and can be effective only together. Yin stands
for the feminine, with quiet, cold, passive characteristics associated with
night. Yang stands for the masculine, with warm, active characteristics
associated with day. Examples of yin foods are tropical fruits and salads.
Examples of yang foods are vegetable and meat broths, and hot spices.
Neutral foods, such as cereals and potatoes, are the easiest to digest.

Malaysian Singaporeans typically eat *satay*, which are small wooden skewers with chunks of meat, pork, or shrimp dipped in spicy peanut sauce. These kabobs are often eaten as snacks. Malay food is flavored with galangal, ginger, fresh turmeric, shallots, garlic, fresh and dried chilies, lemongrass, and dried shrimp paste.

Many Indian Singaporeans practice Hinduism and are vegetarians. They prepare many meals with dried beans and lentils in a variety of ways. Indian Singaporeans have "banana leaf restaurants," known by that name because the meal is served on a banana leaf. Southern Indian Singaporeans eat spicier foods prepared with coriander, cardamom, cumin, fennel, and cloves. They have a largely wheat-based diet. Northern Indian Singaporeans eat milder foods prepared with yogurt or cream and herbs and tomatoes, and they eat a rice-based diet of dishes often prepared with coconut milk.

Eating in Singapore is usually enjoyed in a group, whether with the family or friends. An assortment of dishes is served together, but there are individual servings of rice. They then serve themselves from the dishes with a serving spoon. Eating with fingers is acceptable but only with the right hand and the palm of the hand is kept clean. Hands are washed before and after a meal. Chopsticks are sometimes used, although forks, spoons, and knives are acceptable.

Seafood is quite popular among most Singaporeans. Among the different religious groups some foods are not eaten. Muslims do not eat pork; Hindus and strict Buddhists do not eat beef.

There are several classic dishes in Singapore. Chili crab is considered by many to be the national dish. The crabs are deep-fried and flavored with garlic, ginger, chili sauce, tomato sauce, sugar, soy sauce, and sesame oil. *Popiah* is a spring roll that can be served as a snack or part of a meal. Another popular food is *rojak*, a salad combining fruit and vegetables with a spicy peanut sauce. *Hokkien* shrimp noodle soup, prepared with shrimp and dried prawns, is also very good. *Murtabak* is savory stuffed Indian bread that makes a good lunch or snack. The dough is light and typically filled with fried mutton, although any lamb or beef can be used. Tea-smoked seabass is seabass marinated with soy sauce, sugar, ginger juice and salt, Chinese black tea leaves, star anise, cinnamon sticks, cloves, rice, and garlic. Stingray in banana leaf comes from the Malay population. It is a fish that is covered with chili sambal, wrapped in a banana leaf, and grilled over charcoal.

A traditional drink is Chinese tea, especially with Chinese food. Many older teenagers have beer to complement the spicy food. The local beer that is best known is Tiger. Tiger beer was named because the tiger symbolizes strength to the Chinese.

SCHOOLING

Singapore has among the best-educated citizens of Southeast Asia. The government spends a significant portion of its budget on education. Education is not compulsory in Singapore, although because parents value it highly, almost all the children go to school. In 2003, six years of education will be made compulsory. The overall literacy rate is 92.8 percent, 96.6 percent for males and 88.5 percent for females.

English is the primary language of instruction, although most students also study other languages. There is a national curriculum. At the primary level, more than half of the time the students are studying their mother tongue, English, and mathematics. The other subjects include science, moral education, physical education, and social studies. At the secondary level, the students are divided according to their academic strengths and abilities and take different programs.

There are usually large classes with 40 to 50 students. In special programs, there are fewer students so they can receive individualized attention from specially trained teachers. Some of the programs provided are for students with special needs, that is, learning disabilities, mental handicaps, or physical handicaps, or for gifted and talented students.

Children generally receive at least 10 years of formal education depending on their academic ability. Most children attend two years of kindergarten. Then they have six years of primary school and four years of secondary school. After completing primary school, students take a national exam, the Primary School Leaving Examination.

The educational system has very high standards. Students must pass difficult comprehensive exams to move to the next level. Slower learners can take many years to finish primary school. These comprehensive exams cover material that has been learned throughout primary school. The exams are very difficult, and students study hard to do well on them because their future will be greatly affected by the outcome.

Depending on their scores on the Primary School Leaving Examination, there are three courses of study in which the students are placed: special, express, and normal. Only 10 percent of the students, those who have the highest scores, are in the special courses. Forty percent of the students are in the express courses. Fifty percent of the students score on the bottom end of the scale and are then in the normal courses, which focus on technical studies and computer applications.

After secondary school, many young people go into the workforce. Some attend two years of junior college. After two years of junior college or work, young men must serve in the military for two years. Women do not have to serve in the military. After the young men have completed military service, they can go on to a four-year college in Singapore or elsewhere. Singaporeans are free to study anywhere. Most Singaporeans who study abroad do so in Great Britain or Australia rather than the United States. Ninety-five percent of those who study abroad return to their homeland.

School vacations are from mid-November to early January. Schools also celebrate Chinese New Year, the most festive holiday in Singapore, which falls in January or February every year. In addition, there is a week off in the spring for Easter and four weeks in June. The school year has 200 days. Many schools are crowded because of the young population in Singapore.

Many students go to school on Saturdays for a few hours to participate in clubs, games, and other activities. School administrators are very concerned about the success and future of their students. They see to it that the young minds are cultivated and nurtured so that the children will develop into productive adults.

There are few discipline problems in schools because teachers do not tolerate unruly behavior. Students who misbehave are dealt with strictly. Parents are very supportive of the teachers and strongly encourage their children to do well. In fact, the stress and pressure of achieving academically can be a source of problems and stress for Singaporean youths. Parents and the general public see school as the "work" of the youth. It is their responsibility and duty to do well for their families so they can get a good job and status in the community.

Singaporeans tend to stay in school longer and start to work after completing their schooling. Most teenagers enjoy this privilege and do not work while in school.

In 1993, the country adopted a set of five common beliefs that are ingrained in everything that is done. These shared values are particularly important for the youth. First, they teach youth that the nation comes before the community and society. It is more important than individual needs and wants. Second, the family is the basic unit of society where children grow and learn. The family provides stability and nurtures its members. Third, the community supports and respects the people as individuals. Fourth, it is important to promote agreement and harmony. Reaching a consensus in order to promote unity and peace solves problems. Fifth, harmony is important among the different religious and racial groups that live in Singapore. These values are taught both in and out of school. Teenagers are expected to accept these values and act accordingly.

SOCIAL LIFE

Friendships are very important for Singaporean youth. These relationships help the youth become independent as well as teach them social and emotional skills. Most teens make friends in school or their neighborhoods.

Youth are becoming more westernized as they are more exposed to Western culture. Youths' greater fluency in English gives them greater access to that culture. Many times there are conflicts between traditional Asian values and modern Western values. Usually the traditional Asian values prevail.

Most teenagers choose whom to date. As in many places in the world, different ethnic groups tend to stay together, Chinese with Chinese, Malaysians with Malaysians, Indians with Indians. One determining factor in date selection may be religious beliefs.

Teenagers dress casually. Traditional attire is reserved for specific occasions such as plays or religious holidays. Like people in many Asian countries, Singaporeans remove their shoes before entering a home.

RECREATION

An important part of the education system is extracurricular activities, which encourage healthy recreation and promote self-discipline, teamwork, and confidence. There are a wide variety of sports and games, uniformed organizations, cultural groups, clubs, and societies.

The People's Association is a board established to promote racial harmony and community bonding. Its mission is to build a cohesive, dynamic, and cultured nation through mass participation in educational, social, cultural, sports and recreational, and other community activities. The People's Association Youth Movement is the largest youth organization in Singapore. Its 95 youth groups led by youth volunteers are based at community centers and clubs. Youth from the ages of 15 to 35 participate in self-development courses, adventure and cultural activities, sports, overseas expeditions, and youth exchange programs designed to develop responsible citizens. The youth movement also runs 13 Boys' Clubs for boys from 12 to 15 years of age from lower-income families. The clubs provide educational, cultural, sports, and other activities.

There is also the National Youth Council, which promotes a healthy lifestyle among youth and encourages them to contribute to society. The Singapore Youth Award and Youth Development Fund are run by the council.

Outward Bound Singapore offers adventure training for students, working youths, and young executives who want to experience physically demanding, mentally challenging, fun, and safe outdoor activities.

Teens play many different sports in Singapore. They are encouraged to find some sport that can be enjoyed throughout life. The motto of the Singapore Sports Council is "Sports for All." The most popular sport is swimming; other sports include badminton, soccer, rugby, volleyball, table tennis, gymnastics, softball, and basketball.

The government is very concerned about the recreational lives of the youth of the country and tries to provide many structured activities. Activities youth like to engage in are outdoor sports, popular entertainment such video games, television, music, and travel.

ENTERTAINMENT

Watching television and listening to the radio or to music are the most popular leisure pastimes of teenagers. Other activities include spending time with family, shopping, and visiting friends and relatives. Teenagers also enjoy going to shopping malls and meeting their friends.

One of Singaporeans' favorite pastimes is watching movies. Members of the Board of Film Censors screen movies. They disapprove of films with excessive violence, permissiveness, and glorification of crime and gangsters. Teenagers watch movies from all over the world. Some are produced locally, while others are from different countries in Asia, Europe, and the United States.

Many teenagers and young adults find using the Internet entertaining. They mostly use it to communicate with friends and browse different Web sites rather than make purchases.

There is a very low crime rate in Singapore. The most common offenses of juveniles are shoplifting, robbery, vandalism, and burglary. Rarely are violent, extremely aggressive crimes committed.

Interestingly, in Singapore chewing gum is banned because in the past people would stick chewed gum on the doors of mass transit cars so they would not be able to close. This was a sign of protest because they felt that the government had too many regulations. Antismoking and antispitting laws have also been passed. Although the government has passed these

Teens at a mall in Singapore.
Photo © ASK IMAGES/TRIP.

laws to make the country a better place to live, not everyone agrees with them.

The legal drinking age is 18, although it is not strictly enforced. There is not a significant problem with alcoholism among the youth. This is also related to the religious beliefs held by the Buddhist and Muslim youths, who do not drink alcoholic beverages.

In Singapore, drug possession and drug dealing are handled severely by the police and courts. Drug addiction is common among some young adults, and most addicts smoke heroin. Late adolescence, ages 16 to 21, is the time when young people may initiate drug use. The average age for a first drug experience is 18. The heroin is made in Thailand, Burma, or Laos and then brought to Singapore. Luckily, Singapore is one of the few places where the drug problem is decreasing. This may be partly because of the harsh punishments for buying, using, or selling drugs. Drug dealers are given the death penalty. The country has also made serious efforts to treat drug addicts, and that has reduced the addiction rate as well. There are also preventive efforts that focus on high-risk students and those who drop out of school. The Central Narcotics Bureau works with the National Council against Drug Abuse to organize the National Anti–Drug Abuse Campaigns.

RELIGIOUS PRACTICES AND CULTURAL CEREMONIES

The constitution of Singapore defends the right to religious freedom. The main religions are Buddhism, Taoism, Islam, Christianity, and Hinduism. Usually the Chinese are Buddhist, the Malays Muslims are Muslim, and the Indians are Hindu. About 30 percent of the people of Singapore have no religious affiliation. Depending on their family's beliefs, teens practice the customs of one of these religions.

Buddhism is a religion without scheduled temple services. The goal is to achieve freedom from worldly cares and to attain enlightenment. Buddhist ceremonies are connected to holidays, superstitions, or the need for good luck. A follower of the Buddhist religion passing a temple may enter to burn incense to remember ancestors. One Buddhist celebration is Vesak Day, which is celebrated on the day of the full moon in May to commemorate the birth, attainment of enlightenment, and death of Buddha. Families bring food, candles, and flowers to monasteries and participate in meditation while the monks chant. Houses and streets are cleaned and decorated with flags and flowers. Children make lanterns and cards decorated with lotus flowers, lights, and the *bhodi* tree (the tree under which buddha attained enlightenment).

The major Muslim festivals are Hari Raya Puasa, Hari Raya Haji, and the birthday of the Prophet Muhammad. Strict Muslims recognize two forms of prayer. One form is private, personal, spontaneous prayer. The other form is a ritual that is performed five times at day, at sunrise, at midday, at midafternoon, at sunset, and before going to bed.

The most important Chinese celebrations are Chinese New Year (Chun Jie), Fifteenth Night (Yuan Xiao Jie or Chap Goh Meh), All Souls Day (Qing Ming Jie), Dragon Boat Festival (Duan Wu Jie), Feast of the Seven Sisters (Qi Qiao Jie), Feast of the Hungry Ghosts (Zhong Yuan Jie), Mid-Autumn Festival (Zhong Qiu), and Double Ninth Festival (Chong Yang Jie). The Hindu festivals are Ponggol, Thaipusam, Deepavali, Nava Rathiri, and Onan. Christian festivals include Christmas, Good Friday, and Easter.

The 11 official public holidays include religious festivals from these different religions. The public holidays are New Year's Day, Chinese New

Year (two days), Hari Raya Puasa, Good Friday, Labor Day, Hari Raya Haji, Vesak Day, National Day, Deepavali, and Christmas.

CONCLUSION

Teenagers in Singapore grow up in a modern, industrialized, technologically advanced society. Their primary responsibility is to study and do well so they can be productive citizens in the future. Their sense of duty to family and society prevails in their daily lives and their goals and dreams for the future.

Overall, youth in Singapore have fewer problems with delinquency and drug addiction than youth in other modern countries. There is government support for healthy, balanced lifestyles. The high standard of living in Singapore has helped the youth to enjoy a good education, recreational activities, and a safe place to live.

In spite of the high standard of living in Singapore for most of its citizens, not everyone is content with so much government control. The youth are often the ones to protest, although the government officials step in quickly to suppress any opposing views. As a group, teenagers are not rebellious or deviant.

The youth in Singapore are viewed as presenting opportunities rather than problems. The focus of society is on helping teenagers face an increasingly competitive global system and adjusting to rapid changes that are a consequence of industrialization and modern technological advances.

RESOURCE GUIDE

Nonfiction

Haas, M. (1999). *The Singapore puzzle*. Westport, CT: Praeger Publishers.

Kong-Chong, H. (1994). Singapore. In K. Hurrelmann (Ed.), *International handbook of adolescence*. Westport, CT: Greenwood Press.

Lee, K. Y.; Yew, L. K.; & Kissinger, H. (2000). *From third world to first: The Singapore story 1965–2000*. New York: HarperCollins.

Ling, K. F. (Ed.). (1998). *The food of Asia: Authentic recipes from China, India, Indonesia, Japan, Singapore, Malaysia, Thailand and Vietnam*. Singapore: Periplus Editions.

Ministry of Information and the Arts. (1998). *Singapore: Facts and pictures*. Singapore: Ministry of Information and the Arts.

Wibisono, D., & Wong, D. (1995). *The food of Singapore: Authentic recipes from the Manhattan of the East*. Singapore: Periplus Editions.

Fiction

Burgess, A. (1968). *Time for a Tiger*. London: Heinemann.
Cheong, F. (1991). *The scent of the gods*. New York: W. W. Norton & Company.
Chua, D. (1999). *The missing page*. Singapore: Angsana Books.
L'Amour, L. (1987). *West from Singapore*. New York: Bantam Books.

Web Sites

National Youth Council: http://www.nyc.youth.gov.sg
Singapore Infomap: The National Website: http://www.sg
Yahoo! Singapore: http://sg.yahoo.com

More Information

Singapore Tourism Board
Tourism Court
1 Orchard Spring Lane
Singapore 2477129
Web site: http://www.stb.com.sg
Telephone: 736-6622
Fax: 736-9423

Singaporean Embassy
3501 International Place NW
Washington, DC 20008
E-mail: singemb@bellatlantic.net
Telephone: (202) 537-3100
Fax: (202) 537-0876
Consular: (212) 537-7086 (consular)
Ambassador: Prof. Chan Heng Chee

Pen Pal/Chat

International Penfriends
P.O. Box 1416
East Camberwell Vic 3126
Australia
Web site: http://members.ozemail.com.au/~penpals

World Pen Pals
P.O. Box 337
Saugerties, NY 12477
Web site: http://www.world-pen-pals.com
Telephone: (845) 246-7828

Chapter 12

SOUTH KOREA

Eric Dwyer

INTRODUCTION

When teenagers in South Korea watch the weather on the TV news, they might see two different maps of their country. One map might show just South Korea, indicating temperatures and forecasts for various towns and cities located in the southern half of the Korean Peninsula, roughly the section of land that comes below 38 degrees north latitude. Sometimes, though, a map comes on showing a combination of the entire peninsula, South Korea and North Korea. The two Koreas have officially been at war since 1950, although there has rarely been any shooting since 1953.

There still exist many tensions between the countries today, but there is also great optimism. In 1990, Koreans looked with tremendous interest when the Berlin Wall came down and East and West Germany came together to re-form a nation divided for 45 years. The families on both sides of the North and South Korean border also have been dreaming of such an event, and the breaking of the Berlin Wall re-ignited these dreams. Then in the year 2000, South Korean president Kim Tae-Jung, affectionately known as T. J., met with North Korean president Kim Jong Il. As a result of these talks, a handful of families that had not had contact in over 50 years were finally able to meet, the North and South Korean Olympic teams walked together as one team under a unified flag during the 2000 Olympics in Sydney, and President Kim Tae-Jung won the Nobel Peace Prize.

The teenagers of South Korea have a life different from their parents in that they are now learning to live with the optimism and the reality of these dreams, although their relatives have been waiting for over 50 years.

The situation at the beginning of the twenty-first century is still far from perfect. The border between South and North Korea is still closed, and North Korea remains one of the most isolated and secretive nations on Earth. Furthermore, due to the U.S. military presence in South Korea, U.S. citizens are rarely permitted into North Korea. As a result, while teenagers view the future of their country with optimism, it is a guarded and deliberate optimism. Most people in South Korea, including teenagers, will tell you that it would be wiser to reunify slowly, as recommended by President Kim's Sunshine Policy, rather than quickly, so that the two countries can get used to each other's philosophies and so that the economic strain is not so great. Some South Korean relatives of North Korean families may now travel to North Korea, a new mountain resort run by the Hyundai car company now operates regularly, and there are plans to develop a train between the capitals of the two countries—Seoul and P'yongyang. So, yes, the flag of a unified Korea represents the bringing together of two countries, but many people in Korea see it as a reunion of members of one family.

In spite of its openness to internationalism, South Korea is in some ways just as isolated as it was. South Korea is otherwise surrounded by water, and all access to the rest of the world must be by boat or airplane. South Koreans have not left their country very often and have hosted few visitors from other countries. As a result, the country has been referred to as the "Hermit Kingdom." Furthermore, armies from China, Japan, the Soviet Union, and the United States have struggled for control over this strategic landmark in years past. As a result, South Koreans have long been suspicious of foreigners and their motivations for being in Korea.

Nevertheless, because of increasing internationalism and the communication afforded by the Internet, today's teenagers are more able to comfortably share their heritage with their neighbors, China and Japan, as well as the rest of the world. Young South Koreans are showing the warmth, kindness, and pride of their descendents from Manchuria and Mongolia.

TYPICAL DAY

It is important to understand the age system in South Korea. It starts from the conception of the child. As a result, when babies are born, they are automatically classified as "one year old." They then turn "two years old" on January 1 of the following year. Children born in the last week of December are considered by Korean tradition to be two years old only one week after their birth. As a result, South Korean teenagers are actually a year or two younger than teenagers from other countries.

The focal point of young South Koreans' daily life is school. By law, all children are required to go to school through high school. The principal goal in a South Korean teenager's life is to work toward the university entrance exam. This exam is central to all they do and the decisions they make. Today, over 70 percent of all South Korean teenagers matriculate in universities or junior colleges. (This is in comparison to just 30 percent in 1990.) As a result, South Korean teenagers can spend up to 16 hours a day, Monday through Friday, and Saturday mornings, working on their coursework. Jobs and future income depend almost exclusively on the name of the university one attends. As a result, from as early as children's preschool years, parents and teachers push children toward studying so that they may enter the top universities in Seoul, namely Seoul National University, Yongsei University, and Korea University. Students who attend these universities can expect to be invited to join a top company in a lucrative job that could very well be the only job for their entire lives.

The day often begins with a light breakfast or cleaning of one's room. For teenagers living in boarding schools, dorm room cleaning is part of their grade. While students will be studying or in class for as many as 16 hours a day, there is usually a short morning period and a long evening period when students study on their own. Students often have their own carrels in libraries where they may keep their textbooks and school supplies. These carrels also serve as their study areas during their self-study time. When students are not in their study carrels, they are taking one of seven or eight classes that stretch until around 4 P.M. At that time, though, most students join one of the ongoing teams to clean the school or participate in sporting activities. They may then have dinner at school, whereupon they either return to their study carrel or attend classes elsewhere in their town.

Due to the intensity of studying, teenagers rarely hold part-time jobs. Parents and teachers will not allow it. From the time children start kindergarten, many parents are already pushing them into gaining scholastic advantages. Some parents will spend as much as $600/month to have their five-year-olds study English in private preschools. Even high schools have entrance exams, and students with the best scores therefore attend those schools known throughout the country as "the best schools," regardless of their parents' income or ability to pay. There are several schools throughout the country that claim to be the best because their students have had the best entrance exam scores. A number of these are boarding schools, so the teenagers who attend these schools live away from their families. These boarding schools are also often in rural areas, so the students are less tempted by off-campus activities. As a result, many of the students in the top schools move from Seoul to the countryside to do their high school work. Most teenagers, however, attend public schools.

Parents pay fees to have their children go to school, but the amount of the general fee is essentially the same throughout the country, regardless of the classification of the school. However, it is worth noting that students not attending the top schools are still in full competition with those attending top high schools for those positions at South Korea's best universities. As a result, many students at nonboarding schools will attend cram schools (*haguan*) to gain a competitive edge. Parents actively support their students in the haguan, although it does put an extra financial burden on them to do so.

Teenagers are responsible for their own transportation to and from school. Most students take buses or the subway in larger cities. Teenagers who are running late may take a taxi to school because taxi fare is quite inexpensive. Parents rarely drive their children to school, and teenagers are unable to take their family car because the age for receiving a driver's license in South Korea is 20, the same as the drinking age. Furthermore, students generally enroll in expensive driving schools in order to receive their permits.

Example of a boarding school schedule for a high school student

Time	Activity
6:30 A.M.	Get up, exercise (dancing, aerobics, or jogging), eat breakfast (typically rice, gimchi [see below], soup, yogurt, apples), wash face and hands or take a shower, clean dorm room, take roll call
7:50 A.M.	School officially begins; free study at carrel in student study room, known as a *yaja*
9:20 A.M.	First of four classes, each lasting 60 to 90 minutes
1:10 P.M.	Lunch (typically rice, gimchi, soup, bibimbab, tomatoes, or sometimes spaghetti with a topping of peas and/or fish)
1:45 P.M.	More classes
4:00 P.M.	Students clean the school with their team
4:20 P.M.	One more class
6:00 P.M.	Dinner

7:00 P.M.	Roll call and free study at the yaja (often goes until 11 P.M. with a 30-minute break in the middle, can go until 1:30 A.M. or later during examination periods)

Example of a schedule for a junior high student

Time	Activity
6:00 A.M.	Get up, transportation to school: 15 to 30 minutes by bus, subway, taxi; try to be at school by 7:15; free study until first class
8:40 A.M.	First of six classes for the day
11:30 A.M.	Lunch (school has a cafeteria, but many buy food at nearby restaurants and stores or bring lunch boxes called *toshira*)
12:30 P.M.	Classes resume
5:00 P.M.	Dinner at school
6:00 P.M.	Choice of studying at school at individual study carrels or going to a cram school; study until 10 or 11 P.M., or to well past 1 A.M. during examination preparation time

FAMILY LIFE

In spite of the intensity of daily study, families do manage to show tremendous camaraderie. On weekends, parks and riversides are filled with picnickers. Families make regular outings with their children, often to bookstores, national parks, and beaches. It is not uncommon to see families with sketchbooks, watercolors, and brushes painting in parks on Saturdays. Some families with a lineage of artists have their children study the craft or trade of their family in order to carry on the family line. Such art includes ceramics, masks, knot tying (*maedup*), patchwork cloths, paper design, and calligraphy. The family trades used to include fishing and farming but has given way to South Koreans' thirst for a degree from a top university and a job in industries dealing with semiconductors, communications (related to cellular and mobile phone industries), shipping, and automobiles.

And while many students have their careers decided by their parents, there is seldom disagreement from the children. Most students are proud of the support they get from their parents and say how much they look forward to these weekend outings and other family time.

A boy reading in his bedroom in Kampo, South Korea. Photo © TRIP/TRIP.

There is a hierarchy in South Korean families. As in most families in East Asia, the eldest child is held in highest esteem and holds greater responsibility than the other siblings, especially if the eldest is male. Traditionally, the extended family of aunts and uncles was important, but that has given way to an emphasis on the nuclear family.

South Korea is a very crowded country. As a result, most families live in apartments. Often the apartments are in high-rise buildings provided by major businesses in the country. Even in the countryside, it is common to see a 10-story high rise next to a rice field. As a result, families and teens carry out family activities and meet friends outside of the home. Rarely are guests invited over. There simply is not enough room. In fact, in some houses, living rooms and bedrooms are often the same room, with the mattress and pillows kept in closets, only taken out for sleeping. Nevertheless, if you are invited over, you can expect to take your shoes off at the front door, sleep on a heated floor (*ondol*), and serve yourself from a central set of plates and bowls, from which everyone chooses what to eat.

TRADITIONAL AND NONTRADITIONAL FOOD DISHES

The heart of any South Korean meal is *gimchi*—pickled cabbage with red peppers and red bean paste. Most South Koreans are addicted to it and include it in every meal. Many South Korean dishes are spicy because they contain red pepper, garlic, and onions. Other components of regular South Korean meals are rice, soup, soybeans, seaweed, and other side dishes. Everything is served at the same time. Meat is also integral to lunch and dinner. Common examples include *galbi*—a set of barbecued short ribs brazed in soy sauce, honey, ginger, and garlic; *bulgogi*—grilled beef marinated in mixture of bean paste, grated pear, soy sauce, sesame oil, cooking wine, and sugar; and fish or squid—in raw, cooked, or dried forms. The typical meal has one big plate, a bowl for soup, and several little side dishes. The side dishes usually entail vegetables of some sort, particularly seaweed, soybeans, cucumbers, eggplant, bean sprouts, tomatoes, and of course gimchi. For special plates, there is also usually a stack of lettuce and persimmon leaves. Here, people often use the leaf the same way one would use a slice of bread. They take the leaf in their hand; then they take metal chopsticks and place the meat in the center of the leaf, add a condiment or two, usually raw garlic and hot red pepper sauce, and fold the leaf around the meat and condiments. They then pop the entire concoction in their mouth. Making noise while doing so signals that the food is good. Noodles, served both hot and cold, are also popular. Slurping these noodles and letting them hang from the chopsticks is also considered good manners. *Bibimbap* is the combination of stewed vegetables and rice with red pepper sauce. Found almost anywhere, it is often accompanied by a raw or fried egg. All the ingredients of *bibimbap* are served in a large bowl, and it is considered good manners to stir all the ingredients for a long time before digging in. Finally, in addition to cold noodles, another summertime treat is *boshingtang*, also known as dog soup.

Cafeterias at South Korean schools often serve both lunch and dinner. A typical school lunch consists of rice, gimchi, soup, tomatoes, spaghetti, peas, and fish. Some teenagers will bring their own lunch in the form of a special box, known as a *toshira*. Parents often prepare toshira so that their children can experience some variety in their meals.

South Korean teens also enjoy fast food. In fact, some parents complain that South Korean youngsters' penchant for hamburgers and pizza is making their children fat. However, the most popular hamburgers and pizza have a South Korean twist to them. Hamburgers often have beef stirfry (bulgogi) grilled beef, shrimp, or squid as the main meat. Sometimes, the bread is replaced by two "buns" made of compacted and sculpted sticky rice. Popular pizza toppings include bulgogi, squid, potatoes, peas, gimchi, and corn. Furthermore, pizzas in South Korea typically have only just a touch of tomato sauce. Japanese fast foods have also become more popular.

It is now easy to find restaurants that serve chicken, fish, and pork cutlets, made in the Japanese style, complete with miso (fermented soy) soup and pickled daikon radish.

South Koreans rarely eat dessert. Nevertheless, South Korean junk food has gained tremendous popularity throughout Asia and Australia, and has become an integral part of South Korean desserts. Ice cream, doughnuts, and red bean parfait with crushed ice, fruit cocktail, milk, and ice cream (*patbingsu*) are common sweets eaten as snacks.

SCHOOLING

Junior high school students may take up to 14 or 15 subjects in a single school year, while senior high students may take as many as 18, though never all in one day. Each subject has at least one standardized exam within the school year, and often there are as many as four, often falling in May, July, October, and November. Additionally, most teachers will give mock tests once or twice each month to help students prepare for the major exams. Subjects include South Korean literature, mathematics, English, Mandarin Chinese, music, art, chemistry, physical education, earth science and biology, geography, and ethics.

Students must select their university or college major in their second year of high school. The kind of university they choose, and in effect the kind of university entrance exam they take, will be determined by this important decision. As a result, it is not uncommon for high schoolers to have clear opinions regarding what they want to be when they grow up. The most popular profession mentioned by teenagers is teaching. Many other students aspire to be journalists, diplomats, engineers, architects, designers, doctors, or flight attendants. Many parents will decide the career choices for their children, often asking their children to continue family businesses, although this practice has diminished slightly in recent years.

Traditionally, schools have been divided by gender, although this changed dramatically in the 1990s. Now there are more coed schools. Often there are as many as 50 students in a single homeroom class. In addition to teaching a particular subject, homeroom teachers also serve as guidance counselors for the students in the homeroom. This is particularly important for teenagers new to boarding schools, who are spending their first days away from their families and are living with strangers in narrow dormitory rooms for the first time.

The classroom is often set up with individual desks, aligned in rows and columns in front of a blackboard or whiteboard. The teacher usually stands behind a podium and lectures. Students are not encouraged to ask questions too often, which might appear to mean they do not know the answer.

For each subject, a specific textbook is required. Textbooks are not provided by the schools, so families must buy books for their children. As a result, one may find many bookstores throughout the country. In some bookstores, entire floors are devoted to the selling of textbooks, not only for teenagers' regular schooling but also for their participation in the *haguan*. The bookstores are extremely popular. They are always full of people, and many parents will take their children on regular outings to bookstores.

The school year starts at the beginning of March and goes through mid- to late July. Students then have 40 days of vacation. Students return in September for a second term and go until mid- to late February. There is, however, a brief winter vacation for Christmas and New Year's. After the spring vacation, which usually lasts no more than 10 days, students move to the next grade.

SOCIAL LIFE

In spite of the intense studying, South Korean teenagers do find time to have fun. Often they meet in school at club meetings. Usually these gatherings occur on campus on Friday afternoons, and many schools will sponsor as many as 20 clubs (e.g., drama, radio broadcasting, filmmaking, foreign languages, newspapers, astronomy, cartoon animation).

Off campus, many teenagers jokingly list sleeping as their favorite hobby, although listening to music, swimming, soccer, baseball, tennis, and South Korean billiards are popular as well. As for the best places to meet, many teenagers will meet at fast food restaurants, libraries, karaoke parlors (*noreibang*), and computer game rooms (*PC bang*). The average South Korean teenager spends 17 hours each week in front of a computer. Recently, South Korean-made movies such as *Jingu* have gained international notoriety, so theaters have become more popular.

Teenagers do date one another, though to do so is the exception rather than the rule. In some schools, two teenagers who are going out regularly are labeled a "campus couple." However, discussing dating is not something teens in South Korea regularly do. In fact, to do so is a little tricky. Many teenagers will tell adults that they are too busy to be interested in dating. Some people suggest that silence regarding the discussion of love and dating is founded in the South Korean proverb, "Seven-year-old boys and girls don't sit together in the same room" (*Nam yeo chisae bu tungseop*). Hence, there may be pressure to not date or at least keep quiet about it.

Teenagers expect to get married, but most South Koreans do not get married until they are well out of college or university. Women try to marry before they are 26. Men marry later because they are required to spend 26 months in the military. Still, there is generally significant pressure to get married. Traditional South Korean weddings and church weddings are common, but there are also a large number of "wedding plazas"—large buildings built in the shape of castles where couples may have ceremonies involving both Western and South Korean imagery and have postwedding parties. It is also common to see newlywed couples taking wedding photographs in the city parks on Sunday afternoons. Pre-arranged weddings are certainly part of South Korean history, but that practice has diminished significantly in recent years.

Teenagers, and most South Koreans in general, feel very uncomfortable regarding sexual topics. In fact, it is practically a forbidden subject between parents and their children. As a result, the Ministry of Education has given opportunities for nurses, teachers, and counselors to give sex education in the schools. Many students are directed to additional information resources, principally the Internet and magazines, thereby keeping the topics quiet and personal. Nevertheless, teenage pregnancies are on the rise in South Korea, and adoptions of South Korean children by foreigners from other countries have become more and more common.

While drug and alcohol abuse is rarely reported, or even considered a major social problem, a type of gang violence known as *wang-ta* has received recent attention and given some cause for concern. In *wang-ta*, groups of students find physically weak or passive students to beat up. South Korean teenagers have adopted the practice from Japanese mafia groups' "easy man" activity, which is similar.

However, *wang-ta* is the extreme and certainly not the norm. South Korea enjoys tremendously low crime, and the streets are safe to walk at any time of day. Nevertheless, teenagers do find ways to get into trouble. The most popular way for boys is to smoke. It is not uncommon to see the computer game room *PC bangs* filled with young boys smoking. Furthermore, many schools have smoking rooms for their male teachers. Apart from smoking, students are often reprimanded for coming to class late, having hair that is too long, not eating the food they take at lunch and dinner cafeterias, fighting, breaking windows, or, the worst one, talking back to the teacher. The principal means of punishment is to have students do extra cleaning at the school. Suspensions and expulsions are very rare. Corporal punishment used to be a major form of discipline in South Korea, but it has been recently outlawed; teachers can be put in jail for hitting a student.

CLOTHES

South Korean teenagers wear Western-style clothes. In fact, buying clothes is one of the principal evening pastimes for teenagers, when they are not studying. As a result, in almost any town, central business districts are dedicated to clothing shops. Shopping malls and department stores are also popular. One thing noticeable about South Korean teens is that they strictly follow a color scheme, wearing mainly navy blue, olive, rust, silver blue, mustard yellow, and black. Very few teens, or people of any age for that matter, wear other colors. However, this is not to say that the clothes are boring. Combinations of these colors may exist in the form of pinstripes and plaid. Most teens wear comfortable, slightly loose-fitting clothes, including skirts, shirts, and slacks. Most teens wear black slip-on shoes or sandals. Baseball caps, some worn backward, are common. Shorts, earrings (even on boys), and sunglasses are just becoming popular, though primarily in Seoul.

Brighter colors are reserved for traditional events such as weddings and people representing Korea as a country. In these cases, the same colors as found on temples may be found in South Korean formal dresses—known as *hanbok*—and business uniforms, such as those for flight attendants. (See palette of colors for traditional South Korean events below.)

The same colors, especially gray, navy blue, white, black, and olive green, are often integral parts of student uniforms. Though many schools are discontinuing the use of school uniforms, they are still the rule rather than the exception. Students are generally required to wear uniforms every day and are usually not permitted earrings or other piercings, tinted hair, tattoos, or makeup, although these features are certainly gaining popularity among college-age students. Students are also required to wear a photo ID badge. (This contrasts with North Korean teenagers, who must wear a badge with a picture of President Kim Jong Il.) They also generally wear sandals with white socks as part of their uniform.

RECREATION

Sports also play a major role in South Korean teenage life. There are professional leagues for soccer, baseball, and basketball, and all are popular. Korea was named joint host with Japan for the 2002 World Cup Soccer Championships, for which 10 soccer stadiums and a new international airport were built.

Many teens have been inspired by the success of South Koreans in the Olympics. In 1988, Seoul hosted the Summer Olympics, and South Korean athletes performed well. Sadly, though, athletes from North Korea were not permitted to participate in the Seoul games due to a boycott by its government. Nevertheless, team sports such as handball and hockey and individual sports such as speed skating and cycling have become popular because of the success of South Koreans in these events. School gyms often provide handball goals, almost every school has a soccer field, and many schools have roller-blading clubs. Many schools now also have rooms where students may play South Korean billiards, a game similar to pool known as *danggu* that was outlawed to teenagers until the early 1990s. Skiing is also popular, because the winter months are quite cold and yield tremendous amounts of snow.

Most notable has been the increase in popularity of the marathon. The first South Korean marathon hero was Sohn Kee-jung, who won a gold medal at the 1936 Olympics in Berlin when he ran under the Japanese flag for political reasons (Korea was under Japanese rule at the time). Two more marathon heroes have emerged since, though. In 1992, Hwang Young-jo became the second South Korean to win the gold medal, in the 1992 Olympics in Barcelona, and I Bong-Ju won the 2001 Boston Marathon. As a result, it is now quite common to see people, including teenagers, jogging and running for daily exercise, and competitive marathons are being developed throughout the country, even one called the "Nude Marathon."

South Koreans also admire their fellow South Koreans who have excelled at sports in foreign countries. Women look up to Bak Se Ri, who has had tremendous success in the United States on the Ladies Professional Golf Tour. Bak Chan-Ho is a pitcher for the Los Angeles Dodgers. As a result, both TV and radio stations present Dodgers games whenever he is pitching.

ENTERTAINMENT

As noted earlier, South Korean teenagers jokingly list sleep as their favorite pastime. However, they also list an abundance of activities that occupy their spare time, among them entertainment. South Korean teens list music and sports as their favorite forms of entertainment.

When South Korean teens are not studying, they are often listening to music. There are a number of teenage boy bands and girl bands that have gained popularity recently, and their photographs are often for sale in bookstores. Teen magazines are also popular. However, when asked about their favorite music, most South Korean teens will answer in terms of style rather than artist. Current forms of rock, pop, and even traditional Korean music are popular with teens.

Korean hip-hop, a very popular style, often includes a melodic introduction with a rap in South Korean in the middle. This style is note-

worthy in that it is the base for modern South Korean dancing. On weekend evenings, young people often congregate outside large department
stores where a stage is set up. Here, local school groups can perform a
dance routine they have been practicing before a large audience and with
bright colorful lights behind them. Some stages are so popular that entire
street blocks are closed to traffic because so many people have gathered to
watch the hip-hop dancing.

The importance of English as an international language and the preva-
lence of Western record store chains have helped Western music maintain popularity, but MTV Asia provides time slots devoted to Korean
music each day. As a result, Korean music has become more popular
throughout Asia. Likewise, music from other Asian countries also has
gained tremendous popularity in South Korea. In this respect, karaoke
rooms (noreibang) are extremely popular with teenagers. Karaoke origi-
nates from the Japanese invention of "empty orchestra," in which people
publicly sing popular songs in bars or special karaoke rooms. Additionally,
almost every Chinese video has the lyrics printed across the bottom of the
screen so that people may sing along with the song. As a result, these traditions have passed into South Korean society, and teenagers are regular
customers at noreibang. In fact, noreibang have become so popular that
some karaoke buildings are several stories tall.

RELIGIOUS PRACTICES AND CULTURAL CEREMONIES

Surveys of teenagers show that they comfortably exist amid a variety of
religions. However, unlike some of South Korea's neighbors, South Koreans, teenagers included, practice whatever religion they follow very seriously. While a third of teenagers may mention that they do not follow a
particular religion, even these students usually have a sense of interest in
and respect for those who do practice.

As for Christianity and Buddhism, the intense dedication with which
South Koreans practice these may be in part due to their observation that
religion is not permitted in North Korea. As a result, South Korea is the
second most Christian nation in Asia, following the Philippines.

The emphasis on religion in South Korea is easily observed by the
plethora of churches and temples in the nation. Large Christian churches
may be found in any city or town. At night, one may look into a skyline
and see numerous neon crosses lighting the sky in a single vista. Additionally, it is not unusual to see teenagers wearing T-shirts that say "Jesus"
or make reference to a church outing. Buddhist temples are also abundant. Most neighborhoods have at least one small temple, and ancient

temples dating as far back as the ninth century may be found in many pre-
fectural and national parks.

As with clothing, Buddhist temples follow a specific palette. The bark-
color base of the temple includes images of dragons, tigers, and Buddhist
symbols, drawn in bright purple, blue, green, orange, and yellow. Often
these decorations are separated by black and white outlines. Finally, most
temples add rose pink, scarlet, and black paintings of decorative flowers,
most notably the national flower of South Korea, known as the Rose of
Sharon (*mugunghwa*). (The mugunghwa is so revered that it is also the
name of one of South Korea's national railway lines.) All these colors are
also often displayed in formal hanbok and in uniforms in which the display of South Korean culture is considered important.

Other religions also thrive in South Korea. A form of traditional South
Korean shamanism is practiced, often for purposes of solace and meditation. Confucianism used to be popular, mostly due to its views toward
ethics and respectful politics. However, it has lost popularity recently as it
has become viewed by young people as overly patriarchal and conservative. Islam and Judaism are growing in popularity as foreigners with those
religions have immigrated to the country. Nevertheless, the tradition of
Asia philosophies is still abundantly apparent, as is evidenced in the South
Korean flag. The flag for South Korea, known as *ttagukki*, has its roots in
Eastern philosophy and religion. The circle indicates balance and harmony, known as *yin* and *yang*. The circle is cut into two parts: the red being
the positive *yang*, and the blue the negative *yin*. Surrounding the circle are
four different trigrams, representing the four elements of the universe:
heaven, earth, fire, and water. No matter what religion one practices in
South Korea, these elements are at the forefront of religious thought.

Holidays are important in South Korea. Many are rooted in customs
related to traditional South Korean religion and to farming, but new holidays now honor milestones in South Korean history. There are two kinds:
those set to the solar calendar, such as New Year's Day, Memorial Day (June
6), Constitution Day (July 17), and Christmas; and those set to the lunar
calendar, such as Lunar New Year (the first day of the first moon), Buddha's
Birthday (eighth day of the fourth moon), and Moon Festival Day, known
as *Chuseok* (15th day of the eighth moon), when teenagers can pay homage
to their ancestors. During Chuseok, teenagers celebrate their own version of
Thanksgiving, a day full of food consisting of wine, cakes, jujube berries,
chestnuts, pears, and persimmons; however, many of these foods are then
taken to their family shrines and are offered to their ancestors. Teenagers
also often participate in Children's Day—May 5—by spending the day at

the zoo, amusement park, department store, or ball game with their families. Furthermore, teenagers in South Korea celebrate Valentine's Day in various stages throughout the year: Only girls give chocolate gifts on Valentine's Day (February 14), and only to boys. On March 14, roles are reversed when boys give white cookies to the girls who gave them chocolate on February 14. South Korean teenagers also play with the 14th day of each month throughout the year. May 14 is Rose Day when couples give each other roses, and November 11 is Pocky Day, when couples can give each other chocolate-covered pretzel sticks, called Pocky. The day was moved to the 11th from the 14th because the shape of five pretzel sticks looks like II/II.

CONCLUSION

Today's South Korean teenagers may be the happiest and most prosperous in South Korean history. One of the most isolated peoples on Earth, they are also growing up in an industrialized information center for the world. They aspire to high educational standards, study like crazy, and value both sleep and intense play during their rare spare time. They confront exams and pressures to enter top educational institutions, but they are supported emotionally and financially by their teachers and their parents. They feel they will see a unified Korea within their lifetime, but they are not in a hurry to achieve it, because they want it to be done correctly, not quickly. They are perhaps the first generation ever to demonstrate pride for their roots and comfortably coexist with people traditionally known as their invaders and enemies. They sing rock music and dance at department stores. They love their traditional foods, but they sculpt them in the forms of hamburgers and pizza. They live in close quarters but have learned to deal with responsibility and live with a large number of people. They exude pride for their culture but yearn to express it outside the limiting confines of their geography.

ACKNOWLEDGMENTS

I wish to thank the following people for their kindness, consideration, support, and help in putting together this chapter: Mi-ae Lee, the University of Texas at Austin; Jodi Nelms, the University of Florida, Gainesville; Kirsten Reitan, Korea Teachers of English to Speakers of Other Languages (KoTESOL), Kyung Hee University, Suwon, Korea; Lee Yonghoon, Kyangju English Language School, Kumi, Korea; Kang Byong-hyo, Kyangju English Language School, Kumi, Korea; SangKyu Park, Oracle, Seoul, Korea.

RESOURCE GUIDE

Nonfiction

Adams, E. B. (1983). *Korea guide: A glimpse of Korea's cultural legacy*. Seoul: Seoul International Tourist Publishing Company.

Clark, D. N. (2000). *Culture and customs of Korea*. Westport, CT: Greenwood Press.

Halliday, J., and Cumings, B. (1988). *Korea: The unknown war*. New York: Pantheon Books.

National Statistical Office Republic of Korea. (2000). *Statistical handbook of Korea, 2000*. Daejon: National Statistical Office.

Nelson, L. C. (2000). *Measured excess: Status, gender, and consumer nationalism in South Korea*. New York: Columbia University Press.

Storey, R., and English, A. (2001). *Korea*. Melbourne, Australia: Lonely Planet Publications.

Fiction

Balgassi, H. (1996). *Peacebound trains*. New York: Clarion.

Choi, S. N. (1997). *Yunmi and Halmoni's trip*. Boston: Houghton-Mifflin.

Lee, M. G. (1996). *Necessary roughness*. New York: HarperCollins.

Lee, M. G. (1999). *F is for Fabuloso*. New York: Avon.

Long long time ago: Korean folk tales. (1997). Elizabeth, NJ: Hollym.

Na, A. (2001). *A step from heaven*. Asheville, NC: Front Street.

Pak, S. (1999). *Dear Juno*. Viking.

Park, L. S. (1999). *Seesaw girl*. New York: Clarion.

Park, L. S. (2001). *A single shard*. New York: Clarion.

Films

Dae-seung, K. (Director). (2001). *Bungee jumping of their own* [Motion picture]. CineLine.

Hae-sung, S. (Director). (2001). *Failan* [Motion picture]. CineLine.

Im Sang-soo, I. (Director). (2001). *Tears* [Motion picture]. CineLine.

Kim Sang-jin, K. (Director). (2001). *Kick the moon* [Motion picture]. Cinema Service.

Kyung-taek, K. (Director). (2001). *Jingu* [Motion picture]. CineLine.

Web Sites

Facts and Figures

http://205.124.47.10/Curriculum/korea/index.htm.

http://www.cia.gov/cia/publications/factbook/geos/ks.html
http://www.lonelyplanet.com/destinations/north_east_asia/south_korea/
http://www.marimari.com/content/index.html
http://www.photius.com/wfb2000/countries/korea_south/korea_south_
     geography.html

General Information

Life in Korea: http://www.lifeinkorea.com
Yellow Pages: www.yellowpages.co.kr

Olympics

http://history1900s.about.com/homework/history1900s/library/weekly/aa081000y.
     htm
http://violet.berkeley.edu/~korea/jhmenu9.html

Fashion

http://www.teenwire.com/views/articles/wv_19991008p018.asp

History

http://socrates.berkeley.edu/~korea/history.html

Food

http://asiarecipe.com/kordesserts.html
http://www.foodtv.com/cuisine/korearecipes/0,3200,,00.html
http://www.gergo.com/pauline/korea/recipes.htm
http://www.recipehound.com/Recipes/korea.html

Entertainment

Movies
http://South Koreanfilm.org/
http://members.aol.com/theSensual/movie_e.htm
http://www.cinemakorea.com/

Books
http://korea50.army.mil

Culture, Language, Art, Religion
http://www.geocities.com/Paris/Chateau/5313/frame.htm
http://www.korealore.com

More Information

U.S. Embassy of South Korea: http://emb.dsdn.net/english/frame.htm

Travel

Asiana Airlines: http://flyasiana.com/South Korean/index.htm
Korean Airlines: http://www.South Koreanair.com/index.asp?langid = EN
Youth hostels: http://www.kyha.kr.or

Foreign Chambers of Commerce

http://www.amchamkorea.org
http://www.eucck.org

News Agencies

http://www.koreaherald.co.kr
http://www.koreatimes.co.kr

Pen Pal/Chat

Gyeongbuk Foreign Language High School
1716–24 Daemyeong-dong
Nam-gu, Daegu 705–031, Republic of Korea

Geochang High School
387 Choong-ang Ri
Geochang, Gyungnam, Republic of Korea

Chapter 13

TAIWAN

Chun-Chin Yi and Chyi-In Wu

INTRODUCTION

Taiwan is an island country in East Asia—the largest body of land
between Japan and the Philippines. Shaped like a yam, the island is 247
miles long and 90 miles at its widest point and has a total area of nearly
14,063 square miles. The Taiwan Strait separates Taiwan from Mainland
China.

The most important feature of Taiwan's topography is the central range
of high mountains running from the northeast corner to the southern tip
of the island. Taiwan lies in the path of severe tropical cyclones known in
East Asia as typhoons. An average of three to four typhoons hit Taiwan
every year, usually in July through September. The mean monthly temperature in the lowlands is about 60°F in the winter and ranges between 77°F
and 86°F for the rest of the year. The relative humidity averages about 80
percent. Another significant natural hazard for Taiwan is earthquakes. The
last large earthquake occurred on September 21, 1999. The powerful and
devastating earthquake registered a magnitude of 7.3 on the Richter scale.
In this massive "921 earthquake," 2,415 people died and 11,305 were
injured; 29 are still unaccounted for. More than 5,004 people were rescued
from collapsed buildings, and tens of thousands were left homeless.

The population density of Taiwan stands at 1,567 persons per square
mile, making it the second highest in the world behind Bangladesh.
Taipei, which covers 107 square miles, is Taiwan's most crowded urban
area, with 25,000 persons per square mile. Heavily populated urban areas
have grown outside the official limits of major cities, forming large metro-
politan areas that are now home to 68.37 percent of Taiwan's total popu-

lation. On the other hand, the birth rate has steadily reduced due to increased education, delayed marriages, and comparatively fewer potential mothers between the ages of 20 and 34. Since 1984, the population replacement rate has remained below 1, dropping to 0.7 in 1999.

Interestingly enough, among the 284,073 births registered in Taiwan in 1999, there were 109.47 boys for every 100 girls. Since the global ratio of males to females at birth is about 105:100, the ratio in Taiwan reflects the traditional preference among Asian parents for boys over girls. This preference is reflected in practices that have resulted in an imbalance between numbers of boys and girls. Many young Taiwanese newlyweds plan to have only one child because of economic concerns as well as lifestyle preference. In the early 1960s, 72 percent of Taiwanese parents favored two children, but the percentage had decreased to 24 percent by 1991. However, the dominant cultural preference for male descendants has resulted in parents' desire to have one boy rather than one girl.

History

Large tribes of indigenous peoples as well as migrants, mostly Han people, from Mainland China, had been residents in Taiwan for several centuries when Europeans first visited the island in 1590. Portuguese navigators were the first visitors. Struck by the beauty of Taiwan's green mountains rising steeply out of the blue-green waters of the Pacific, they named the island Ilha Formosa, or "beautiful island," the name Taiwan was known by in the West for centuries. The next groups of Europeans arriving in Taiwan were the Spanish and the Dutch. In 1622, Taiwan became an important trading and shipment center for goods from a number of areas, such as Japan, China, Indonesia, and Holland. In addition to trading, Dutch missionaries were also active in converting the Taiwanese to Christianity. Protestant missionaries established schools where religion and the Dutch language were taught. By 1650, the Dutch had converted approximately 5,900 of the island's inhabitants to Christianity.

In 1895, Japan seized Taiwan. Unlike the Dutch, who colonized Taiwan in the seventeenth century mainly for immediate commercial gains, the Japanese aimed at establishing effective political control over the island at the start of the twentieth century. Thus, the Japanese policeman rather than the missionary became the most important tool in the exercise of colonial goals. During its 50-year rule of Taiwan from 1895 to 1945, Japan developed programs designed to supply the Japanese empire with agricultural products, created demand for Japanese industrial products, and provided living space for emigrants from an increasingly overpopulated home country. In short, Japan intended to build an industrial homeland and an agricultural Taiwan. Despite the relative success in transforming Taiwan into a society that, economically, was rather modern in comparison with its neighbors, resistance against alien rule never ceased on the island. Liberation was accomplished vis-à-vis a total defeat of Japan in 1945.

In the post-1949 era, Taiwan has experienced well-known economic success, with consequent significant rise in income and living standards. At the same time, steady social transformation has followed the lifting of martial law in 1987. The legalization of labor strikes and street demonstrations, and the formation of new political parties, gave rise to the enhancement of freedom and power. Lifted restrictions on newspapers and publishing have resulted in an explosion of media growth as well as in a broadened perspective for an increasingly sophisticated audience.

Economy

Over the last half-century, Taiwan has completed the transformation from an agriculture society into a service-based modern economy. Back in the 1950s, agriculture had a higher share in the gross product than industry did (32% vs. 21%). But the importance of agriculture declined rapidly and became almost nil by 1999 (2.5%). The industry sector growth first steadily elevated to almost half of the national gross product in the 1980s (45%–47%), then slowly decreased to approximately one-third of the product. The service industry, on the other hand, has experienced continuous growth, from 46 percent in 1951 to 64 percent in 1999, and has become the major industry in Taiwan.

With the impressive economic progress, the annual per capita income has thus grown from less than U.S.$500 before the 1970s to more than U.S.$13,000 since the mid-1990s. It is now the third highest in Asia.

Taiwan's ability to thrive and sustain a high level of economic growth can be attributed to various effective export-oriented policies adopted by the government since the 1960s. Since the early 1990s, political democratization and economic liberalization have brought about a more prosperous Taiwan. As a result, the spending power of both the government and the private sector has increased immensely.

Despite the generally lackluster performance of the domestic economy in recent years, Taiwan's hardware information technology industry still enjoys significant growth. Taiwan is now the world's third largest producer, next to the United States and Japan. As to the production of notebook computers, monitors, motherboards, and scanners, Taiwan ranks first, supplying over half of the world's market. With the encouraging performance of Taiwan's high-tech industries in recent decades, Taiwan has truly become what many had wished for: a "green silicon island" in Asia.

Religion

Religion in Taiwan takes many forms. First, almost all Taiwanese, even those without formal religious belief, engage in religious practices stemming from one or a combination of traditional Chinese folk religions. It is very common for homes and shops to furnish lighted shrines with incense burning to honor a deity, hero, or ancestor. Most families perform filial duties of ancestral worship. At important occasions, such as getting married or taking an entrance examination, a visit to the temple is expected to bring luck or to solicit divine assistance. Even taxi drivers will put charms, amulets, statuettes, or religious slogans inside the car for protection against accidents and harm.

Another important characteristic of the Taiwanese religion is its nonexclusive nature. Most religions currently practiced in Taiwan are for the most part combinations of several religions. Taoism, for example, is rooted in traditional Chinese philosophy but has absorbed many aspects of non-Chinese dogmas. Unlike Muslims, Jews, and Christians, whose religions require believers to worship the religion's own God, most Chinese seldom felt it necessary to exclude other faiths from their personal or collective religious life. For instance, the popular Taiwan folk deity Matsu, Goddess of the Sea, and Kuanyin, the Buddhist Goddess of Mercy, are often worshiped together in the same temple. The Chinese religion can accommodate seemingly contradictory beliefs.

The rituals of many polytheists and nonrevelatory religions in Taiwan—such as burning incense sticks and chanting—have more or less merged with each other.

The latest figures, released in 1999, indicate that about 10.8 million people in Taiwan (almost half of the population) are religious believers, and about 49,000 temples and churches are spread around the island.

Religious groups have traditionally been the backbone of community services in Taiwan. Organizations affiliated with specific religions establish or operate hospitals, schools, retirement homes, as well as other social welfare agencies such as homes for people with mental retardation or rehabilitation centers. In addition to sharing a common concern for the poor and disaster victims, religious groups in Taiwan have also taken the lead in organizing cultural and recreational activities. Whereas the Protestant Church has focused on promoting youth activities, Taoist organizations have channeled much of their efforts into preserving and staging traditional Chinese dramas, and Buddhist groups have offered a wide range of self-improvement seminars.

Juvenile Services

As of December 1999, Taiwan's population aged 12 to 17 totaled 2.08 million. Most Taiwanese adolescents finish the nine-year compulsory education by age 15. After graduation, these young people have to face difficult circumstances. While most take the competitive examinations for senior high school or senior vocational school (if failed, enrolling in cram school to prepare for the exams the following year is an option), a minority of them need to look for employment due to their family's economic needs. Since drafted military service starts at age 18 for young men not at school, the job search is thus considered a temporary career route that lasts almost three years. With increased pressure on youths, general social provisions, such as counseling and psychiatric services, are readily available at community health centers and psychiatric health clinics at major hospitals. However, the most noticeable accomplishment in this respect is the hotline service, especially the so-called Teacher Chang, which was set up by the China Youth Corps in 1969. A free counseling service that recruits volunteers from all walks of life to counsel youths over the phone on such issues as dating, sex, drugs, and pressure in achieving academic success, Teacher Chang has gained trust and respect.

Teenage Prostitution

In Taiwan, any person who has sexual intercourse with an individual aged 14 or under is guilty of statutory rape and is subject to a mandatory sentence of at least five years in prison. A person who has sex with an adolescent aged 15 or 16 is also guilty of rape and must be sentenced to one to seven years in jail. Halfway houses for rescued adolescent prostitutes provide shelter, food, clothing, medical care, and counseling, but they are mostly in the Taipei area. Private foundations, such as the Good Shepherd Sisters and the Garden of Hope Foundation, not only operate several halfway houses for teens they help rescue but also are the main contributors to the legalization that led to the prosecution of those guilty of rape.

Social Strife

At the beginning of the twenty-first century, Taiwan continues to face challenges from within as well as from outside of the island. While political corruption and money politics remain the two most serious problems in Taiwan, major national efforts have been put into the process of reconstruction after the disastrous 1999 earthquake. For perhaps the first time in Taiwan's history, the general public developed a strong sense of sympathy toward others and their suffering. Reports on youth and children from the damaged areas have also garnered considerable attention, and various support groups pour in resources to help the personal and social rehabilitation of these youngsters and their families.

Another persistent threat that Taiwan faces is its complex relations with Mainland China. Although economic, social, and cultural interactions continue to grow, the cross-strait political relationship remains quite tense. In recent years, Taiwan has invested over U.S.$16.8 billion in Mainland China, with direct and indirect employment opportunities for millions, yet the Chinese communist government refuses to renounce the use of force against Taiwan. The main argument is about nationalism: whether Taiwan should be a province of China or an independent nation. While Mainland China insists on the former, a substantial proportion of Taiwanese favor separation—either maintaining the separated status or establishing an independent nation. This discord with Mainland China greatly affects the people of Taiwan. Many of them feel unnamed stress, fear, and uncertainty about their own future because of the Chinese communists' threat of force. Needless to say, young people experience this turmoil as well.

TYPICAL DAY

Education has long been cherished above all else in the Chinese culture. Parents value education and are expected to gather all family resources to help youngsters attain the highest education possible. A few relevant statistics will reveal the present educational development in Taiwan: the total enrollment rate of the population ages 6 to 21 was 84.83 percent in 1999 (i.e., more than one-fifth of the total population was attending an educational institution of some type). In 1999, there were 7,915 registered schools, with an average of 35.91 students per class and a student-teacher ratio of 19.96:1. Compulsory education was extended to nine years starting in 1968. As a result, the number of high school students increased from around 34,000 in the 1950s to more than 400,000 in the 1990s. The national illiteracy rate has dropped to its current 5.08 percent. Literacy is a major focus of the Ministry of Education.

Over the last decade, higher education has been the government's priority. The number of colleges and universities has increased, as has the number of people who receive a higher education. This, of course, increases Taiwan's human capital. On the other hand, it means that young people are now expected to complete higher education. Taiwanese teenagers know that to thrive in the future they must study hard today.

Therefore, a typical day for a teenager in Taiwan involves going to school, going to a cram school, and then going home and continuing to study. Due to the normative values of education and the consequent keen competition for higher education, the priority for almost every teenage student (grades 7–12) in Taiwan is to prepare for the high school and college entrance examinations. Each teenager has to pass these highly competitive entrance examinations to attend a high school or a college. Since these exams are held in the hottest months of June and July and in non-air-conditioned classrooms, it is common to see a nervous student surrounded by anxious parents and friends holding cold drinks and fans during breaks in the exam.

A typical day for a ninth grader before exam time would start by waking up at 6 A.M. or even earlier depending upon the distance between home and school as well as traffic. Most teenage students in urban Taiwan take public buses to get to school, while their rural counterparts usually ride bikes to school. In the worst situation, a teenage student who lives in the suburb but attends schools in downtown Taipei may spend two hours in traffic in the morning in order to be present when school starts—usually 7:30 A.M. It is estimated that only about one-fourth of teenagers are able to have their breakfast at home before heading for school. More than half of them have to buy and eat their breakfast on the way to school or in their classrooms. After arriving, there may be morning tests of various classes arranged by the headmaster, followed by morning rituals, including singing the national song and saluting the national flag, or sweeping and cleaning the campus. For those absentees without reasonable excuses, oral warnings or more severe punishments may be given.

The morning tests are rigorous. To push for higher scores for the exams to come, the headmaster may set different standards for each student. Teenagers must meet the score criteria and do well enough to avoid further punishment, such as being publicly scolded or, on some occasions, even being physically battered by the teacher.

There are seven 50-minute class periods in a typical school day and a 10-minute break between class periods. Morning classes go from 8 A.M. until noon. After lunch time, which lasts from 50 minutes to 1 hour, another three classes last until 4 or 4:30 P.M. The major curricula for teenage students in Taiwan are Chinese, English, mathematics, social studies, physics, chemistry, and biology. According to survey reports,

Mathematics is Taiwanese teenagers' least favorite subject. But in prestigious high schools, students usually take advanced math courses that in the United States would be available only in college. More tests and more homework are assigned during each course. In sum, a typical school day for a teenage student in Taiwan is highly strained and stressed.

After school is dismissed, most ninth graders do not go home directly. Rather, there are several after-class activities waiting for them. The most common requirement for students to attend is "the study-after class." Ninth graders and twelfth graders are usually asked to stay in their own classrooms for more studying. In general, this after-class period lasts for about one hour at the beginning of the fall semester but may last until 9 P.M. in the spring as the entrance examination approaches. Teachers may use this period to give tests or to strengthen the weak part of the main curricula. After the study-after class finally ends, can these students go home and have dinner? Unfortunately, most of them have scheduled cram school until 9 P.M. or 10 P.M. An average dinner is thus fast food eaten in a hurry on their way to the cram school. According to adolescent survey research, more than 60 percent of teenage students in contemporary Taiwan are involved in some kind of cram schools. Teenagers attend these cram schools to strengthen their skills for the examination as well as to learn more information that is not covered in the regular school.

After different cram schools for different courses on different nights, 15 hours of schooling since waking up, students finally go home. By the time they arrive home, it is usually after 10 P.M. Can they take a bath and go to bed right away? Most teenage students in Taiwan dare not do so since they need to do homework. From the survey report, the typical bedtime for these exam takers is after 1 A.M., and the 6 A.M. wake-up call is not far away.

In short, as long as you are a teenage student in Taiwan who does not drop out from school, there is almost no escape from this nightmare study cycle. For obvious reasons, the existing education system has been criticized for its inflexibility and failure to address the needs of Taiwan's rapidly changing society. As a result, support for educational reform is spreading. Government programs aimed at solving educational problems have been established, but sometimes they lack adequate evaluation and have been instituted under the public pressure. Specific measures include more comprehensive compulsory education, the improvement of higher education, diversified and refined vocational education, a system of life-long learning and information education, additional channels for continued study, a new student counseling system, and a program for fostering pedagogic talents and on-the-job training for teachers. Perhaps Taiwan's future teenagers will benefit from these programs.

FAMILY LIFE

One salient feature of the Taiwanese family is that while the nuclear family (parents with unmarried children) remains the dominant type, stem families (married couples residing with elderly parents) and extended families (2 or more married siblings residing together and/or with elderly parents) constitute at least one-third of the households. Needless to say, the nuclear family is more prevalent in urban areas, while stem families and extended families are more often found in rural areas. Owing to the patriarchal heritage of the Chinese culture, children are expected to obey elders, showing their respect in daily interaction. Although teenagers may not live with grandparents, they have frequent opportunities to see them, especially during major holidays or festivals. Therefore, the concept of family or clan is kept intact in the socialization process of Taiwanese youth regardless of their living situation.

Within the context of a strong family, the internal division of labor for Taiwanese families may not necessarily reflect the stereotyped male-female roles. For example, it has been repeatedly shown that most couples make decisions about family matters together. Variations are found to associate with the difference in background (rural vs. urban), in education, in personal income level, as well as in sex role attitude held. Teenagers in this environment have also observed how parents resolve conflict and how household chores are shared. However, because studying is the top priority for most teenagers in Taiwan, few household chores are assigned to them at home. Parents want children to save their energy for study.

This common practice is reinforced by society: it is agreed that a tight and regular schedule is good for teenage students. Hence, teenagers do not need to worry about what to do at home since their schedules are already assigned. And the cost? Perhaps no real relaxed family life at all.

As to the daily family life, typical urban families such as those settled in the Taipei area generally require two salaries. (It is estimated that more than 80% of households in Taipei belong to this category.) Because all family members have hectic and conflicting schedules, there are fewer family dinners together. Benefiting from the many convenient eating places in urban areas, a lot of families in Taipei do not eat at home anymore. For these families, the kitchen is not functional and may be used for

Friends riding on a motor scooter in Taitung, Taiwan. Photo © H. Rogers/TRIP.

storage. It is not uncommon to see teenagers communicating with parents by written notes (e.g., to pay school fees, to sign school forms) or simply not having any in-depth discussion.

The situation in rural areas is different. Teenagers are more likely to be raised by grandparents while parents work in cities. They are also more likely to help aging relatives with simple household chores since the school competition is less severe. However, they too experience a lack of full family life. The crisis of parent-child relations among teenagers has aroused much attention in Taiwan, and many intensive professional workshops aimed at alleviating the undesirable situation receive funding from both the public and the private sectors.

Unlike other teens in the world, who often admire U.S. culture, teenagers in Taiwan admire Japanese culture. This trend began in the 1980s. Japanese movie stars, teenage TV stars, and singers quickly become idols for Taiwanese teenagers. The allowance from parents is used to collect products from Japan. Consequently, Japanese cartoon figures, comic books, electronic products, notebooks, pens, and so on are always on the lists of most popular goods among teenagers in Taiwan. In addition, Taiwanese teenagers dress and behave like Japanese teenagers, and for them, the first choice of countries to visit is Japan. Because family life in Taiwan is usually constrained by daily schedules and school requirements, it has become customary for middle-class parents to arrange family trips abroad during summer or winter breaks. A trip to Japan is thus considered a high priority among Taiwanese teenagers. According to government statistics, Taiwanese teenagers are among the most likely in the world to visit a foreign country before the age of 14 (10% of the population). In short, the pro-Japanese phenomenon among teenagers in Taiwan involves both cultural dissemination and cultural assimilation.

TRADITIONAL AND NONTRADITIONAL FOOD DISHES

Rice is still the staple for meals in Taiwan. Nevertheless, there is a significant difference in the food preference between older people and teenagers. A recent survey revealed that the first choice of restaurant among Taiwanese children 12 years old and under is McDonalds. Fast food, including fried chicken, pizza, and hamburgers, has gradually merged into teenagers' daily life and may be regarded as a natural and "traditional" choice someday.

A conventional practice for Taiwanese used to be to go to the marketplace to get fresh food for preparing daily meals. Besides rice, the meal usually included fish, fried or stewed meat with soy sauce, bean curd of some sort, a variety of vegetables, and a pot of hot soup. Although traditional Taiwanese cuisine is Fukienese, dishes from other provinces of China (including hot dishes of Szechuan) have been accepted as traditional food in Taiwan. No matter what traditional food is favored, it may take hours to prepare a single meal; only a full-time housewife has enough time to do this. Ever since the Western-style supermarket was introduced in urban areas, consumers, especially dual-earner couples, have been attracted by its convenience and the guaranteed quality. With the increasing demand for quick preparation for meals, the supermarket offers home-style dishes that take only minutes to fry. The menu also changes daily to attract more buyers. Furthermore, since on weekends or holidays families have more time to do home shopping, in few urban areas, going to the supermarket has become an important recreational activity for families with young children. However, teenagers are generally not involved in this type of shopping due to their tight schedule as well as lack of interest.

A recent longitudinal survey (1991–96) on the nutrition and health conditions of Taiwanese by the Institute of Biomedical Sciences of the Academia Sinica points out that the average Taiwanese consumes too much protein and fat and too little calcium. Teenagers have the same problem as the average Taiwanese, if not a more serious problem. Most teenagers like high-fat foods, such as fried potatoes, hot dogs, hamburgers, fried chicken, and steak, and they tend not to eat vegetables. They also prefer bread, toast, and cheese to the traditional rice and noodles. Interestingly, while teenagers prefer high-fat foods, more than half of them think of themselves as overweight. To address this concern, Taiwanese teenagers tend to take diet pills rather than exercising and eating right.

Another food revolution currently taking place is the introduction of food from other parts of Asia, such as Thai food and Vietnamese food. These nontraditional cuisines are considered exotic. Young people are more open than older people to trying these new foods.

SCHOOLING

As mentioned above, almost all Taiwanese teenagers have to attend schools of some kind. Generally speaking, in Taiwan, public elementary schools, junior high schools, and senior high schools are community based. Teenagers attend neighborhood schools up to the ninth grade. Nonetheless, students from wealthier families are more often registered in private schools for better educational quality. For senior high schools, attendance is based on the entrance examination or the comprehensive test scores for all students. Those top schools are what most teenage students dream about, but only 5 percent or less of them will get permission to enter. The heated competition for attending top high schools is one reason for the high anxiety and depression among teenage students in Taiwan.

Unlike American schools, which value the development of the individual student's potential and talents, schools in Taiwan emphasize homogeneity and discipline. Consequently, there is not much liberty, independence, or self-determination on the school campus. Most schools require students to wear uniforms. Taiwan's teachers are trained at colleges and universities that emphasize conformity, order, and thrift, and is not surprising that they transmit the same values to their students.

The dropout rate in Taiwan was once low but has been rising in recent years. Based on the data gathered by the Ministry of Education of Taiwan, the dropout rate for elementary schools, middle high schools, and high schools has jumped up to 0.3 percent in 2001. Part of the reason is due to the economic recession, which has put a higher proportion of families under the poverty line. Nevertheless, the main reason lies in the schools' failure to keep students at school. One of the main goals of the ongoing educational reform in Taiwan is to make school a fun place to learn and thus reduce teenage students' antagonism toward school. However, the challenge arises from the school system itself. Taiwan's secondary schools lead students to their future career routes: further academic schooling or vocational training. While the former requires long hours of studying, the latter schedules long hours of field training. Acquiring a balanced knowledge of science and humanity as well as having fun on the campus never appears to be a major priority. It may take years to change the existing values and expectations of middle school education. Until then, schooling for teenagers in Taiwan will remain stressful and sometimes frustrating.

SOCIAL LIFE

Most Taiwanese teenagers do not understand the concept of a social life. As stated earlier, the only mission that teenage students have is to study as hard as they can. Only adults have a social life, although there are a few school-based activities during the year.

On campus, one of the most welcomed social activities among high school students is perhaps the annual school day or the graduation dance. Because it is sponsored by the school itself implies that the principal is open-minded, the school counselors do not object to it, student clubs are active, and the school atmosphere is lively. In most elite single-sex high schools, inviting students (usually of the opposite sex) from other schools is of course a novel and exciting experience. Being able to wear casual attire, rather than uniforms, at a formal event on campus is a reward in itself. Therefore, large-scale social events between schools are becoming more common in recent years.

Since dating or making friends of the opposite sex is not encouraged in the society, teenagers in Taiwan find other ways to meet. One recent development is making "net friends" through the Internet. Today, it's a very popular activity. Teenagers log on to the Internet to chat with somebody else online or to try to ask net friends out on dates. These behaviors may cause serious problems because teenagers do not know how to protect themselves when meeting with strangers. Parents often prohibit their teenage children from having access to the Internet at home. As a consequence, teenagers search for access to the Internet outside of the home. This makes Internet coffee shops extremely popular. As in other Asian countries, Internet coffee shops in Taiwan are mostly in urban areas. In the coffee shops, teenagers can engage in various activities online that are forbidden at home. Interestingly, concerned adults, especially anxious parents, have tried harder to force the government to set up strict regulations to ban these Internet coffee shops.

One last point worth mentioning here is about teenage pregnancy in Taiwan. In the 1990s, teenage pregnancy went from being extremely rare to being a severe social problem in Taiwan. A new phenomenon called the "September abortion boom" has gotten much attention. Obviously, quite a few teenagers have become involved in premarital sex during the summer vacation between July and August. With inadequate knowledge of birth control, pregnancy almost becomes inevitable, resulting in abortions when the school semester begins in September. In Taiwan, the fertility rate among adolescents between the ages of 15 and 19 was 13 per 1,000, higher than in some other Asian countries in 1999. The birth rate for married teenagers in this age group was even higher than that of the United States: 7.64 per 1,000 in 1999 (more than 12,300 children are born annually to teenage mothers in Taiwan). Unexpected pregnancies and pregnant brides perhaps contribute to this high birth rate. According to a Taiwan Provincial Government study, between 1984 and 1994 there was a 264 percent increase in premarital sexual activities among teenagers. Specifically, in 1994, approximately 10 percent of teenage girls in Taiwan had had sexual intercourse. Two-thirds of those who had engaged in sex for the first time did not use any form of contraception, and 11 percent became pregnant. Among pregnant teenage girls, 8 percent chose to have an abortion, but the vast majority became teenage mothers. As social values and sexual behavior have changed, the number of unwed teenage mothers has reached a new high.

RECREATION

Chinese traditionally value diligence and hard work. This cultural norm helped create the economic miracle for Taiwan from the 1970s to 1980s. A playful attitude toward life is generally looked down upon and is certainly not encouraged among teenagers. Due to the demanding study schedule, holidays and weekends are supposed to be spent attending cram classes or working on exam exercises. Taiwanese teenagers actually do not have much time for recreation. It is fair to say that for them, recreation is a luxury.

Some Western notions about enjoying life and taking breaks have gradually been accepted as possible alternatives, as long as the main personal responsibilities are not forsaken. Hence, high school teachers start to encourage students to play ball or to do physical exercise during breaks so that they can concentrate better, and parents let teenagers go to the movies with their friends after the monthly school exam is over. All in all, for most teenagers, as long as the proposed recreational activity does not conflict with their learning, adults may allow it.

Hence, when spare time is available, such as during major holidays or after the final examination, teenagers will plan their favorite recreational activities. Boys may play basketball for the afternoon or play online electronic games, while girls may shop with friends or get together at someone's home. Going to the movies is certainly a priority for both genders. For example, the Harry Potter film that was shown right after the first monthly exam of fall 2001 was booked for its entire opening week. But this type of relaxation is not regular.

Under the prevailing value of study, athletes or teenagers with considerable athletic ability do not necessarily enjoy a high status among their peers. Although baseball stars, for instance, attract much attention in the society, few parents would wish most of all for their children to become professional athletes. Those who are good at sports may even be thought of as poor students, incapable of academic achievement. To be a member of the school team is thus not a high honor. Lacking the social support from peers and parents, students actively engaged in various athletic pursuits usually decline to be on the school team in the last year of their school in order to prepare for the entrance examination. Consequently, although Taiwan is well suited to hiking and fishing, few teenagers are involved in these time-consuming pastimes. In fact, besides basketball for teenage boys, there are few popular sports among teenagers in Taiwan.

ENTERTAINMENT

In addition to the movie theater, the most important place of entertainment for Taiwanese teenagers is perhaps karaoke TV (KTV). It provides customers with entertainment with friends or acquaintances through singing and gathering. It is usually located in the urban center. Snacks and drinks are served, and fancy Kuroki (auto-singing machine) equipment allows customers to select all kinds of popular songs from the huge song reservoir of each store. Fees are calculated according to the time periods occupied, the number of persons present, the amount of food ordered, and the size of the room. Teenagers in Taiwan are most likely to gather at KTV on weekend or holiday afternoons, when the lowest fee applies.

Entertainment at KTV usually proceeds as follows: groups register at the reception desk, then wait to be seated in private rooms. Once in the room, they order drinks and snacks from waitstaff and select their songs. When a person's selected song appears on the screen, that person starts to sing in front of the group by following the words at the bottom of the screen.

When KTV was first introduced to Taiwan about a decade ago, critics pointed out that as people who are introverted, Taiwanese feel a release by singing aloud in a public place and receive rewarding feedback from friends if their performance is good. Whether it is indeed a healthy entertainment or not, being able to sing has gradually become an important social skill in Taiwan. Therefore, KTV nowadays is a serious industry in Taiwan. However, due to the relatively high cost (still much higher than eating at McDonalds, for instance), not all Taiwanese teenagers have adequate opportunities to entertain themselves at KTV.

Although KTV is enjoyable for many Taiwanese teens, it has gradually become a place of criminal activity. Due to the privacy afforded by KTV, with people gathered together in a completely closed space that is not easily monitored, deviant teenagers find it to be an ideal place to have illegal drinks or to do illegal business. Some of them even use KTV for drug transactions. Occasionally, the media will report on date rapes or forced premarital sex at KTV. For adults (including those who have been to KTV), KTV has become a potentially dangerous place for teenagers in Taiwan. However, due to the scarcity of entertainment for teenagers, if they stop going to meet at the KTV, it will be most likely due to economic reasons rather than safety concerns.

RELIGIOUS PRACTICES AND CULTURAL CEREMONIES

According to the General Social Change Survey in Taiwan (2000), religious beliefs claimed include Buddhism (27%), Taoism (20%), folk religion (21%), and Christianity (4.8%); 23 percent claimed no religion (and 4.2% did not respond). Since Taoism assumed a minor role (less than 10%) for the last 15 years, the reasons for its sudden rise are unclear. Among Buddhists, a large majority (86%) are not serious believers and may have similar religious practices as those of the folk religion. One of the characteristics of folk religion in Taiwan is that it tends to sanctify objects and thus worship all gods in order to avoid hardship and to attain happiness.

Religion in Taiwan is used to help ensure success in secular affairs. For example, before the annual high school entrance examination, thousands of parents bring their teenage children to a temple to ask for a blessing from supernatural powers. If the teenager does well on the test and is able to attend a good school, it is customary for the parents to go back to the temple to give financial offerings. Since religious belief has been documented to have direct intergenerational transmission, the respect toward all gods and the common religious practices may continue in the future.

There is a unique cultural ceremony in Taiwan that involves youth in the transition from childhood to adolescence. Every year on September 28, the birthday of Confucius, 64 seventh graders from a nearby middle school are invited to perform an ancient Chinese dance in front of the Confucius Temple to celebrate the greatest teacher's birthday. The 64 students line up in rows of 8 and hold a feather in their hands symbolizing the quills used to write with during Confucius's time. It is regarded as the highest honor for teenagers to participate in this unique cultural ceremony. Because of its cultural meaning, this grand ritual always attracts many Taiwanese as well as foreign tourists. The highest moment of the cultural ceremony is "picking hairs of wisdom" which takes place inside the temple. It is believed that if teenage students are lucky enough to pick the wisdom hair from the sacrificed pork (any hair left on the pig), the wisdom hair will make these fortunate teenagers wiser and bring them the good luck to enter the prestigious high schools, universities, and graduate schools. This again signifies the importance of education in the value system among Taiwanese: even a traditional cultural ceremony must bear the responsibility to provide teenagers something practical. No wonder anthropologists argue that the religious belief in China has always been utilitarian, not purely for religious worship only.

CONCLUSION

There are two major structural factors affecting teen life in Taiwan: the political uncertainty with Mainland China and the omnipotent value of study. The political dispute between the two sides of the Taiwan Strait is an inevitable source of tension for the society. Teenagers socialized in this context may become interested in politics at an early age. Because of the political instability and the achievement orientation of the culture, Taiwanese parents regularly send teenage children abroad for study. Regardless of one's social status, education (or, more accurately, diligent study) remains a significant part of the daily life as well as the future plan of teenagers in Taiwan.

Due to the strong emphasis on attending good educational institutions, teenagers are expected to make studying their top priority. The system also provides a series of mechanisms to facilitate this recognized goal, such as morning tests, after-school classes on the campus, and cram classes in the evening and on weekends. The stress on studying is shared by other Asian countries heavily influenced by Confucian thought—Confucius being an honored and respected teacher figure (e.g., Japan, Korea). Nevertheless, the situation in Taiwan may appear to be more condensed or more serious due to its geographical density and the resulting higher competition for the same number of school spots.

The importance of study in Taiwanese teens' daily agenda has certainly reduced their participation in other aspects of life, including family life, recreation, and social life. As described above, to have fun or to relax is not encouraged because of the potential conflict with study time. Playing basketball during breaks, getting together with friends after examinations, playing computer games on weekends, and doing other non-study-related activities is gradually becoming accepted—but as a means to enhance one's concentration while studying.

In general, teens in Taiwan get little sleep, do lots of studying, face enormous pressure to excel academically, and have relatively little fun. However, the convenient access and affordable cost of KTV and Internet coffee shops have attracted teenagers eager to extend their dull life into the outer world. Undesirable side effects from these locales have been noticed, and some preventive measures have been taken to protect teenagers' safety.

Since the dropout rate is low, almost all teenagers under 15 years old and more than 90 percent of those between the ages of 15 and 18 attend school. This chapter on Taiwan has thus focused on teenage students only. Teens not at school are often neglected by the society as a whole. Because males will be drafted for the army at age 18 if they are not students, their work activities are considered temporary. Only after the military service will Taiwanese males be regarded as reaching full maturity. In other words, although the ancient ritual of transition into adulthood no longer exists, the mandatory military service serves as the demarcation between being a teenager and being an adult.

In addition, this chapter has discussed the cultural influence from America and Japan. As members of the global village, Taiwanese teenagers eat American fast food, watch American movies, and admire American sport heroes, and they wear Japanese-style clothes, collect Japanese show business and music personalities, and sing Japanese pop songs. A survey on teenagers showed that Japan rather than the United States has the heaviest cultural influence on Taiwan. Similar survey results are found among adults island-wide.

From a Taiwanese teenager's perspective, what are the most important aspects of life? Familial support, school performance, and basic personal security are what matters most for teens in Taiwan.

RESOURCE GUIDE

Nonfiction

Davison, G. M., and Reed, B. G. (1998). *Culture and customs of Taiwan*. Westport, CT: Greenwood Press.
Hsiau, C. (2000). *Contemporary Taiwanese cultural nationalism*. New York: Routledge.
Marsh, R. M. (1996). *The great transformation: Social change in Taipei, Taiwan since the 1960s (Taiwan in the modern world)*. Armonk, NY: M.E. Sharpe.

Fiction

Carver, A. C., and Chang, S.-S. Y. (Eds.). (1991). *The Bamboo shoots after the rain: Contemporary stories by women writers of Taiwan*. New York: Feminist Press at CUNY.
Huang, C.-M. (2001). *The taste of apples: Modern Chinese literature from Taiwan* (H. Goldblatt, Trans.). New York: Columbia University Press.

Web Sites

Bureau of Education, Taipei City Government: http://www.tmtc.edu.tw/~tainet/english.htm
Chinese Taipei Film Archive: http://www.ctfa.org.tw/
European Union Study Association—Taiwan: http://eusa-taiwan.org/cnglish/index-e.htm
Ministry of Education: http://www.edu.tw/english/index.htm
Science and Mathematics Education Information System: http://smeis.ntnu.edu.tw/esmeis
Taiwan Economic Data Center: http://www.edu.tw/moecc/rs/pkg/tedc/tedc2.htm

More Information

Government Information Office: http://www.gio.gov.tw/
Humanistic Education Foundation: http://hef.yam.org.tw/
National Palace Museum: http://www.npm.gov.tw/
National Taiwan University: http://www.ntu.edu.tw/
Tourism Bureau, Ministry of Transportation and Communications, Republic of China: http://www.tbroc.gov.tw/

Pen Pal/Chat

http://www.geocities.com/SoHo/Lofts/4897/

Chapter 14

THAILAND

Harriet L. Amato

INTRODUCTION

Thailand occupies approximately 198,114 square miles (513,115 square kilometers) in Southeast Asia. It is bordered by Myanmar (formerly Burma) on the north and west, Laos on the northeast, and Cambodia on the southeast. The long, narrow peninsula to the south and west is surrounded by the Gulf of Thailand on the east, Malaysia to the south, and the Andaman Sea to the west. In school, young Thai students are taught that the map of Thailand resembles an ancient axe whose handle is the peninsula, but the country's shape can also be seen as an elephant's head with the peninsula as the trunk.

Thailand has three seasons that vary by degree of warmth and humidity. The hottest weather is from March to June, when temperatures rise to 100°F. The summer monsoon winds bring in the rainy season from July to October, during which parts of Thailand will get over 200 inches of rain. This extraordinary amount of rain is relied on heavily for growing rice, the staple of Thai meals. During the cooler season, from November to February, there is an occasional dip in temperature to as low as 65°F.

Geographically, Thailand's 76 provinces are divided into four natural regions. Each region contains at least one major city, but none of these cities are as large or as westernized as the capital of Thailand, Bangkok, whose population is approximately 6 million. The northern region is made up of mountains, fertile valleys, and teak forests. Farming villages, nomadic tribes, and hill tribes characterize this area, and each has its own culture and dialect, similar to some southern states in the United States. It is common to see domesticated elephants being used for transportation, farm work, and moving raw teak to processing in the teak forests. In fact, the elephant training camp is located in this northern region. The major city here, Chiang Mai, is the hub of local trading for the farmers.

The Central Plains region has been called the Rice Bowl of Asia. This rich, fertile valley of rivers and canals is one of the world's major rice- and fruit-growing areas. It is no surprise that it is the most densely populated region of Thailand. It is the home of Bangkok as well as the other major cities such as Ayutthaya and Nakhon Pathom.

The northeast region of Thailand is noted for its hilly terrain and its extreme weather conditions causing floods and droughts. Most of the approximately 20 million inhabitants of this vast region are cattle, rice, and maize farmers.

The southern region contains mountains, thick rain forests, and beautiful beaches. This region is the center of Thailand's tin, rubber, and natural gas industries as well as being an attractive tourist area.

There are conflicting theories regarding the origins of the Thais. Some historians say the Thais originated in northwestern Szechuan in China and migrated south. Most recently, archeologists have uncovered artifacts in the Village of Ban Chiang in northeast Thailand that indicate Thais may have originated in Southeast Asia, migrated from there to various other parts of Asia, and then slowly migrated back to Thailand. A large number of Thais remained in southern China, where they eventually organized the Kingdom of Nanchao in 650 and remained independent of Chinese rule through 1000 C.E., when the Chinese made Nanchao a tributary state.

Prior to this, discoveries indicate that Southeast Asia contained two large and influential empires that date back as far as the first millennium B.C.E.: the Mon or Davaravati Empire (it is not certain if this was an actual empire or a civilization) and the Khmer Empire. As each of these grew in power, it expanded and took over most of what is today considered Thailand. The Thais who were migrating back to central Southeast Asia settled in two basic regions that they eventually referred to as kingdoms: Lan Na or Lanna (Million Thai Rice Fields) and Sukhothai (The Dawn of Happiness).

In 1253, the Moguls led by Kubla Khan invaded Nanchao and the Thais living there fled south, many of them settling in Sukhothai, which was still part of the Khmer Empire. By 1260 the Thais had overtaken the Khmers and established the first independent Thai Kingdom, with Sukhothai as its capital. From 1260 to 1350 the Sukhothai Empire continued to expand. To many Thais this period is considered the golden era of Thai history. It was a peaceful time of plenty that saw the beginning of the first formal Thai writing system, the establishment of Theravada Buddhism, which remains the leading religion in Thailand, and the beginning of many Thai art forms, including painting, sculpture, architecture, and literature. After the death of King Rama Kamheng, Sukhothai began to decline and the capital was eventually moved to Ayutthaya.

From 1350 to the beginning of the seventeenth century, the Thai Kingdom (Siam) with its capital at Ayutthaya flourished, but not without some serious setbacks. During this period the Kings of Siam attempted to expand their kingdom's borders through conflicts with Laos, Cambodia, and Burma (currently known as Myanmar). Burma posed the biggest threat to Siam, and in 1569 Ayutthaya fell to Burma. In 1584, the Thais overtook Ayutthaya, but war with Burma continued. In 1767 the Burmese again took Ayutthaya, this time virtually destroying the city and sending the spoils of their victory back to Burma. In less than a year, however, the Thais were back in control of Ayutthaya. Because the city was so badly ravaged, the capital of Siam was moved to Thon Buri. When Chakkri (Rama I) became ruler, he moved the capital to Bangkok and established the Chakkri Dynasty, which remains the ruling house of Siam today.

Siam's relations with the West and subsequent Western influence on Siam began as early as the 1500s with Portuguese traders and missionaries. By the seventeenth century, Siam expanded its Western trade to include the Dutch, British, and French. It was during this time that these Western powers, realizing the value of the resources Southeast Asia had to offer, began moving toward colonizing the area. Siam very skillfully averted colonization by negotiating trade agreements with Western countries in such a way so that no one outside power would gain too much influence in the country. In fact, Siam is the only Southeast Asian country that has never been colonized by the West. In this way the Thais were able to reap benefits from Western culture while remaining autonomous. In 1886, the French in Laos and the British in Burma forced Siam to relinquish some of its territory to them. To ensure that no further expansion into Siam would occur, on October 23, 1886, Rama V (King Chulalongkorn) declared Siam an independent kingdom.

The eighteenth and nineteenth centuries saw many changes in Siam. Agricultural production increased, and new roads, railways, and waterways were created. The first printing press and post office were established, and a civil service system was set up. Schools were introduced and the first primary school system was established. New laws were enacted to improve the rights of women and children. The government of Siam saw changes ranging from allowing officials to sit on chairs (rather than stand) during royal audiences, to a cabinet form of government with 12 ministers. Under Rama VII (1925–35), the absolute monarchy of Siam was replaced by a constitutional monarchy based on the British system of government.

During World War II, Japan's close proximity to Thailand caused increased pressure on the Thai government to ally itself with Japan. In addition, Thailand's Premier Phibunsongkhram (Phibun) saw the possibility of recovering some of Thailand's lost territories if the country sided with Japan. In 1942, Premier Phibun declared war on Great Britain and the United States. The Thai Ambassador in Washington, however, refused to deliver the declaration, and in 1944 pressure from the Thai underground resistance forced Phibun to resign. It was Phibun who, in 1938, first changed the name of the country from Siam to Thailand. After his resignation, the name of the country was changed back to Siam and a few years later the name Thailand was reinstated. Finally, on May 11, 1949, an official proclamation changed the name of Siam to Prathet Thai, or Thailand, which means "land of the free."

Thailand opposed the expansion of communism and sent troops to Korea in support of the United Nations' efforts there. In 1954 Thailand, along with seven other nations, including the United States, signed the defense treaty establishing the Southeast Asian Treaty Organization (SEATO). Thailand also aided the United States' efforts in Vietnam by providing bases and troops and was a leader in establishing the Association of Southeast Asian Nations (ASEAN) in 1967.

During the 1970s and 1980s, Thailand's focus turned more toward internal problems. The people began to demonstrate against the military monarchy that had been established in 1971, claiming there was far too much military influence in the government and not enough civilian influence. At this time, military politicians were favoring economic expansion of Thailand while civilian politicians urged increases in funding for social services and economically disadvantaged areas. Although civilians were allowed more participation in government, tensions between the military and civilian factions continued for almost three decades. During this time there were many street demonstrations, some resulting in military intervention and fatalities, several new constitutions, and an increase in political corruption. It was not until the Asian financial crisis of 1997, including the collapse of the Thai stock market and currency and the resulting fall of the government, that a new constitution was instituted. This constitution included actual input from the Thai people for the first time, and it is this constitution that governs Thailand today.

Although Thailand is economically and politically more stable today than it was in the late 1900s, like most countries, it still has its share of problems. There are continuing efforts to fight corruption, end drug trafficking, control pollution, preserve Thailand's natural resources, and ensure that the people's voice continues to be represented in government. History, topography, politics, religion, socioeconomics, and climate all play a significant role in understanding the daily life of Thai teenagers.

TYPICAL DAY

A typical day in the life of a Thai teenager varies depending on whether he or she lives in an urban or a rural area. It also varies somewhat depending on socioeconomic status. Basically, teenagers from wealthy families, whether in urban or rural areas, will be responsible for less work around the house because their families can afford hired help. These teens will then be required to spend more time on their studies.

During the week, a teenager in Bangkok gets up early to get ready for school. Before leaving the house, teenagers shower, eat breakfast, get their school books together, and often attend to household chores, including helping a younger sibling get ready for school. Teens get to school by public bus, motorcycle taxi, tuk tuk taxi (a three-wheeled, open, motorized vehicle that holds four or five people), or tricycle (*samlor*), or they are driven to school. The public bus is usually teenagers' transportation of choice if they are not driven because it is less expensive, more dependable, and safer to ride in during rush hour. Bangkok has serious traffic congestion problems not only during rush hour but all day long.

Teens are at school from 7:50 A.M. to 3:30 or 4:30 P.M. After school there is usually a mandatory activity such as a school club or Scouts that they are required to attend. After that, some teens will have tutoring, others will stay to play some basketball or soccer (commonly referred to as football in Thailand), and others will return home. Once they are home, homework and chores need to be done. If a teen returns home late, he or she often picks up something for dinner at a take-out stall or eats dinner out. This depends on each family member's schedule for the day. Teens in urban areas usually do not work outside of the home while they are attending school. Often in Bangkok both parents work so it is the responsibility of the children in the family to take on many of the daily household chores and to keep up with their schoolwork. Household chores could include any or all of the following depending on socioeconomic status: dusting and sweeping the house, washing and drying dishes, doing laundry by hand or taking the laundry to a Laundromat, watering plants, and feeding pets. Also, many parents prefer to give their children an allowance so they will not have to work and can spend more time on their schoolwork. If a teen does work outside of the home it is usually in a department store and this would be only on the weekends to ensure that the job does not interfere with schoolwork.

The weekend for teens means not having to get up as early as they do during the week. A typical Saturday might include school in the morning (to prepare for a post–high school entrance exam), then work if the teen works at a job outside of the home, homework, house chores, and finally time with friends playing sports, going shopping at a mall, going to a movie, or just hanging out and watching television. Sundays may include visiting grandparents or other extended family members and the usual homework and house chores. Most of the population in Bangkok is Buddhist, and practicing Buddhists pray twice a day, once in the morning and once in the evening. Since Buddhists are not required to pray in the temple, many families set up a room in their homes with an altar in the Buddhist tradition. This enables them to pray at home rather than having to go to a monastery.

In rural areas of Thailand, teenagers spend the same amount of time at school. The household chores are more extensive since many rural areas do not have a lot of the conveniences that are in urban areas. For example, homes may not have running water, electricity may be very limited, and help may be needed on the farm. Thai children take on family responsibilities in these areas at a very young age so that by their teenage years they are considered adult laborers and are expected to carry their weight. After school, teens often go directly home to do their homework and work on the farm. Sometimes, in the evening, after all work is done, villagers will congregate around a bonfire. Teens get together during these times to sit around and talk, play cards, play chess, or play takraw (played by passing a woven rattan ball to one another without using hands).

FAMILY LIFE

One can understand family life in Thailand today only by looking at the most rural areas first. In the villages, extended families live together in several houses in the same compound. A typical village home usually consists of two wooden structures, each containing a single room, that are connected by a simple wooden balcony. The home is raised on pillars to protect it from flooding during the rainy season, and beneath the home domesticated animals such as pigs and chickens are kept. One of the structures might be the sleeping area and the other the living area. This type of living environment affords little privacy and, at a very early age, instills a strong sense of unity and tolerance. As soon as children are old enough, they are given responsibilities based on their ability. These could range from feeding livestock to sweeping the house or watching younger siblings while both parents are working in the field. As children get older they are given more responsibility, thereby reinforcing their importance within the family unit. By the time a child reaches the teenage years, he or she is an active participant in important decision-making discussions. All residents of the compound know what their jobs are, and all work together. The elders of the family are highly respected for their experience and wisdom. It is their responsibility to advise their children and to teach their grandchildren and great-grandchildren Thai traditions and values. It is also the children's responsibility to care for their aging parents. This they willingly do out of respect.

The way these people live is very much the same way Thais lived for decades before Western influence. Buddhism, the primary religion in Thailand, reinforces harmony, tolerance, compromise, and respect for elders and those of higher status. These teachings have extended beyond the family. For example, when Thais greet each other they use the "wai" by putting their hands together in a prayer-like manner in front of the face. This is a sign of respect as well as a greeting: when one greets an elder or someone of higher status, one's fingertips will be closer to the forehead. When one greets a child, the fingertips will be closer to the chin, indicating a lower hierarchical status. It is also considered rude to criticize or challenge other people, to raise one's voice, or to exhibit angry or aggressive behavior. In fact, any display of extreme emotion is considered ignorant, crude, and immature.

Urban family life is very different in Bangkok than it is in any other major city in Thailand since no other city is even close to the size of Bangkok. Approximately 6 million people live in Bangkok and its suburbs, and there are over a million registered motor vehicles in this area. In fact, 90 percent of all motor vehicles registered in the country are in Bangkok. Cities such as Chiang Mai in the north, Nakhon Ratchasima in the northeast, and Hat Yai in the south, although continuing to grow, are still considered provincial by Bangkok standards, and family life in these cities more closely resembles family life in rural areas than in Bangkok.

Bangkok is a very large, westernized city with numerous high-rise office buildings and apartments, town houses, condominiums, hotels, factories, shopping centers, universities/colleges, and cultural centers. The average middle-income family owns a modest home in the outskirts of the city. This is typically two floors with two bedrooms, two bathrooms, a kitchen, a living room, and a balcony outside the second floor. The homes on the same lane are very often attached and all of the same style. Parents sleep in one bedroom and all of the siblings sleep in the other bedroom. It is common for siblings to sleep in the same bed, and the beds are large enough to accommodate three or four people. There is no front or back lawn, but potted plants are kept in the small area between the gate and the front door and just outside of the gate. The extended family or at least the grandparents usually live nearby. Although appliances such as washing machines, microwaves, and vacuum cleaners are readily available in Bangkok, many families do not own them. The price of electricity is high and these may not be considered as necessary as a refrigerator and stove. Cars are very expensive in Thailand and usually only rich families own a car. You will not see families with two or more cars as you do in the United States. Although Thai teens can get a driver's license at the age of 15 or 16, they are not anxious to drive. Public transportation is the least expensive, safest, and quickest way to get around Bangkok and its suburbs. Older teens may, at some point, be able to afford a motorbike, but it is still difficult to get around because of the traffic. In Bangkok, rich people live in more spacious dwellings and, for the poor, there is low-rise public housing in the city and simple single-story dwellings throughout the suburbs. As is true of most major Western cities, in Bangkok there are many shops, restaurants, and so on that are three or four stories high. The shop owners, their families, and sometimes even the hired help live above their shops. The city is where you will find fast food restaurants, take-out food stalls, open fresh food markets, and grocery stores. Bangkok also offers museums, theaters, movie houses, and nightlife.

When families migrate to Bangkok, some of the Thai traditions have to be compromised because they are not practical. Although families try to live close to each other, this is not always possible. They do stay in touch via telephone and will make sure their children see their grandparents regularly. For a family to be able to live in Bangkok, it is often necessary for both parents to work. Men usually aspire to positions of prestige such as civil service, police, or army, while women pursue more business-oriented careers. As a result, family members have very different schedules and the families spend much less time together than in the villages. Another difference between village life and living in Bangkok has to do with the role of religion (Buddhism) in family life. In the village, each wat, or Buddhist monastery, is situated on a large grassy area that is often used by villagers to congregate in the evening and to celebrate holidays or other festive occasions together. In Bangkok, because of overcrowded conditions, the wat is not as easily accessible to families and, as mentioned earlier, often families have an area in their home set aside for daily prayer and meditation.

Westernization has had positive and negative effects on Thailand. The positive side includes the increase in the number of schools, which has increased the literacy rate; the availability of more goods and services, including such things as medical facilities; and more diverse employment opportunities and cultural centers. On the negative side is the availability of illegal drugs, alcohol, prostitution, pornography, and gambling. The Thai government has recently turned its attention to these problems through strictly enforcing laws controlling drinking and possession and use of illegal drugs; strengthening laws governing night spots; and regulating Internet use. Recently, parents living in Bangkok met to discuss ways to control and/or eliminate adverse temptations that affect teenagers.

TRADITIONAL AND NONTRADITIONAL FOOD DISHES

Thailand provides an abundance of food for its people. Although it is known for being one of the largest rice producers in the world, Thailand's fertile fields also offer a variety of seasonal fruits and vegetables that are available in its markets all year long. From the Andaman Sea and the Gulf of Thailand come fish, crab, shrimp, lobster, squid, and mollusks. Thais are traditionally not large beef eaters; pork, chicken, eggs, or fish/seafood appear in most of their main dishes. They are also famous for spicy dishes. Among the most common spices used in cooking are ginger, garlic, a variety of chilies and curries, cumin, coriander, pepper, basil, and lemongrass. These are used in different quantities to create combinations specific to each recipe. It is common at meals to have several small bowls of sauces such as curry paste and fermented fish sauce (*ram pla*) available to dip food into before eating in order to accentuate the flavors of the food.

Food varies slightly from one region of Thailand to another based partly on the availability of different foods in different regions. The Central Plains, which includes Bangkok, the capital city of Thailand, is believed to have the most appealing combination of flavors. Generally, food from the Central Plains can be described as hot, salty, sour, and slightly sweet. In the South one will find more fish dishes and food is usually very hot and salty with a slightly sour flavor. In the North more pork, more chicken, and a lot more vegetables are included in dishes. People in this region tend to use fewer spices and more condiments to achieve a hot, spicy, and slightly salty flavor. Rice is the main dish of every meal in all regions. Sticky rice (*khao niaw*) rather than steamed rice (*khao suay*) is prevalent in the North. It is usually cooked and served in a wicker basket made from bamboo splints or palmyra palm leaves and eaten with the fingers. Some-times it is rolled into a small ball shape, pressed against other food that will stick to it, and then eaten.

Thais typically eat three small meals and enjoy snacking. Breakfast in the Central Plains could be slow-cooked rice porridge with pork (*joke*), an omelette (*kai jee-o*), or chicken with rice (*khao mun khai*). A typical lunch in this region might be egg noodle soup with pork and vegetables (*ba-me*), fried vegetables (*pad pak*), or chicken with vegetables and rice (*Khao mun Khai* with different types of vegetables). In the North, break-fast and lunch are often simply sticky rice. Soups and salads are very pop-ular in Thailand; unlike in the United States, the soup or salad is the main meal, not a side dish. A Thai salad could contain meat, seafood, fresh vegetables, herbs, and fruits, all spiced and often topped with peanuts and slices of chilies. While breakfast and lunch consists of one dish, dinner usually consists of four or five main dishes set out on the table for everyone to share. A traditional dinner will include a large bowl of rice, then possibly a soup dish (*tom yam*, made with shrimp, tomatoes, spiced coriander, lemongrass, and chilies), a fried dish (*phat thai*, Thai-land's national dish, a mixture of rice noodles fried with bean curd, vege-tables, egg, peanuts, and dried shrimp), a steamed dish (some type of fish or seafood steamed in a curry sauce), and a hot salad (sliced pork on a bed of greens with onions, mint, chilies, and lemon juice) along with a variety of sauces and condiments. Water is served with the meal and tea or coffee, either hot or iced, is served after the meal. Thais also enjoy fruit juices and beer. Dessert is not necessarily a part of the daily Thai meal the way it is in the United States. For something sweet, people eat fresh fruit. For spe-cial occasions and in restaurants in the cities, desserts will be prepared; these are usually carved fruit or are fruit based. Two popular desserts are *khao niaw mamuang*, mango with sticky rice sweetened with coconut cream, and bananas coated with sugared coconut and deep fried.

It is considered rude in Thailand to fill your plate with a lot of food at once. Instead, Thais take small portions at a time. Each meal contains some form of rice (e.g., steamed rice, sticky rice, rice noodles), which becomes the base for the meal. Rice is served first and is commonly used to cool the mouth when eating very hot and spicy foods. All food is cut into bite-size pieces before cooking so there is no need for knives at the table. In urban areas, chopsticks are often used to eat rice noodle dishes, and everything else is usually eaten with a fork and spoon. The fork is used to push the food onto the spoon and the food is actually eaten from the spoon. In the north and in other rural areas, chopsticks are more common utensils and, although breakfast may be eaten in the house, lunch is usually eaten in the fields during working breaks. In these areas, dinner is a family function. It is interesting to note that in urban areas of Thailand, the family often does not eat dinner together on a daily basis. With both mother and father working and children having their individual schedules, it is difficult for the family to be together for meals.

For Thais, communal meals are an informal social event in all regions. When families gather for a special event such as a wedding or holiday, the focus of the event is the meal and it can last several hours. Many main dishes are prepared. On these special occasions it is typical for Thais to carve fruits and vegetables into elaborate flower and leaf shapes, making their plates very decorative and attractive. Thai chefs are famous for their carving, which is an ancient Thai art form dating back to the time when a woman's ability to carve fruits and vegetables secured her position in the royal court, because it was important for their royalty to display this art form at its best on special occasions.

In rural Thailand, meals are often prepared by the woman but cooking is not necessarily considered "women's work." Families work as a team, each family member doing his or her part to help out. In Bangkok, which is the largest, most modern, and most densely populated city in Thailand, many middle-class families, because of their busy schedules, do not cook lunch or dinner at home. For teenagers, lunch is served at school during the week and on the weekend they will get take-out food from stalls that sell typical Thai food and bring it home to eat. Food stalls are common in most cities in Thailand. In Bangkok there are also a number of fast food restaurants such as Burger King, Kentucky Fried Chicken, and McDonalds, and most of these places have modified their menus to include Thai-type food. While you can still get a double cheeseburger with fries at McDonalds, you can also get a pork burger. Kentucky Fried Chicken has fish burgers and Burger King in Bangkok is now offering two different fish meals and three different chicken meals. The food at these restaurants is more expensive than at the food stalls and, according to many adults, not as nutritious as Thai food. Despite the objections of the elders, fast food restaurants are still a first choice for many Thai teenagers.

SCHOOLING

The development of the education system in Thailand is a good example of how education grows out of necessity. Prior to the establishment of the Department of Education in Thailand in 1887, it was believed that only the royalty and Buddhist monks required formal education. Princes needed to be educated in order to run their provinces effectively. Monks had to be able to read and interpret religious texts for the people. For the rest of the population, most of whom were farmers, formal education was not considered a priority. All of their time was devoted to working in order to provide for their families and to the practice of Buddhism. For these people there was little need to read or write and no time to sit for instruction. Also, the only schools available besides the school at the Royal Palace were in the Buddhist monasteries, and these provided only a very limited education.

The 1900s saw Thailand's cities expand and their populations grow. Thailand began making the transition from an agricultural society to an agricultural/industrial society. In fact, when the Government of Thailand established the Department of Education to be responsible for the education and religious affairs of the entire country, it was trying to satisfy a need for better-trained personnel in government. As the cities continued to grow, there were more jobs for which education was essential. In 1917 the first university, Chulalongkorn University, was founded. It included four colleges: medicine, law and political science, engineering, and arts and science. In 1918 the Private School Act formalized the responsibilities of and regulated the participation of the private sector in public education. The 1921 Compulsory Primary Education Act made primary education compulsory for all children. In 1932, a National Education Plan acknowledged the right of each Thai citizen to an intellectual, moral, physical, and practical education regardless of sex, economic or social background, or physical handicaps.

Currently, Thailand's education system is the primary responsibility of the Ministry of Education, the National Education Commission, and the Ministry of University Affairs. Students are required to attend six years at the elementary or primary level and three years at the lower secondary level (middle school). Thai schools also provide three years at the upper secondary level (high school) and four years at the tertiary level, which could be vocational/specialized school, college, or university. In addition, Thailand provides special education schools for children with physical and mental handicaps and welfare schools for children that are poor and, as a result, would be considered socially and/or culturally handicapped. These schools are equipped with special facilities to enable the children that attend them to receive an equal opportunity education. Today Thailand is home to some 42 universities and 36 teacher colleges as well as many vocational schools and specialized training institutions.

For the Thai teenager the new school year begins in May, after a recess lasting approximately two months. The Thai teenager gets ready for the school year by getting a haircut and the proper uniform. Long hair at school is considered impolite, and if your hair is not cut to the required length the school will cut it for you (purposely too short according to some Thai students). Students must wear their school uniform or they can wear their club uniform (Boy or Girl Scouts, Red Cross Youth, Girl Guides) to school on days that they have these meetings or activities. Unlike in the United States, all students are required to join Junior Red Cross and Boy or Girl Scouts. Children entering first grade join the Scouts and continue with scouting until they graduate from secondary school.

Students use public transportation to commute to school, or, in the case of wealthy families, students are driven to school. Schools in Thailand generally do not provide free transportation for students. There are, however, some organizations such as the military and government welfare (especially in rural areas) that provide free transportation for students. The first class begins at 8:30 A.M. and the last class ends at 3:30 P.M., but students have to sign in by 7:50 A.M. Prior to the start of the first class, the Thai flag is raised, all sing the Thai National Anthem, and there is a prayer period. There is also a 10- to 15-minute homeroom session before classes begin. During this time the teacher makes the daily announcements, which include the names of about 10 students in the class (there are usually about 50 students in a class) who are assigned classroom cleaning duties at the end of the day. Each class is 70 minutes long, with a 70-minute lunch break at about 11:00 A.M. for grades 7 to 9 and 12:10 P.M. for grades 10 to 12. Most students buy their lunch in the canteen (school cafeteria) because school lunches are inexpensive and the school provides different hot meals every day. Some typical school lunches are noodles with gravy and meat, chicken fried with basil and chili, chicken curry with bamboo shoots, fried pork and meat balls, and fried fish cakes with rice.

Unlike U.S. high schools, which are usually housed in a single building, Thai schools in urban areas are made up of five or more buildings, each containing approximately four floors and each floor containing about five or six classrooms. Students often remain in the same classroom for all subjects except labs, and different teachers go to the students to teach their subject specialty. Depending on the school, specialized subject area teachers will begin rotating into classrooms as early as the fifth grade. In rural areas, the school is usually located on the outskirts of the village and is often a single-room building where several grade levels are taught simultaneously.

The lower secondary school typically has seven main programs: English, science, business, physical education, arts, social studies, and home economics. Courses such as hygiene, Buddhism, and electronics are all either part of the required courses for a particular main program or can be selected to satisfy the school-required number of elective credits. The upper secondary school offers only two main programs: science and arts.

Requirements for both main programs include the Thai language, social studies, and physical education. Other subjects such as science, math, and arts (including foreign languages) are considered electives. A certain number of electives are required, and students select which electives they will take based on what they will be doing after they graduate. The school day consists of seven periods, and often there is an eighth period after 3:30 P.M. in which students are required to pursue a club interest such as a math, science, chess, or Scrabble, to name a few. Not all subject classes meet every day. For example, math might meet three or four times a week, and physical education might meet twice a week.

Although the Thai government's compulsory education requires students to attend grades one through nine, many Thai families in urban areas send their children to kindergarten from age three or three and a half to age six or seven, at which time they begin first grade. Most Thai students not only remain in school for grades 10 through 12 but also attend tutorials after school and on Saturdays to help prepare them for the entrance exams to universities, colleges, and vocational/specialized schools.

SOCIAL LIFE

Teens in Thailand would be considered shy compared to American teenagers. When children enter school at age six or seven, they begin wearing uniforms. Not only is the clothing they wear standardized, but boys and girls must have their hair cut to a certain length and similar style. It is almost as if everyone starts out the same; there are no visible differences related to socioeconomic status. In lower and upper secondary school, there are different uniforms, but there is no feeling of having to impress or make a statement by what you wear. Boys' uniforms consist of slacks and a cap-sleeve, button-down shirt, while girls wear dark skirts that come below the knee and a cap-sleeve, button-down blouse. Uniforms may vary slightly from school to school, but the standardization and lack of competition to outdress each other remain. This feeling about clothes may set a tone for how Thai teens dress outside of school. Also, in the Thai culture, wearing suggestive or sloppy clothing indicates a lack of respect for the people you are visiting or that visit you. For example, it would be insulting to show up at a good friend's house in wrinkled, oversized clothes. You will not see the typical teenager wearing torn clothes or clothes that are too tight, skimpy, or see-through.

In the villages, teens are able to meet other teens at school, and very often one school serves several villages. Schools do not have socials or dances like they do in the United States, and outside of school there is little time for teens to socialize since they are busy working on the farm. During planting and harvesting, when villages pool their manpower, teens have opportunities to work together, and when one or more villages get together for a celebration, teens are able to socialize. They dance together, participate in games together, or just go for walks together. The kind of dating that teens do in the United States does not occur in the villages. If a young man is interested in a young woman for marriage, the courting is usually restricted to chaperoned visits to the girl's home.

Bangkok provides more opportunities for teens to meet other teens at school, shopping centers, and movie theaters as well as in the neighborhood where they live. Since more than half of the approximately 6 million residents of Bangkok are under the age of 30, most of the city's shopping centers are geared toward younger people. Even though shops carry a much wider variety of styles of clothes, you will rarely see the average teen wearing the type of suggestive clothes worn by teens in the United States. Although most teens in Bangkok do not hold a job, their studies take up a considerable amount of time. Therefore, dates are probably once a week and might consist of a movie and something to eat at one of the many food stalls around the city, or shopping at one of the malls. A special date might be dinner at McDonalds or Burger King, which is much more expensive than the food stalls.

Parents of Thai teenagers express many of the concerns that parents in the United States do regarding their children. Teens are attracted by the expensive clothes, electronic equipment (including cell phones), and night life available in the city and look for quick ways to make some money (e.g., gambling, selling drugs) so they can afford some of these luxuries. There are problems related to premarital sex as well as the availability of drugs and alcohol, and the fact that in most families both parents work and are not around to monitor what their children are doing much of the time. Recently, the Thai government set a 10 P.M. curfew in the city for teens under the age of 18, has begun to require mandatory drug testing in all schools, including colleges and universities, and has begun enforcing more control over night spots in Bangkok. Meanwhile, parent groups are organizing to come up with suggestions for keeping teens out of trouble.

RECREATION

Leisure activities are a very important part of the Thai culture. They believe that fun (*sanuk*) is as important as hard work and that physical sanuk helps keep the individual in balance. Kickboxing (*muay thai*) is Thailand's national sport and dates back to the thirteenth century.

Although both men and women practice muay thai, the actual competitive sport is better left to the professionals. Contestants use their fists, elbows, shoulders, knees, legs, and bare feet against their opponents. Before a match begins, the ringside band begins playing traditional martial arts music and the boxers perform *wai khru*, a short ritual dance paying homage to their teachers. The band plays during the fighting and changes its tune and tempo to suit the action. The boxers wear certain charms for spiritual protection, and women are not permitted into the canvas ring because it is believed their presence would destroy the strength and skill of the boxers. In Bangkok, professional muay thai is played every night at one of the many stadiums and can be seen on television at least once a week.

Another popular participant and spectator sport is *takraw*. This is played by using basically any part of the body except the hands to keep a hollow woven rattan ball five or six inches in diameter in the air. There are many versions of this game, of which the most common among teens is the tossing takraw and the circle takraw. Tossing takraw is almost like a

Thai boxing. Photo © N. Ray/TRIP.

free for all; the goal is just to keep the ball in the air. Circle takraw usually has five or six players. The ball must remain in the air inside the circle created by the players. Hoop takraw is played using a lot of players but no fewer than six on a team. Players on each team take turns hitting the ball into a basket that is about 19.5 feet above the ground. Each team has 40 minutes to hit the ball into the basket as many times as possible. Sepak takraw is the international, competitive version of the sport. It is played with a net on a court similar to a badminton court with three players on each team. Since players do not use their hands, points are scored based on the complexity of the kick or block as well as when the ball hits the ground in the opponent's court. The team to reach 21 points first wins.

Kite flying is a favorite pastime in Thailand as well as a competitive sport during the hot, breezy season. There are two opposing teams, one using male kites (*chula*) and the other female kites (*pakpao*). The smaller pakpao kites try to get the larger chula kites to fall to the ground, while the chula kites try to surround the pakpao kites and force them into the chula side of the playing field. Although soccer (Thai football) and basketball are not played competitively among schools the way they are in the United States, teenagers enjoy playing these and they play them at school more because the schools provide the equipment and playing areas. If a school happens to have a soccer or basketball team, it may play other schools that have teams, but this is not necessarily the formalized type of competition among schools that exists in the United States. Soccer has also become a very popular spectator sport for teens, and, as in the United States, teens follow the games and their sports heroes to the championships.

In recent years, tourism in Thailand has become big business. With the increase in tourism has come an influx of more modern, less traditional sports. Although many of these have expenses involved that prohibit the average teen from participating, they are nevertheless becoming more popular among Thais. In addition to about 50 golf courses, some of which were designed by world-famous golf pros, volleyball, cricket, rugby, snooker (similar to billiards), tennis, and badminton are increasingly available. Many of the beach resorts located in southern Thailand also offer canoeing, surfing, scuba diving, snorkeling, and deep sea fishing. There are also several amusement parks on the outskirts of Bangkok that offer a day of fun for teens as well as their families.

In addition to the more physical activities, teens enjoy playing cards, playing board games such as chess or Scrabble, and, in urban areas, listening to the radio and watching television. Although Thai teens learn how to use computers at school, most teens do not own their own computer. As a result, a popular gathering place for teens in Bangkok is the shops that, for a fee, allow people to use computers. They are a type of Internet cafe. In more rural areas, fish, cock, and goat fighting are more popular among teens.

Thailand has many national and regional celebrations throughout the year. These give Thai families the opportunity to gather with relatives and friends, pool their resources, and have a big party with music, dancing, entertainment, and games. In the villages there are no televisions, computers, or CD players, but there are spacious fields for playing. As mentioned, teens in the villages, when not in school, are working on the farm, and often there is little or no time for leisure activity outside of school. Village festivals and celebrations tend to be even more extravagant than in the city and can sometimes last for several days. In fact, even when there is no festival or holiday, villagers may just decide to get together for a big party. For teens, these serve as an opportunity to interact with other teens outside of school.

One of the concerns parents living in Bangkok have is that their children are spending too much time at sedentary activities and are not getting enough exercise. They feel part of this problem is caused by the lack of open spaces such as parks that would provide safe areas where children and teens could engage in physical activity. Cell phones, very common in Bangkok, enable teens to communicate without having to leave the home, while television keeps teens home watching their favorite programs. Another "teenage" problem parents feel is indicative of Bangkok is gambling. This is interesting since this is a favorite adult pastime. Thais enjoy betting on everything from soccer games and muay thai matches to boat races and cock fights. The Thai government and parent groups in Bangkok have been meeting to try to address these problems.

ENTERTAINMENT

Traditional Thai theater is a combination of dance, literature, drama, and music. The two main forms of classical drama are *khon* and *lakhon*. Both involve lavish costumes, including masks or heavy makeup, and slow, angular dance movements, with lakhon being the more graceful of the two. In khon, the audience can differentiate between demons and heroes by the costume: demons wear masks and heroes, usually depicted as heavenly or divine beings, wear crowns. The stories portrayed are primarily taken from Thai Buddhism and set to traditional Thai music. Classical Thai music is played by a *phiphat*, which is made up of percussion instruments, or a *mahori*, which includes stringed instruments, and depending on the performance, one of these will accompany the drama. *Likay* is a satirical version of lakhon and khon. Likay might be considered Thailand's traditional form of drama-dance comedy. The plot is derived from ancient Thai stories and is portrayed in a satirical manner incorporating improvised jokes and puns. Actors typically wear gaudy costumes to enhance the satirical comedy of the performers. It is common to find these performances in outdoor areas, especially during holiday or festival celebrations.

Bangkok is home to several museums and art galleries, a planetarium, and a cultural center. A variety of visiting opera, ballet, and folk dance troupes from other parts of Asia, Europe, and the United States appear in Bangkok on almost a regular basis. However, these performances are frequented more often by upper-class residents and tourists than by the average Thai teenager. The many modern, air-conditioned movie houses are more attractive to the average teen because they are less expensive and offer a wide variety of Thai as well as Western movies. Most movies made in Thailand are purely for entertainment rather than to promote a social message. The films usually contain a major plot and several subplots and are intended to evoke as many emotions as possible. Thai filmmakers are also involved in the production of films from other countries that are shot in Thailand. Among some of the most well-known are *The Man with the Golden Gun*, *Killing Fields*, and *The Deer Hunter*. Teens also have their favorite pop, rock, and country singing stars and groups and, if there is a concert scheduled, teens will wait on line for hours to buy tickets. For those that like to shop, Chatuchak Park on the outskirts of Bangkok is where the Weekend Market resides, containing acres of stalls selling everything from fresh fruit and vegetables to used books and records, clothes, and household goods and appliances.

Although Bangkok is well known for its varied nightlife, teens are discouraged from frequenting discos because of the expense and the availability of drugs, alcohol, gambling, and prostitution at many of these places. Instead, you will find teens listening to their radios or CD players, watching television (especially local soap operas), going to soccer or other sports games, or meeting friends to play such games as takraw, soccer, or basketball.

In the rural areas, much of the entertainment is created by the villagers themselves. During the communal village parties there is always music, dancing, and lots of food and drink. For special occasions a formal band might be organized and a likay troupe hired for entertainment. Thais also enjoy traveling and, when they are able, will take a few days off to explore various parts of Thailand with the family. In rural areas where CD players and televisions are not readily available, teens will play takraw, cards, or board games together.

RELIGIOUS PRACTICES AND CULTURAL CEREMONIES

Buddhism was introduced to Thailand from India during the third century B.C.E. At this time Thailand had just established itself as a kingdom separate from the rest of Southeast Asia and there was a period of peace and prosperity for the people. Some of the reasons the Thais adopted Buddhism as their state religion may have been because it was similar to what they were practicing but was more tolerant and flexible regarding sacrifices and rituals and did not emphasize a distinction between social classes. Thai Buddhists believe in karma—that life is a progression of reincarnations where each current life is affected by actions from previous lives. Nirvana or enlightenment is the only way to achieve true happiness and end the reincarnations. To attain nirvana one must be able to overcome such traits as greed, craving, and violence, which bring unhappiness, and try to develop the "three pillars" of morality, meditation, and wisdom. The tenets of Buddhism are actually rules on how to live your life in order to achieve the ultimate happiness, nirvana. Widespread among the Thais is the belief in spirits, astrology, and the power of amulets for protection. If one is experiencing bad luck, this could be the result of something from a previous life, bad karma; and wearing a particular amulet, sprinkling the item causing the bad luck with lustral water (water blessed by a monk), or "making merit" can help overcome the bad karma.

Making merit refers to paying homage. It is a way of reinforcing one's belief in and commitment to Buddhism and of paying respect to the person or concept for which one is making merit. On the Buddha's birthday (Visakha Bucha), the May full moon, people make merit to the Triple Gem—Buddha (the teacher), the Dhamma (truth—the teachings), and the Sangha (followers of Buddhism—the students)—by bringing flowers, candles, and incense to the temple. When a person dies, it is common for the family members to make merit for that person as a way of helping the deceased get to paradise. This indicates that he or she was admired and respected. Ways of making merit consist of making thin leaves out of gold and affixing them to images of Buddha and other sacred objects, donating food to the monks, helping build or renovate a temple, and creating elaborate sculptures and paintings. As a result of the Thai people's unanimous acceptance and practice of Buddhism, this religion has been the focus of most of Thailand's cultural development throughout the decades. It is found in architecture, literature, painting, and sculpture.

The wat is an enclosed complex containing many buildings, including the Buddhist temple, often a library of religious texts, a bell tower, and various housings for elaborate Buddhas or other sacred images. The living quarters for the monks are usually next to the wat but separated from it by a wall. Although the temple's primary objective has always been to teach Buddhism in order to help people achieve nirvana, throughout Thailand's history, the village wat has also served as a school, community and recreation center, hospital, hotel, and so on, and the village monks have been teachers, arbitrators, doctors of herbal medicines, and counselors. Currently, most of Thailand's 30,000 wats are located in the villages, where they still perform many of the same functions they did decades ago. In the urban areas, wats often provide temporary homes for students who have come from the villages to attend school in the city, for orphans, and even for troubled teenagers.

Traditionally in Thailand, when children are born they are given a nickname by which they will be referred to by family and close friends for the rest of their lives. After a month and a day there is a ceremony during which the monk cuts the child's hair (first haircut) and the father finishes by shaving the child's head. It is believed that after this period of time the child is free of danger from illnesses that might be inflicted on the newborn by spirits. Usually, at the same time, the child is given an official name. Sometime during their teens and before marrying, all Buddhist males become monks for at least one rainy season in order to make merit for themselves and their parents. This represents the boy's transition to adulthood. The actual ordination after the three-month period is an elaborate ceremony followed by a big party. In some villages girls will not even consider marrying a man who has never been a monk. These traditions have continued in urban areas. Even for those Thais that do not consider themselves practicing Buddhists, much of the teachings of Buddhism make sense to follow as a practical way to a happier life. Also, many of the traditions associated with Buddhism carry with them some form of superstition that these people may not be willing to reject completely.

At one time, marriages were arranged by parents, but now prearranged marriages are rare. In the villages, older teens select their own marriage partners. They are usually married by the age of 20, but in cities this is not the case. The wedding ceremonies are very different from those in the United States. They are made up of traditional and religious elements. For example, in one part of the ceremony, wai phee, the couple says prayers to show respect for their dead ancestors. Another part of the ceremony, khan mark, is a procession made by friends and relatives coming to the house for the wedding ceremony, each one carrying a gift. It is customary in the villages for the newly married couple to move in with the wife's family; the husband works on the wife's family's farm. This also avoids any conflicts between the wife and the husband's mother that might have occurred had the couple moved in with the husband's family. In the cities it is more common for the newlyweds to move into their own home. Before doing so, they make sure there is a spirit house on the property. This is about the size of a doll house and is placed on the property in order to provide any spirits that might be living in the house an alternative place to stay. Though women perform most of the household chores, they also work in the fields on the farms or hold a full-time job if the couple lives in the city. The man's primary responsibility in the village is running the farm, but it is not uncommon for a man, whether he lives in the city or the village, to do the laundry or cook.

Thais enjoy getting together for parties. Each year they celebrate three New Years. The Songkran Festival, which is the Buddhist New Year, marks the beginning of the solar year. This three-day celebration is also referred to as homecoming. Families get together and go to the temple to make merit offerings. At the temple, children ceremoniously pour water blessed by the monk into the hands of their parents and older relatives to show their respect. After temple come the celebrations during which it is customary for people to throw water (sometimes buckets of water) at each other in a good-natured way. Thais also celebrate the Chinese New Year since about 15 percent of the population of Thailand, the largest minority there, is Chinese. And the Thais celebrate the calendar New Year on January 1. They celebrate both the Chinese and the calendar New Year with fireworks and parties.

In Thailand, holidays are celebrated based on the monarchy, Coronation Day, the King's Birthday; Buddhism, The Buddhist New Year, Ok Phansa (Buddha's reappearance on Earth after having spent time preaching in heaven); and the growing season, the Royal Ploughing Ceremony marking the start of the rice-growing season, and the Fruit Festival marking the start of the fruit-picking season.

CONCLUSION

Thailand is a country rich in culture, religion, and national pride. You will never see public criticism of the monarchy or Buddhism in the media, theater, or literature. In the United States, comedians pride themselves on clever political jokes, but this is something that simply would not occur in Thailand. In fact, the movie *Anna and the King* was banned in Thailand because the government felt it did not accurately depict Siam.

The Thai people value their freedom as a country, as a family unit, and then as individuals. They understand the importance of working as a team, and their respect for the hierarchy of that team is part of their daily lives. Buddhism, for the Thai people, reinforces these feelings not only through its teachings but by the physical presence of the wat and its ability to take on responsibilities based on the needs of the community where it resides. Thais can be characterized by such words as *krengchai*, which means one does not criticize others because it will upset the person's personal balance, and *phuan ta*, which means a friend for whom one would die if necessary. *Mai pen rai*, which means "never mind," might be interpreted by someone in the United States to be derogatory, but in Thailand this expresses the feeling that problems should not be overemphasized because life should be enjoyed.

The question now is whether the children growing up in Bangkok will be able to maintain the same values that their parents and grandparents have had for centuries. The strong family unit needed for survival on the farms is not needed in the same way in the city. Having "things" may gradually become more important to teens than associating with people. Many people feel that Thai history confirms the fact that their culture and tradition are strong enough and, at the same time, flexible enough to overcome troubled times and times of change. They cite in particular the student demonstrations that led to the current constitution of Thailand.

Teens in Thailand today are faced with many of the same issues that teenagers in the United States face. Their worlds are changing and they need to become educated enough to be able to make well-informed decisions about their present and future.

ACKNOWLEDGMENT

Special thanks to Nantapa Posrinak.

RESOURCE GUIDE

Nonfiction

Background notes, Thailand, Government Documents Collection. (1994). Washington, DC: U.S. Department of State, Bureau of Public Affairs, Office of Public Communication.

Brown, D. (1997). *Thailand, Eyewitness Travel Guides* (P. Cornwel Smith, Ed.). New York: DK Publishing.

Mulder, N. (2000). *Inside Thai society.* Chiang Mai, Thailand: Silkworm Books.

Smythe, D. (1994). *Thailand.* Santa Barbara, CA: Clio Press.

Wyatt, D. K. (1984). *Thailand: A short history.* New Haven: Yale University Press.

Fiction and Poetry

Barrett, D. (1999). *Kingdom of make believe*. New York: Village Easy Books.

Ho, M. (1996). *Hush, a Thai lullaby*. New York: Orchard Books.

Kepner Fulop, S. (Ed.). (1996). *The lioness in bloom: Modern Thai fiction about women*. Berkeley, CA: University of California.

Masavisuth, N. (Ed.). (1999). *The SEA Write anthology of Thai short stories and poems*. Chiang Mai, Thailand: Silkworm Books.

Read, M., & Vathanaprida, S. (1998). *The girl who wore too much: A folktale from Thailand*. Little Rock, AR: August House Little Folk.

Somtow, S. P. (2000). *Dragon's fin soup: Eight modern Siamese fables*. Northridge, CA: Babbage Press.

Web Sites

http://www.bangkokpost.net
http://www.encyclopedia.com/html/section/thailand
http://www.encyclopediaamericana.com
http://www.escati.com
http://www.experiencethailand.com
http://www.hoteltravel.com/thailand/guides/thailand_sports.html
http://www.mahidol.ac.th
http://www.nationmultimedia.com
http://www.nectec.or.th
http://www.sunsite.au.ac.th
http://www.thailandgrandfestival.com
http://www.thailandlife.com
http://www.thaiways.com

Pen Pal/Chat

http://www.bangkokpost.net
http://www.sakdipat.com
http://www.sriwittayapaknam.ac.th/suthiphong
http://www.student-weekly@Bangkokpost.net

Chapter 15

VIETNAM

Judy Chin

INTRODUCTION

The Socialist Republic of Vietnam is a long, thin country that curves southward from China with its coastal line traversing the Gulf of Tonkin, the South China Sea, and the Gulf of Thailand. Like Burma, Laos, and Thailand, Vietnam was once included in an area called Indochina because it is located between the much larger countries of China and India. Both Indonesia and China left their marks on Vietnam, as did other countries.

The Vietnamese people have a history of being ruled by others and until very recently have not been able to govern themselves without direct external influences. Although it has an old and established culture, as a sovereign nation the newly formed Socialist Republic of Vietnam is in its adolescence—in a transitional stage of growth and development, full of conflicts and contradictions. Vietnam continues to struggle internally and externally as it carves its new identity and makes the decisions that will shape its future and determine its place in Asia and the world.

The ancient roots of Vietnamese culture are located in the Red River Delta in northern Vietnam. It is thought that the first Indonesians arrived from the south in about 1500 B.C. and established a kingdom named Champa on the eastern coast. The explorers who settled in this area, and later Indian explorers, along with Thais and Chinese, mixed with the indigenous people of the region, who were Negroid pygmies, and created a distinct group of people identifiable as Vietnamese. Descendants of these early Negroid pygmies can be seen in the much darker skinned tribal people who make up one of the larger minority groups, the Montagnards. They live in the mountainous regions.

The kingdoms that followed the first one in Champa were much more closely tied to China than anywhere else. The land now known as Vietnam was ruled for over one thousand years by the Chinese. Their influences on Vietnamese culture are great and permeate almost every aspect of art and culture. Although dominated by the Chinese, the Vietnamese continued to want freedom. After years of trying to break free from the dominance of China, Vietnam was finally able to establish its own independence in about 900 A.D., but this was achieved only by pledging strict loyalty to China. In effect, Vietnam could be independent only because China let it be and expected Vietnam to cooperate with the Chinese in all ways.

For the next several centuries, Vietnam enjoyed self-rule. Various aristocratic families controlled Vietnam, but there was no centralized government and the north and south were constantly fighting. Eventually they divided the country into two sections, north and south. This was the situation the explorers found when they first came to Vietnam in the early sixteenth century. By the early 1500s European explorers were arriving and trading in Vietnam. The Portuguese were first, followed by the Dutch, the British, and then the French. It was this final group that decided to colonize Vietnam. After many years of extensive battles, the French ended Vietnam's independence in 1883. Its domination over the next hundred years would reap more benefits for the French than for the Vietnamese. There would be some positive aspects of France's being in Indonesia, but not many. The French introduced different customs and, most important, influenced the Vietnamese with a Western approach to learning. While the French grew richer from the plantations they owned, the Vietnamese worked long hours for minimal pay and did not improve their life circumstances appreciably. In fact, when the French domination of Vietnam began, almost 80 percent of the Vietnamese population could read; when the French finally left the country nearly a hundred years later, only about 20 percent of the population could read. Like most groups, the Vietnamese did not want to be dominated by another culture and strove for liberation. There were frequent battles with the French. The country finally got its opportunity for independence after World War II.

During World War II, the Japanese were one of the Axis powers, the group that fought against the United States, Great Britain, and France. They fought the war from the Pacific side of the world. They invaded China and then moved southward to Southeast Asia. Since France was a member of the Allied forces, the Japanese arrested all French officials and declared Vietnam independent. Although supposedly it had autonomy, it was really supervised by the Japanese armies. They chose the head of its government too. But Japan was not on the winner's side at the conclusion of World War II. The course of the war changed, and Japan surrendered. This left an opportunity for the Vietnamese people to take control of their own land. The Vietminh, which was a communist organization of various liberation groups, took over in August 1945. Once again, Vietnam claimed itself an independent nation. It was named the Democratic Republic of Vietnam and led by a man named Ho Chi Minh. Despite having declared itself a sovereign nation, Vietnam was not able to begin the necessary steps to independence. Battles continued with the French. World War II was over, but the French wanted to regain control of their Indochinese colonies. They wanted to continue to exploit the region for their financial gain. So a war broke out, once again between Vietnam and France. The war raged on for over eight years. By 1953, France controlled the major cities, but the rural areas in northern Vietnam remained under the control of the Vietminh, Ho Chi Minh's party. Intervention was necessary to bring peace to the region. It was decided that in order to end the French-Indochina War, Vietnam should be divided into two parts, north and south. Historically, whenever there was separation of governments in Vietnam it had been along these lines. This division was supposed to be temporary until elections could be held that would form a unified Vietnam. However, the elections did not occur, and struggle began among the Vietnamese people themselves. There was continued fighting between north and south, and the situation in Vietnam worsened. U.S. military advisors were brought in to assist the South Vietnamese in fighting the North Vietnamese. By 1962, the United States had more than 12,000 military advisors in South Vietnam. They were not allowed to enter the war, but finally, in 1964, after a naval ship was reportedly attacked off of North Vietnam, the United States was allowed to take part in the war. By 1967, there were over half a million American soldiers serving in Vietnam. In 1969, the United States began its gradual withdrawal of troops. The military involvement of the United States lasted 10 years; in the end, North Vietnam defeated South Vietnam. Saigon fell to the North Vietnamese in mid-1975.

In 1976, once again, the country of Vietnam was formed into and represented by one government. The formation of the Socialist Republic of Vietnam created a one-party communist government. In this type of government, everything is state controlled, which at a basic level means that people are not free to own their own businesses or use their farm to produce food for sale for themselves. The people in the south were not used to this type of political or economical system and so they were quite resistant to it. To try to bring everyone to the same economy, the new government did three things that caused a great deal of concern and dissatisfaction among the South Vietnamese: they changed the currency, they sent major resisters to reeducation camps, and they displaced entire families. The currency change occurred overnight. People who had one day had money woke up to discover their money was now worthless paper. Imagine what it would be like to realize the money you saved yesterday to buy something today, no longer had any value. This caused extreme panic. Now people who had been wealthy were no longer. They were now in a position where they had to accept and do what the government asked. This was part of an attempt by the government to make everyone equal. People who resisted or disagreed with the new socialist government were sent to re-education camps so they would accept the new government structure. Basically these were concentration camps. Some people spent three or more years in them, separated from their families. For a culture that is so family oriented, this was an extreme event. War had already torn at the heart of families; the placement of many mothers and fathers into these camps only deepened that tear. Additionally, in the same year, the government moved over 600,000 people against their will from Ho Chi Minh City (formerly Saigon) into new economic zones to boost agricultural production and help prevent starvation, as well as to disperse possible dissenters so they could not unify and resist together. It was evident to those who lived in South Vietnam that the government of Ho Chi Minh intended to control with an iron hand. These three events spurred a massive migration out of the country.

Because the state controlled everything, the only way people could leave was to pay large sums of money (as much as two thousand dollars per person) to the government for permission to leave. That gave them passage to sail on an unsafe boat and risk death at sea. If the boat did not sink, they still had to deal with lack of food and water, leading to possible starvation and dehydration. Worst and most ominous of all, there were sea pirates from neighboring countries who robbed and committed violent acts against those who came to be known as the boat people.

The exodus of anticommunists, over 2 million people, continued for nearly four years. Vietnam lost many of its professional, managerial, and skilled workers. For the most part, it was the elite and well-educated classes that left Vietnam at this time. This massive migration had a major effect on the country that has lasted even up to now, leaving a large hole in the Vietnamese economy. The removal of professional and skilled labor meant that people moved into positions they were not qualified for. For years, the communist economic and political system has made foreign investment difficult and kept Vietnam from developing more rapidly. It is only recently that the country has begun to move toward a more open economy.

Following the declaration of independence, Vietnam received a large amount of assistance from what used to be known as the Soviet Union, but since its dissolution, economic times have become much harder. Besides having an economical and political system that makes it an unappealing trading partner for some countries, Vietnam's human rights record has deterred foreign investment. The Vietnamese government itself is struggling with its economic situation: the leaders would very much like to be a member of the World Trade Organization, but because of their political beliefs they do not yet feel they can open their state sector to outside competition. They do not want to give up their control of business. They have made certain concessions and adjustments, like allowing farmers to sell some of their crops for personal profit. However, the government still maintains a strong hold on business. This internal conflict causes much strife and hardship within the country.

TYPICAL DAY

A typical day in the life of a teenager in Vietnam will vary depending on his or her region of the country and social class. The south is more urbanized than the north; in cities, there are more activities and goods available than in villages. Ho Chi Minh City (formerly Saigon) in the south is a more developed and thriving city than Hanoi in the north. Part of the reason for this has to do with the governments that were there prior to reunification of the country: the north was communist and state controlled, whereas the south was capitalist and driven by a free market. Although independence came more than 25 years ago, there are still roots beneath the surface that stretch to that time and affect the way people think about business and the economy.

There are approximately 76 million people living in Vietnam. Only a quarter of the population lives in cities; the rest live in villages in the rural areas. Where people live dictates, to a certain degree, how they live. In the rural villages of Vietnam, fresh running water and electricity are still luxuries, so living conditions are more difficult. Agriculture, especially rice production, is the main industry in this area, so teenagers usually spend some part of their day helping to increase production in these farming areas. Even though they are in school six days a week, since their school day is much shorter than the American school day there is time left over to help the family with chores. Because there is no running water in some areas, it may have to be brought to the village from local canals. Those canals may provide the water for the kitchen as well as the tub for bathing. The lack of water means that the daily things that most American teenagers take for granted, such as washing machines and indoor toilets, are not to be expected in many homes in the rural areas. Nevertheless, clothes and dishes still get washed, and meals still get cooked. Without electricity, meals must be prepared on an open fire and food must be secured the day of cooking and usually eaten at that time, since refrigeration is limited and leftovers cannot be stored. Without good roads, transportation of goods is hampered. That means fewer supplies can reach these areas easily or rapidly. One mode of transportation that a teenager might use besides walking or riding a bicycle is taking a boat. For centuries the rivers have been the major thoroughfares of Vietnam. Boats are more readily available than bicycles or cars, and though waterways may be congested, they are still more dependable than the road system.

The number of children in the rural family and their ages affects how much responsibility each child has around the house. For instance, older teenage children are often asked to look after younger siblings. Since many homes house more than two generations, teenagers may also need to help take care of an elderly grandparent, uncle, or aunt.

Teenagers who live in the more urbanized areas have more distractions than their peers in the villages, but many of their activities are the same. School days in the urban areas are the same as in the rural. That leaves time to go to the market for fresh produce. The market in a major city or large town is a more thriving and interesting place: there is more going on and a larger variety and abundance of goods. Since cities have more roads there is not only more foot traffic due to the density of the population but also more vehicular traffic, particularly bicycles, motorbikes, and bicycle rickshaws. There are movie houses and different types of stores and shops, so teenagers have more opportunities to be exposed to more things. It is in the cities where the street children go to live. These are children who have come to the city to try to have a better life. Many times they are encouraged by their parents to go since life in the farming communities provides fewer avenues for their financial security and success in the future. Unfortunately, these children frequently end up begging on the street or become involved in criminal activity, such as prostitution. Many of them fall victim in some way to the drug trade. In the year 2000, Vietnam estimated that it had approximately 4,800 child addicts. This is one of the reasons for an emphasis by the government on combatting drug abuse through educational programs and family involvement. Life in the cities may offer more opportunities but can also be dangerous for teenagers on their own.

FAMILY LIFE

Prior to reunification, the family was considered to be the primary socioeconomic unit in Vietnam. Now the role of the family has changed somewhat. In many places you can see as many as three generations living under the same roof. This has always been the norm since family and filial piety has always been valued. It used to be thought that large families were better, so couples had many children. One of the advantages of so many children was that as people got older there would be more family to care for them. By tradition a married couple would care for the man's parents. If there was only one son in the family, he and his wife would go and live with his parents. If there were no sons in the family, at least one daughter would remain unmarried to care for her parents. The government now advises married couples to have no more than two children. Before, most families would have preferred more boys than girls since there was more value placed on males than females. That attitude has been changing over the last 50 years. Of course, in the rural mountainous areas, change is more gradual. The socialist government has tried to make the sexes more equal and change traditional roles for men and women. A famous slogan that was used to promote this idea was "As good in running society as running the home, women must be the equals of men." Currently over 60 percent of the workforce is female and employed in a variety of jobs. Fewer women are thought of and treated as second-class citizens.

Dire economic circumstances and a country that is struggling to develop mean that in most families both parents work. The average annual income is only $240. Even though the cost of living in Vietnam is lower than in the United States, this is still very little money. Unemployment is nearly 25 percent. There is a growing gap between the rich and the poor that the government is aware of and trying to address by developing agriculture and bringing in foreign investment. There are factories that make Nike shoes and ones that make the toys for McDonalds Happy Meals. There is more emphasis on war-related tourism, with travel agencies offering tours of the underground tunnels used by the Vietcong during the war with the Americans. Another business that is war related is the production of artificial limbs. There are land mines, artillery shells, and cluster bomblets that lie underground in areas in Vietnam. Most of them are in the Quang Tri province, where some of the worst fighting occurred. These munitions have killed almost 3,000 people, and more than 1,600 others have lost their eyes, arms, or legs. The war is over, but it still affects life today. Even though the government does not like Western influences, particularly American influences, its leaders realize that in today's global climate, some westernization is inevitable.

In America most teenagers look forward to driving or getting a car. In Vietnam, however, less than 20 percent of all roads are paved. Most of those are located on the coast. Motorbikes are more accessible and affordable than cars. They are also involved in many road accidents, causing the government to require helmets to cut down on injuries. If a teenager is fortunate enough to have some form of transportation, more likely than not it will be a bicycle; a really lucky teenager might have a motorbike.

TRADITIONAL AND NONTRADITIONAL FOOD DISHES

Vietnamese food is a blend of foods from the cultures that have dominated it historically. The influence of Chinese, French, and to a lesser extent, Indian cuisines can be found in Vietnamese cooking. Unlike American meals, Vietnamese meals are not served in courses. All the food is usually served at once and is shared from common dishes. There is usually some form of starch, either rice or noodles. Most meals have a soup, a stir-fry, or another main dish. Bowls and chopsticks are used instead of plates and forks. In cities, many people eat *pho* for their breakfast or midday meal. It is a soup made of noodles, onions, and organ meats or beef. Another type of lunch in the south might be *banh xe*. This is a sort of crepe filled with vegetables and meat. In rural areas breakfast will usually be *xoi*. This is sticky rice steamed in a leaf wrapper. Sometimes peanuts or mung beans will be steamed in the rice. Large portions of meat are not served like they are in the United States; instead, meat is sliced or chopped into smaller pieces that do not require cutting at the table. Since Vietnam has a long coastal line, fish and seafood are important components of meals. Fish is often dried since refrigeration is scarce. The lack of refrigeration is also a reason that food is obtained on the same day that it is prepared. Just as American teenagers love their ketchup, Vietnamese teenagers love their *nuoc mam*, a fish sauce made with lime juice, sugar, garlic, and hot chiles. They use this for dipping all sorts of finger snacks. Vegetables and fruits are an important part of the Vietnamese diet. Vegetables are often served fresh or after very little cooking. Most workers eat their main and largest meal in the middle of the day. This is especially true if someone lives in the rural area, since in a subtropical climate the midday is the hottest part of the day. Many village people have a larger meal halfway through the day and take time to rest when the temperatures are most extreme. In villages or cities, the females in the household still usually do the cooking. Additionally, in rural villages it is customary for the women to serve the men first. Tea is the beverage that everyone drinks all the time. Usually, however, it is drunk not with a meal but before or after it. Another drink is sugarcane juice. Of course, sodas are always available and quite popular. Teenagers in America love fast food and like hanging out at places like McDonalds or Taco Bell. The only fast food outlet the government permits in Vietnam is Kentucky Fried Chicken, and the average student or worker cannot afford to eat there.

The Vietnamese diet, a mixture of fresh produce and meat, is a fairly healthy one, but the problem is a continuing scarcity of meat and an insufficient number of calories. Although there is no obvious threat of starvation now like there was 25 years ago, many in the Vietnamese population are undernourished. Protein sources are more limited in the mountainous regions. An effort had to be made by the government to educate people to include it in meals for children since two-thirds of children under 3 are malnourished and nearly 40 percent of all children ages 6 to 18 are undernourished. There is far more food in the south of Vietnam than there is in the north. Although Vietnam is the third-largest exporter of rice in the world, there is not an abundance of food within the country, and there are few ways to store it or transport it, so this remains a serious problem for the nation.

SCHOOLING

Almost 40 percent of the population in Vietnam is under the age of 15, so there is an intense need for education. Children start school at the age of 5 and can continue their education for 12 years. All levels of schooling used to be totally free, but because of severe economic problems the government now requires that parents pay a minimal tuition fee, pay for books, pay for school uniforms, and contribute to parent-teacher organizations, which helps to raise the teachers' low salaries. For most students, the school day runs for four hours, six days a week, all year long. The government has restructured the educational system and now requires children to complete nine years of compulsory education and three additional years in secondary schools. Once students have graduated from a secondary school they are ready for any type of employment requiring skilled labor. They are also able to apply to colleges or vocational schools. One of the differences between schooling in the United States and schooling in Vietnam is the inclusion of manual labor at the primary and secondary

Students in Ho Chi Minh City, Vietnam. Photo © H. Bower/TRIP.

levels. Students are required to spend about 15 percent of school time engaged in some form of manual labor.

One of the things that American students take for granted in their schools is variety in their curriculum. In Vietnam, students study the same thing across the nation. There is an emphasis on socialist ideas and vocational training. The other subjects taught include history, geography, mathematics, and literature. Literacy for the entire population is almost 95 percent. Both Confucianism from the Chinese tradition and the French influence gave the Vietnamese a high regard for education and learning. Most Vietnamese see education as a way to improve themselves. The Vietnamese system, like the American system, educates the gifted students and those who have physical disabilities. Unlike American schools, Vietnamese schools face extreme shortages of equipment, buildings, and teachers and in some areas an alarmingly high dropout rate. One of the big problems facing the country is the number of secondary students who are staying home. It is mainly the teenagers in the villages who are not attending school. Approximately 50 percent of them are remaining at home because their parents cannot afford to pay for books. Another reason students are not going to school is that they no longer see it as a road to financial security or success. Nearly three-quarters of Vietnamese live in rural areas, but the chances for opportunity exist only in the urban areas; there are not enough jobs to go around, so teenagers in the villages prefer to work to try to improve their circumstances. The government wants to continue to improve schooling for the nation's children and to develop a stronger and more skilled workforce. Because of the previous high literacy rate, the prospects of being able to create highly skilled and educated workers are quite high, but students must first go to school and stay there to get an education.

SOCIAL LIFE

Different cultures interact and express themselves in some ways that other cultures may misinterpret. For instance, in Vietnam it is quite common to see friends of the same sex, either girls or boys, holding hands or walking arm in arm. A young American male might find it uncomfortable to have another male hold his hand or place his arm around him, but a Vietnamese boy would not. Also, American teenagers like to show their affection for members of the opposite sex publicly. This is not considered acceptable behavior in Vietnam for anyone, including teenagers. Dating in Vietnam is different from in the United States. On a first date a Vietnamese boy would usually ask a girl to have a cup a coffee or something to drink, or to go for a ride around the town in a rickshaw. He would never ask a girl to go to the movies on the first date. This would imply that he thought a girl was "easy." Any girl who wanted to protect her reputation would decline this kind of invitation. If they continued dating and decided to go steady, the boy would ask to meet her family. He would usually go over on a weekend and meet the entire family, which could mean not only the nuclear family but also all its extensions: uncles, aunts, and very important, grandparents. He would then visit them weekly. Because of the Vietnamese culture's ties to former Chinese cultural traditions, the family still has a great deal of say about whom their teenager can see and date. Many of the parents of today's teenagers were the first generation to have the freedom to choose their own marriage partners. Their own parents had had that decision made for them by their families. Arranged marriages and the importance of the family in making decisions is a part of Vietnam's recent past. In the last few years, more and more young people in the rural areas have been marrying earlier and earlier. The reason for this is financial. If they leave their parents' home to begin their own family, the government gives them land. Many teenagers end up being parents themselves at an early age and miss out on being a teenager almost completely because of economic factors.

The government does not want there to be American or Western influences in Vietnam. The traditional dress for Vietnamese women has always been the *ao dai* outfit: a blouse with long panels worn over a pair of long loose-legged white or black pants. In an effort to produce social equality, the government initially encouraged the wearing of simple clothes made from black, white, or gray cloth since the type of fabric and the color of the fabric had once been an indication of a person's position in society. Still, it is not uncommon in the urban areas to see jeans and T-shirts. Western styles are most often seen in the south, in the cities, and on younger people.

RECREATION

A Sony Walkman, a CD player, or toys for younger teens are almost out of the reach of the average Vietnamese youth. It is not unusual in a city to see street children scrounging through a diner's discards to retrieve metal cans. Most of these cans are sold for scrap metal, but many can also be used for amusement. There is not a lot of time for play or recreation for many of the teenagers of Vietnam. It is one of the poorest nations in the world, so reality dictates that people work and save whatever they have. Most teenagers in America spend a lot of time on the phone chatting with their friends. Most teenagers in Vietnam cannot do this since the majority of the population lives in the rural area and only about 10 percent of the villages have phones. Watching television usually requires going to someone else's house. Electricity is extremely expensive and in many rural areas it is not available; there are also frequent blackouts that interrupt viewing.

Beyond a doubt, the most popular sport in Vietnam, both to watch and to play, is soccer. There are many teams throughout Vietnam, and informal games often occur in the afternoons. When Vietnam plays in the World Cup competition, everyone watches. All those who own a large television may open their doors so their less fortunate neighbors can have the joy of watching their country's team play. One of the victory celebrations when the national team wins is motorbike drag racing. This is a dangerous and often deadly way to celebrate the team's win, but it is common.

Along the coastal areas, teens may be involved in some form of water sport, such as swimming, snorkeling, or diving. Fishing is more of an industry than a recreational sport. For a few adventurous people who like spelunking, the exploration of caves, there is a set of spectacular caves known as the Pon Nha River Caves.

ENTERTAINMENT

Like teens almost everywhere, Vietnamese kids like music, music, music. It could be traditional or more contemporary, like jazz or pop. The most contemporary popular Vietnamese music is quite diverse since it may combine ancient and modern forms of music. Regional and ethnic differences across the country can add unusual patterns and sounds to the music. More and more, this is a global society and popular music from around the world affects contemporary Vietnamese music.

Vietnamese music is remarkable in one sense because it has managed to survive as a recognizable musical form despite nearly one thousand years of Chinese domination, a hundred years of French rule, and ten years of U.S. military occupation.

One of the most popular performers in Vietnam is Tranh Lam. She has recorded many albums that have been released in the United States as well as across Asia. She frequently tours Asia. She is known for her unusual singing style, which is very expressive and powerful, very different from the lyrical, ballad-like singing of typical Asian female singers. Another very popular female singer is My Linh. She is totally different from Tranh Lam but has a very large following. Her music is lighter and more pop-oriented. Her voice is light and sweet, much like the more traditional singers of Vietnamese music. Many of the more popular musicians, composers, and singers born in Vietnam now live abroad, most often in the United States or in France.

Another form of entertainment is *cai luong*. This is a form of musical theater. It combines traditional music, dance, and theater in a form that is similar to opera. It began in about 1920. It was created by musicians of the south, using the traditional theater styles of the north, *hat boi* and *hat cheo*. It then combined southern chamber music and some elements of French music. It remains quite popular today.

If teens cannot go to concerts, buy CDs, or attend performances in the theater, they still can see these types of entertainment on television. There are now seven channels offering a variety of types of programming, including films that are directed and produced in Vietnam. However, since there is limited electricity throughout Vietnam, there are only about 3.7 million televisions in a population 20 times as large. This is quite a difference from many American homes, where teenagers may even have a television in their own bedroom.

RELIGIOUS PRACTICES AND CULTURAL CEREMONIES

Vietnam has had many cultural influences throughout its history, so religious practices and traditions vary for teenagers depending on whether they practice Confucianism, Buddhism, Taoism, Catholicism, or Cao Daism.

Confucius was a Chinese teacher and philosopher who developed a set of guidelines for behavior. He thought that education, ethics, and an honest government were necessary and should be valued. He taught that an orderly society was dependent on the ability of the emperor to rule justly and fairly. If he did, then all else would follow and the cosmic, natural, and human order would maintain balance and harmony, receiving approval from heaven; without it, there would be social disorder and no approval from heaven. Although through the centuries Confucianism has changed, certain values and beliefs have stayed the same. Teenagers who are Confucianists have a strong sense of family and tradition. They are very loyal to the family, both nuclear and extended, and demonstrate through their relationships a respect for traditions. They also have a deep devotion to their parents, as well as a strong belief that they must practice personal self-restraint. These ideas are found wherever there are believers in the teaching of Confucius.

If a teenager is a Taoist, he or she believes in the teachings of Lao-Tsu, who was a philosopher and believed in a spirit world. Taoism is a religion that stems from the Chinese domination of Vietnam. It is similar to Confucianism but is more concerned with religious issues. Teenage Taoists are interested in harmonizing with the fundamental energies in the universe. They will read and be familiar with the Tao Te Ching, a book of Lao-Tsu's writings that is as important to understanding Taoism as the Bible is to understanding Christianity, for instance. Teenagers will worship their ancestors and concentrate on geomancy: how things connect and align themselves with Earth, an important part of this religion.

Most teenagers will probably be a follower of Buddhism since this religion is the most widely practiced in Vietnam. It originated in India. Buddhism is not based on an idea or belief in God. It also does not have a specific set of written beliefs, which is one reason that Buddhism in one country might be somewhat different from Buddhism in another. The life of Siddhartha Gautama, the man who became Buddha, is very important to understanding this religion since it explains most of the basic teachings of Buddhism. Teenagers who believe in Buddhism hope to reach nirvana, the attainment of perfect peace, perfect knowledge, and ultimate truth. They will maintain a shrine in their home that has an image of Buddha and usually burn incense and candles to show respect and appreciation for his teachings.

Some teenagers in Vietnam are Catholics. This is a Christian religion that was brought to Vietnam by French missionaries. Teenagers who practice Catholicism believe that Jesus was the son of God and follow the writings in the Bible. They believe in heaven, hell, purgatory, saints, and the Virgin Mary. Most of the Catholics in Vietnam live in cities, and many of them left after the reunification of Vietnam in 1976.

In the rural villages one is more likely to find animism, although there are probably very few teenagers who practice this religion. Those who do practice are more likely to live in the mountainous tribal areas than anywhere else. They believe that rivers, trees, and many other things in the world have souls. Since most tribes have disappeared or been driven out of the country, there are few animists left.

There is one religion that is peculiar to Vietnam. It has taken ideas and beliefs from various religions and mixed them. Teenagers who believe in Cao Dai worship a variety of religious figures and historical people as their saints: Buddha, Christ, and Joan of Arc (a French peasant girl who led a revolt against the English in the early fifteenth century). It is an eclectic religion. Even though there are many religions present in Vietnam, they still need government approval to be practiced or they are considered to be unlawful superstitions.

No matter their religion, all Vietnamese people celebrate Tet. It is the single most important holiday in Vietnam. It is difficult for an American teenager to understand how immensely special this holiday is. There is no American equivalent. It is like Christmas, Independence Day, and Thanksgiving all rolled into one. A three-day holiday, Tet is the celebration of the lunar new year. Most Vietnamese end up getting a week of holiday time to prepare for and celebrate this day. During Tet, peach tree branches and strips of red and gold paper can be seen decorating homes. Every night there are fireworks. Special meals, which include more meat and confections than normal, are eaten. The Vietnamese go to great lengths and expense to celebrate this holiday in style and in spirit. Items made out of paper that represent jewelry, televisions, motorcycles, or money are sold for home altars. These items and food will be burned as sacrifices for ancestors. In Vietnamese tradition it is important that ancestors know how much they are worshiped. It is a matter of great pride that they not be ashamed of their progeny. The theme of ancestor worship and devotion to family tradition remains strong in the Vietnamese people no matter what their religious beliefs.

Another holiday that all teenagers would love is a holiday that celebrates them. That is what Tet Trung Thu is. It is the Children's Festival, sometimes called the Mid-Autumn Festival. One of the most famous activities on this day is the lantern procession. Many youth groups participate in this parade, holding lighted lanterns as they proceed down the streets. Teenage groups usually perform and compete for prizes. It is a symbolic procession. The translation of the name for the parade is "a carp (a type of fish) that transformed itself into a dragon." It is supposed to represent the hard work and accomplishments that young students have achieved.

This celebration dates back thousands of years and was originally a celebration of autumn, but its main purpose now is to celebrate education, arts, crafts, and, most important, affection and appreciation for young people. The food that is eaten on that day is of the sweeter variety, with moon cake, lotus seed cake, and mung bean cake being among the most popular. Of course, as always, tea is drunk by everyone. This is a time for families to be with one another and enjoy their young people.

Even though the country of Vietnam may be poor economically, it is rich in family and in the spirit of celebration.

CONCLUSION

Being a teenager in Vietnam is difficult because life in Vietnam is difficult. It is hard for American teenagers to comprehend how different their lives are from those of Vietnamese teens and many other kids across the globe. Even the poorest Americans are better off than many other people around the world. Field trips, football game pep rallies, proms, and yearbooks are the stuff of American high school. All of these are most likely taken for granted, and they have become so because of the abundant wealth of the United States. Economy and history shape the directions of countries. There is tremendous poverty in Vietnam that affects everything else: availability of food and fresh drinkable water, transportation, health services, telecommunications, education, and so on. All the factors necessary for a society to function well and go forward are in one way or another dependent on a viable economy. Vietnam is still struggling to complete reunification, to define itself, and to figure out the direction it wants to go. It is pulled in many directions and limited by its lack of development and resources. Teenagers are limited by their lack of opportunities and are pessimistic about their prospects for the future. The most important issue for the Vietnamese people at this time is making enough money to survive adequately. Crime, prostitution, AIDS, drug use, and the number of street children are major problems for teenagers and all of Vietnamese society. The Vietnamese teenagers of today are luckier than their parents. They are living not in a war but in its aftermath. Fortunately, they are part of the rebuilding process. The positive side of the current situation is that the majority of the population in Vietnam is quite young; most were born after 1975. They are energetic, talented, optimistic, and inventive. The Vietnamese people are used to struggling for independence, and their indomitable spirit keeps them going, despite extreme adversity and dire living conditions. On a monument on the Ben Hai

River is a quote by Ho Chi Minh: "Vietnam is one. The Vietnamese people are one. Rivers dry up, mountains crumble, but that truth will remain forever." Vietnam is finally becoming one nation after years of domination and devastation.

RESOURCE GUIDE

Nonfiction

Kamm, H. (1996). *Dragon ascending*. NewYork: Arcade Books.

Karrow, S. (1997). *Vietnam: A history*. New York: Viking Penguin.

McLeod, M. W., and Nguyen, T. D. *Culture and Customs of Vietnam*. Westport, CT: Greenwood Press, 2001.

Pham, A. X. (2000). *Catfish and Mandala*. New York: Picador.

Vu, T. (1988). *Lost years: My 1,632 days in Vietnamese reeducation camps*. Berkeley, CA: University of California, Institute of East Asian Studies.

Fiction

Hanh, T. N. (1995). *The stone boy and other stories*. Berkeley, CA: Parallax Press.

Huong, B. T. (1994). *Paradise of the blind*. New York:Viking Penguin.

Luu, L. (1997). *A time far past*. Amherst, MA: University of Massachusetts Press.

Thong, H. S. (2001). *An anthology of Vietnamese poems: Through eleventh to the twentieth century*. New Haven, CT: Yale University Press.

Vu, T. (1999). *The dragon hunt*. Westport, CT: Hyperion.

Vuong, I. D. (1992). *The brocaded slipper and other Vietnamese tales*. New York: HarperCollins Children's Books.

Web Sites

http://coombs.anuedu.au/WWWVLPages/VietPages/WWWVL-Vietnam
http://vietgate.com
http://www.asiarecipe.com
http://www.vietlin.com/english
http://www.vietline.com
http://www.vietnamembassy-usa.org
http://www.viettouch.com

Pen Pal/Chat

http://www.iec.org/
http://www.kidlink.org
http://www.penpal.net
http://www.penpals.com

INDEX

ABOUT THE EDITOR AND CONTRIBUTORS

JUDITH J. SLATER is a Professor at Florida International University, Miami, where she researches curriculum theory, evaluation, organizational analysis, and women in higher education.

HARRIET L. AMATO teaches mathematics at Broward Community College, Fort Lauderdale, Florida.

RIMJHIM BANERJEE is a graduate student from Calcutta, India, at Florida International University, Miami. She is an accomplished dancer and singer in the Indian classical culture.

LEIPING BAO is an Assistant Fellow Professor of Psychology at the Institute of Juvenile and Youth Studies, Shanghai Academy of Social Sciences, Shanghai, China.

LAURA BULLOCK is an educator who has traveled extensively and spent considerable time in Nepal.

DAVID CALLEJO-PEREZ is the co-director of the Urban Education Teacher Initiative and Assistant Professor of Curriculum Studies and History at the University of Nebraska, Lincoln.

JUDY CHIN teaches English to speakers of other languages in Miami.

LILIA C. DIBELLO is an Assistant Professor at the Adrian Dominican School of Education in the Graduate Pre-K/Primary Program of Barry University, Miami Shores, Florida.

ERIC DWYER is an Assistant Professor in Modern Language Education at Florida International University, Miami. He has lived, taught, and traveled extensively throughout Asia.

VERONICA GESSER is an academic dean at the Centro Universitário de Jaraguá do Sul, UNERJ in Jaraguá do Sul, SC, Brazil.

DEBORAH HASSON is an Assistant Professor in the Multilingual Multicultural Program in the College of Education at Florida State University in Tallahassee.

MYUNG SOOK HYUN is a doctoral candidate in Adult Education and Human Resource Development at Florida International University, Miami.

RISAKO IDE is a Visiting Assistant Professor of Japanese Language and Culture at Vassar College, Poughkeepsie, NY. Her specialty is linguistics anthropology, particularly the ethnography of speech in Japan, the United States, and South Korea.

TAI-LOK LUI is a Professor in the Sociology Department at the Chinese University of Hong Kong, Hong Kong.

ONEYDA PANEQUE is an Assistant Professor at Barry University Adrian Dominican School of Education, Miami, Florida.

AIXA PEREZ-PRADO is an Assistant Professor in the TESOL (Teaching English to Speakers of Other Languages) program at Florida International University, Miami. She has lived and worked overseas teaching English and cross-cultural communication for international organizations and schools.

CHYI-IN WU is an Associate Research Fellow of Sociology at the Institute of Sociology, Academia Sinica, Taipei, Taiwan.

CHUN-CHIN YI is a Research Fellow of Sociology at the Institute of Sociology, Academia Sinica, Taipei, Taiwan.